**A storm of suspicion threatens Billy Graham's health, his mission, and his dreams.**

The first charge came from a Charlotte newspaper: "The Billy Graham ministry has amassed $22 million in land, stocks, bonds, and cash it has carefully shielded from public view." Despite Graham's immediate denial, the attacks continued and seemed to avalanche. Word was spread that the Billy Graham Evangelistic Association sold securities illegally and that it was not approved by the Better Business Bureau. Graham himself stood accused of plagerism, mobster connections, and false representation.

Billy Graham has a profile of great importance to our own position at a time when our beliefs and ministries must withstand tests of criticism. Is he a saint or a sinner? Curtis Mitchell knows the answer and the implications of the answer on our lives. Now we can know it too.

# BILLY GRAHAM:
## *Saint or Sinner*

CURTIS MITCHELL

**SPIRE BOOKS**
FLEMING H. REVELL COMPANY
Old Tappan, New Jersey

Unless otherwise identified, Scripture quotations are from the King James Version of the Bible.

Scripture quotations identified RSV are from the Revised Standard Version of the Bible, copyrighted 1946, 1952. © 1971 and 1973.

Scripture quotations identified LB are from The Living Bible, Copyright © 1971 by Tyndale House Publishers, Wheaton, Illinois 60187. All rights reserved.

Photos provided by Russ Busby.

**Library of Congress Cataloging in Publication Data**

Mitchell, Curtis.
  Billy Graham, saint or sinner.

  1.  Graham, William Franklin, 1918–
2.  Billy Graham Evangelistic Association.
I.  Title.
BV3785.G69M468    269'.2'0924[B]    79-13037
ISBN 0-8007-8387-5

TO my father
Charles Albert Mitchell
1855–1924

# Contents

# Preface

IN RECENT MONTHS A FIRE STORM OF SUSPICION AND DEROGATION has threatened Billy Graham's health, his mission, and his dreams.

This conflagration has been fueled by newspaper stories, magazine articles, television broadcasts, and books purporting to be factual or fictional.

*Billy Graham: Saint or Sinner* is my effort to describe those attacks and to explain the evangelist's reaction of relying on God's sovereignty as his major defense.

As a reporter who had written about Graham over the course of twenty-five years—the major years of his ministry—I believed that I knew the evangelist better than any contemporary journalist.

So I committed myself to one more project, an endeavor in depth that would probe all those allegations (and more) and, if possible, discover their sources and determine their accuracy.

I was at the beginning of a trail that would lead through countless interviews, newspaper files, magazine stories, books, radio and TV scripts, transcriptions, diaries, tapes, and letters.

I was searching for the answer to the question: Is Billy Graham a saint or a sinner?

My search is finished. I know the answer.

I want the world to know it, too.

CURTIS MITCHELL

# BILLY GRAHAM: SAINT OR SINNER

# PART ONE
## *The Year of the Locusts*

# 1

# The Year of the Locusts

*Thou shalt carry much seed out into the field, and shalt gather but little in; for the locust shall consume it.*

Deuteronomy 28:38

The assault on the financial integrity of Billy Graham began on Sunday, June 26, 1977. The first salvo was a front-page story in the *Charlotte Observer*, a member of the Associated Press and part of the Knight-Ridder chain of newspapers.

The story's first four paragraphs told stunned readers that:

- The Billy Graham ministry has amassed $22 million in land, stocks, bonds, and cash it has carefully shielded from public view.
- Graham spoke publicly about the fund for the first time this past week after the *Charlotte Observer* discovered its existence and asked about it.
- Graham and his associates have never wanted to talk about their assets because they worry that people will think the ministry is too rich. Graham conceded in an *Observer* interview Thursday that another reason for that secrecy was to avoid being inundated with requests for help.
- This accumulation of wealth appears perfectly legal. And, in fact, is simply prudent money management. However, the two million contributors a year whose gifts to

Graham's ministry average $10 each never have been told
of the fund, which makes the ministry far wealthier than
ever reported.

The *New York Times,* also a member of the Associated Press
and one of America's most prestigious newspapers, repeated the
attack under the heading: BILLY GRAHAM FUND DISCLOSED. Re-
working the report from Charlotte, the paper stated that: ''An
arm of Billy Graham's ministry has amassed almost $23 million
over the past seven years in land, stocks, bonds, and cash holdings in a fund that has been shielded from public view.'' By the
end of the week, hardly a paper in the land had failed to echo the
charges. The original mention of ''carefully shielded'' wealth
quickly became ''Graham's secret fund.'' The article stated
clearly that no illegality was involved; yet its effect was to cast
suspicion on the financial aspect of the evangelist's life and
work.

This attack was strange, because Charlotte was Graham's
hometown, where he had on several occasions been paraded,
feted, and given the city's keys. Only four months earlier, the
*Charlotte Observer* had published a heartwarming, five-part
series on its famous native son.

What could have happened?

## A Year of Successes

Few people have been granted so many honors and so much
public respect as has Billy Graham. His Billy Graham Evangelistic Association (BGEA), established in 1950 to spread the good
news of the Gospel of Jesus Christ ''through every means possible,'' includes ministries via radio, television, movies, books,
magazines, evangelistic conferences, and scores of crusades on
every continent.

In late March 1977, Graham had come home to his beloved Appalachia for a short crusade in Asheville, North Carolina. His home lay twenty miles across the foothills, in rustic Montreat. The idea of this crusade had originated first with Asheville's black ministers. Swiftly, the idea was extended to embrace all races and all evangelical creeds. The opening-night crowd filled the new civic center, the Thomas Wolfe Auditorium next door, two banquet halls upstairs, and the Saint Lawrence Catholic Church across the street. Closed-circuit television blended them all into one gigantic sanctuary.

In the month of May 1977, he had brought off the coup of preaching on the campus of the famous Notre Dame University, in an unprecedented joining of Protestant and Catholic interests. His final service was moved from the university's Athletic and Convocation Center to its huge stadium, where it attracted the largest nonfootball crowd in the stadium's history.

Graham's 1977 itinerary carried him to a crusade in Gothenburg, Sweden—home of the impassive Norseman—where less than 2 percent of the city dwellers, and only 5 percent of the country folk, go to church. Experts anticipated failure. "Nobody will come," they predicted. "This nation is too blasé, too sophisticated."

But the Swedish people did come, to a series of standing-room-only meetings. They responded to Billy's invitation to repent and accept Jesus Christ, tears running down their cheeks. On their own, Gothenburg teenagers, carrying banners and torches, streamed through snow-covered streets one night, chanting "Jesus is the Way, the Truth, and the Light."

By midyear of 1977, Billy Graham could look back at an unprecedented succession of personal triumphs. His ministry included the longest winning streak in the history of evangelism. For a dozen years, he had been considered one of the world's most admired men. A famous editor had once called him the

American Pope. An astute politician is alleged to have said: "In my district you can be against motherhood, but you cannot be against Billy Graham."

There were other successes.

His motion-picture company, established early in his evangelistic ministry, had recently produced the successful *The Hiding Place*, an award-winning dramatization of the experiences of Corrie ten Boom, a heroic Christian woman who fought the holocaust in Holland by making possible the escape of countless Jews. Experts said that more people had seen the movie, and more young persons had been led to accept Jesus Christ through it, than by any religious film in history.

To the surprise of many people, his 1975 book *Angels* had made the best-seller list. His latest book, *How to Be Born Again*, was breaking new ground in the publishing business, where its first printing of 800,000 hardcover copies was reported to be the largest first edition ever issued.

By 1977, Graham's voice was being heard regularly on more than 900 radio stations in a score of countries, and each crusade provided a series of prime-time television programs. His newspaper column was appearing regularly in 160 important newspapers, reaching millions of readers.

In 1977, he would return to Wheaton College, in Wheaton, Illinois, from which he had graduated in 1943, to realize a dream: the ground-breaking ceremony for a four-story brick structure which would house an international institute of evangelism, a library, an advanced-study center for students in communications, and the archives of his multipronged ministry. The building, along with an endowment for its upkeep, would be a gift to Wheaton College from the Billy Graham Evangelistic Association—a $15.5 million commitment—to include construction costs and the endowment of the building. Despite his objections, it would be named the Billy Graham Center.

In the back of Billy Graham's mind in 1977, there must have been some awareness that his endeavors were pleasing to God. The evidence of heavenly approval lay in many things: in his reknown, his acceptance by most of the nation's ministers, and by the rising curve of evangelistic successes. One particularly reliable indicator was the torrent of supportive letters that arrived daily at his Minneapolis headquarters. An offer of a free Living Bible had produced more than a million responses several years ago.

Graham was content. Other evangelistic organizations were bigger, but he was big enough. His vision of tomorrow perceived the means by which fresh ministries could be raised up, generation after generation, so that the fires of evangelism would never go out and Christ's Great Commission could finally be executed. His program would cost money, but so had his crusades, movies, magazines, international conferences, and every other evangelistic enterprise; yet, the Lord had always provided.

Minneapolis aides, who monitored income and outgo of BGEA funds, assured him that the average contribution had risen steadily over the last several years, to $10 to $12. The combined income of BGEA and its affiliates from 1977 earnings and contributions would probably hit a new high of about $40 million.

His personal finances were no problem. While other charity association heads drew far more handsome salaries—often up to $75,000 annually—Graham's salary was $39,500 plus $200 monthly for unreimbursed expenses. When he traveled, tickets and accommodations were provided by the association. Income from his early books is in trust for his children. The book *Angels* was a best-seller and a big money-maker. All of Graham's royalties from that book were given to Wheaton College, his alma mater. He writes a newspaper column that is read by millions. He inherited a share of his father's farm which, thanks to urban sprawl, became a real-estate development occupied by office buildings, supermarkets, and so forth. His home, atop a mountain near Montreat, North Carolina, is surrounded by 200 acres of spectacular scenery. He has also invested in some Carolina farmland.

According to *Corporation Report*, a financial magazine, for June 1977, Graham has had many invitations to go into politics and at least as many offers to go into personally profitable motion picture and television deals. He turned them all down. He evidently is more than content with his present economic base.

For sure, Billy Graham had it made.

Or did he?


### The Locust Swarms

Satan's snares were already set and waiting. The locusts were massing to swarm. The *Charlotte Observer* story was their first blitz.

As that story of the "carefully shielded" fund was repeated in newspapers from coast to coast, insinuating headlines blossomed. Most of them seemed to confirm the secret fund by using such provocative words as *admitted* and *discovered* and *leaked out*. Thus, a single article released the locusts to devour the fields which had been so carefully planted and nurtured. The evangelist's immediate denial went unheard. The *New York Times* story said, "one of Mr. Graham's closest assistants," speaking for Billy, called the report "grossly inaccurate." Nobody listened.

In the following months, one Satanic foray followed another, as if by plan. Soon, distressed friends began to wonder if the work of the evangelist could survive the shock. It seemed inevitable that a considerable portion of his following would fall away. The withdrawal of any large number of contributors could have serious consequences for Graham's ministry.

The assault on his integrity in the *Charlotte Observer* had hurt him deeply.

Equally punishing was the revival of the almost-forgotten rumor involving the evangelist and Mickey Cohen, a Hollywood hoodlum and gambling czar of the 1950s and 1960s. A book published in the autumn of 1977 exposed again to public scrutiny the mildewed charge that Graham had offered a $10,000 bribe to Mickey, if he would be converted to Christianity. The caper was supposed to have happened in the full glare of Madison Square Garden's spotlights in 1957. Thousands believed what the book said.

The roughest books came in 1977 and 1978. Within eighteen months, Billy Graham would shudder under a barrage of five books, most of them hostile. In them, he was characterized as being a White House hanger-on, power mad, a money huckster, and a high roller. In one fictional account of a renegade evangelist, the main character used such favorite Graham phrases as "may the Lord bless you real good" and "every head bowed and every eye closed."

It could have been chance, I suppose, that the book's setting included two of Graham's hometowns, Charlotte and Minneapolis. It was not by chance that its pages described the evangelist participating in explicit sex scenes that surely must be among the most offensive writings in modern "literature."

The parody might have remained unnoticed, except that its author toured the nation in a series of radio and TV interviews. His brisk disclaimer that Billy Graham was not his model was quickly obscured by his chatter about a certain evangelistic association's tax-dodging, gimmick-ridden method of operation. Naming Graham over and over, he left no doubt in this listener's mind that all big-money ministers were birds of a feather, intent on extracting a fortune from an audience of born-again suckers.

There were lesser locusts, too, operating locally but making news that spread quickly across the nation. For a number of years, the Billy Graham Evangelistic Association, with proper authority from the Securities Division of the Minnesota Department of Commerce, had been offering annuities in its home state and elsewhere and had been filing annual reports with the proper authorities. Because of an oversight—plus the sudden death of the head of BGEA's development department—an annual report was not filed. When BGEA discovered this omission, they immediately prepared the report and delivered it to the Minnesota Securities Division, only to be told that additional information was required.

When they filed this extra information, they were told that still more was needed. Local newspaper reporters with connections in the statehouse heard of the situation. Almost anywhere in the world, Billy Graham news is important news. The Minneapolis stories blew the incident up to incendiary proportions. The national press picked it up. Fortunately, it fizzled after a two-hour session between state authorities and BGEA executives. Face-to-face, they pinpointed and pinned down what the state wanted. On the double, the information was provided. End of problem! But damage had been done by ever-spreading circles of misinformation.

From out of the blue, another city released its swarm of locusts. The Better Business Bureau in Washington, D.C., issued a statement saying that it had tried for years to obtain information from the Billy Graham Evangelistic Association, and failed. Therefore, they could not certify that the BGEA was a charity approved by the BBB. By implication and by saying that the BGEA had not responded to their requests for information, they were suggesting to many casual readers and listeners that Billy Graham was hiding something.

Another complaint—more technical—seemed to ask, "Why is

Billy Graham stealing?" The "theft," it turned out, was of words taken from one of his own out-of-print books that he had written in 1965, and which he had added to the chapters of his 1977 best-seller, *How to Be Born Again*. The charge was very legal and very involved, and came from a publishing company that had lost its bid to publish *How to Be Born Again*. Regardless, it made headlines: not because it was big news, but because Billy Graham was being zapped, and zapping the big boys was the new national pastime.

One day, Billy picked up a copy of *McCall's* magazine. It advertised an article entitled "I Can't Play God Any More." That wordage jolted him. The text from which the words were lifted delivered an even heavier blow. Saying that Graham now holds a more modest view of his role in God's plan for man, the author quoted him: "I used to play God, but I can't do that any more. I used to believe that pagans in far-off countries were lost—were going to hell, if they did not have the Gospel of Jesus Christ preached to them. I no longer believe that."

Millions of readers were stunned and stumped. How could Billy Graham deny the Gospel tenets he had supported all of his life? Hardly a broadcast on the "Hour of Decision" had failed to emphasize that Jesus Christ is the *only* way to salvation, the *only* way to God. Letters poured into Minneapolis.

Late in June 1978, *Human Behavior* magazine printed an article describing how a four-member research team from Arizona State University had infiltrated the Graham organization during the 1974 crusade in Phoenix.

They reported that Graham's advance men had come to the city about six weeks ahead of the crusade, to advise the locals. "By the time Graham arrives in town to make his altar call, an army of 6,000 awaits with instructions on when to come forth at varying intervals to create the impression of a spontaneous mass outpouring."

The article claimed that Graham used "goats" to lead his converts forward. (In stockyards, goats have been used to lead sheep to slaughtering pens.) Their duties in the Phoenix audience, it was charged, were threefold: to prod reluctant sinners into activity, to herd them down the aisles to Graham's platform, and to swell the stream of inquirers, so the crusade would look good on television.

What the magazine did not report was that these human *goats* all wore highly visible, blue and silver badges naming each of them a counselor, and that they sat on chairs reserved for counselors. Nobody in any crusade audience could have any doubt of their function, which was to provide a friendly and informed companion for an inquirer in a moment of possible need.

The falsity of the magazine article did not prevent a national news service from spreading its lies from coast to coast, or editors from headlining it in their papers. Thus, another smear was added to Graham's burden.

When criticizing Graham became endemic in 1977, my gorge rose, slowly but irresistibly. Other conditions abetted my discontent. Since Watergate, we have been brainwashed by printer's ink and electronic bad-mouthing. Let a personality climb to the top rung of the success ladder and the public, led by the media, dubs him a closet crook. Courage, strength of character, and personal integrity are vanishing American virtues.

I subscribe also to the belief that ordinary mortals have a need for authentic heroes. When a people loses its heroes, it loses its heroism. Without models, it descends to mediocrity. Today our heroes are in short supply, while our problems remain unsolved, and our writers (who create heroes, in the first place) are forced to reach into outer space to find men who are larger than life (*Star Wars* is an example).

By any standard, and in the most improbable of circumstances, Billy Graham became a hero to millions. Aside from the intrinsic value of his message, he represents a cultural, even a national, asset.

Certainly when I wrote my first story about young Graham's extraordinary success in Great Britain in 1954, I had no intimation that he would grow so tall. Old-timers may recall that he shocked conservative churchmen by moving out of the tents of rural evangelism, into the sweaty palaestras of sport. A hockey arena in London became his tabernacle, and his final service caused such a colossal traffic jam that the British Broadcasting Corporation interrupted its programs to urge Londoners to stay away unless they had reserved seats.

As a writer, I had wanted to know more about the thirty-six-year-old Baptist evangelist. A few months later, I cornered him in a trailer parked a few yards from his pulpit at Vanderbilt University's football field. He was beginning his 1954 Nashville crusade. Every day of that memorable crusade, and throughout the subsequent one in New Orleans, I listened to him, talked with him, lunched with him, and interrogated members of his team.

I have known Billy Graham since 1954, and I have probably studied him and every element of his ministry for a longer period than any other practicing journalist. I can therefore claim a unique degree of acquaintance with him and with the personnel of his association. Never once has he or any of his representatives misled me or given me false or doctored information.

As an author and journalist whose interviews have brought him face-to-face with hundreds of celebrities, statesmen, and scientists—from Dwight D. Eisenhower to Clare Boothe Luce, from Irving Berlin to Dr. Paul Dudley White—I have never talked to a more open, candid, and responsive celebrity. Color me biased, if you will, but also color me honest. I believe in the man.

But what did I know about all the new charges and allegations?

Someone has used the analogy of the machine. A machine sits there, shiny and complex, and you can describe it from front, back, and both sides. You can name its levers and calculate its potential. But there is knowledge of a different kind: the knowledge that comes from personal involvement. Until you sit in that machine and use those levers and feel the engine's vibrations, you really don't know much about it.

From the day I felt the tides of rancor that the *Charlotte Observer* article initiated, I knew that important issues were at stake and that I had to get involved. For years, I had described and analyzed every facet of the Billy Graham machine from without. Now I had to get within. Could I, an outsider, manage to find a way to probe the fears and joys of the legions of Billy Graham association supporters, laborers, and executives? Would they speak freely? Would I understand?

A thrilling impatience gripped me. The Bible says that God has a plan for each life. His plan had once used my skills to supplement Billy Graham's ministry of preaching. What was God's plan now?

I was semiretired, full of years, and busy with other literary projects. On the other hand, I knew the man so well. My instinct told me that every question could be answered honorably.

In my file room, a dozen cabinet drawers are laden with the debris of twenty-five years of association. The thousands of papers there are yellowed and crumbling. I had been tempted a hundred times to haul it all to the dump. With a reporter's instinct, I knew that this serendipitous assortment could be my launching pad.

I spread ancient manila folders on tables and floor. I reread full-page sermons from a dozen crusades, relics of the days when newspapers printed every word Graham spoke. There were dictaphone belts holding addresses he had once delivered to Yale students, plus magazine articles from long-dead issues of *Look* and *Life*, and first drafts of my own interviews with him. I reread typed notes of early impressions and notes jotted down while in transit with him.

Some memos seemed to invite me to pick them up, as if eager to demonstrate the qualities of the young man who had become a famous evangelist.

Finally, I uncovered a yellowed, unbound chronicle that Billy Graham had dictated fifteen years ago, describing the key events and the spiritual experiences on which his life had turned. The document was lengthy, but vibrant with the realization that God was opening doors before him. A magazine had asked him to write his autobiography, and he had dictated these memoirs. I had been commissioned to edit them into a series. This forgotten manuscript was what I had been unconsciously seeking all the time, guided by the feeling that somewhere among those musty papers was the key to Billy Graham's essential nature.

The manuscript had been dictated in the early 1960s, but its author was remembering how he had felt earlier, upon deciding to give himself to full-time evangelism. To read its faded pages was to take part in a remarkable spiritual adventure:

I knew that to be a successful evangelist, I would have to be set apart by divine consecration. Those who handle the Word of God in evangelism must have pure hearts and clean hands.

"Consecrate yourself this day unto the Lord" is still God's command. "As I am, so must ye also be in the world" is still Christ's ideal for His servants. Separation from the world's mind, method, and way had to become a part of my life.

"Be ye not conformed to this world but transformed."
"Wherefore, come out from among them and be ye separate." "If any man loves the world, the love of God is not in
him." I interpreted these passages to mean that the spirit of
evil that is in the world must have no part in my life.

My life must be an open book from now on and for all to
read, and it must be wholly God's.

From this moment on, I must have no other master, no
other desire, no other goal, no other ambition. I must become God-intoxicated.

That was Billy Graham, age forty-four, remembering how he
felt on a very special evening when he was barely thirty.

Some said he had changed.

The day I read those words, he was involved in a crusade in
Cincinnati, a city once called the "cemetery of evangelists." A
visit there would renew my friendships with old team members
and introduce me to younger ones. I wondered if, after so many
years, they were still eager to walk that extra mile.

Next, I could make a quick trip to Minneapolis. It had become
Graham's headquarters in 1950, when the fledgling BGEA rented
600 square feet of space, hired a secretary, and installed a young
business manager named George M. Wilson to mind the store.

My instinct told me that the swarm of locusts now surrounding
Graham was more than an attack on him; it was an attack on all
Christians.

The prospect of uncomfortable travel, of interrogating strang-
ers, and of playing the role of a self-appointed Inspector Maigret
or detective Lew Archer was not particularly appealing. But I
knew I could wait no longer.

As I packed a suitcase, my father's voice whispered, in memory, the ancient warning that whenever Christ accomplished a

mighty work, the devil invariably redoubled his own efforts.

I wondered if Satan and his devils had finally penetrated the mighty work represented by the Billy Graham Evangelistic Association. I wanted desperately to know.

A few days later, I was in Cincinnati.

# 2

# An Investigative Committee of One

*Be sober, be vigilant; because your adversary the devil, as a roaring lion, walketh about, seeking whom he may devour.*
1 Peter 5:8

Once it was said that the sun never sets on the British Empire; today, it never sets on Billy Graham's ministry. In 1977, he circled the earth twice and added to his record of having preached face-to-face with more people than any evangelist in history.

Simultaneously, he supervised the production of movies, wrote books, participated in TV specials, published magazines, and carried out all the administrative and policy-making duties of a chief executive. The pace was killing. He was fifty-eight years old. As his remaining years decreased, his eagerness to get his job done seemed to increase.

By the time I became involved, he had made a statement to the press denying secrecy and explaining why the World Evangelism and Christian Education Fund (WECEF) had been separated from the Billy Graham Evangelistic Association (BGEA). Copies of the statement were mailed to many of his supporters.

He had also addressed his followers through his "Hour of Decision" broadcast. He explained that the fund had been announced to the press in 1971, although reporters generally had not considered it important enough to mention.

Speaking to the issue of financial integrity, he said, "We believe we are accountable to God. . . . We consider ourselves stewards before the Lord." And he told how BGEA had asked "one of the most distinguished law firms in America to assess our organization and its affiliates in every possible detail to see if there were any financial safeguards we were overlooking." After studying BGEA for two years, this firm (which specialized in nonprofit organizations) reported that they "had rarely found an organization with higher standards or better financial control than yours."

As for WECEF, Graham said, it was administered by a dedicated board of directors "made up of some of America's most outstanding Christian businessmen." No board member received financial benefit from WECEF. No employees worked for it, except an occasional part-timer.

Its purpose was to accumulate money to build two important educational projects, one at Wheaton College in Illinois, and one near Asheville, North Carolina.

What the public could not know—indeed, they had little reason for even being interested—was the extreme care with which WECEF had been divorced from BGEA, how its board of directors was appointed, its administration entrusted to an unimpeachable group of Christian business leaders, and its headquarters settled in Dallas, where it was most convenient for them to exercise their wholly voluntary stewardship.

As for secrecy, many public meetings had been held and countless solicitations made. Over a score of cities were visited by Graham and other speakers, where they met with specially invited groups who met openly for the purpose of hearing about Graham's ideas. Funds were contributed or pledged over a seven-year period. While feasibility studies were going on and architectural plans were being made, those monies were prudently invested by the businessmen who had volunteered their experience and advice. Several of them, including their chairman, lived in the Dallas area.

The Wheaton Center turned from dream to reality when a ground-breaking ceremony was held at Wheaton College in September of 1977. At that time, several million dollars that had been raised were transferred to the college.

Twice during 1977, Billy had accepted invitations from David Hartman to appear on the American Broadcasting Company's "Good Morning, America" telecast. In the course of an interview in August, Hartman mentioned the furor in the media about big-money religion, and asked, indirectly, about the veiled charges of hanky-panky by Graham's organization.

The weary evangelist summarized his earlier statements:

The fund was not a secret, but had been announced at a news conference in 1971.

The fund was not a holding company. Its money had already been pledged to the building of two educational institutions, the first at Wheaton College and the second in western North Carolina.

Between its founding and the present, its funds had been prudently invested and profits given away, wholly or in part, to needy work across the world.

Since the beginning, its records have been on file with the IRS in Washington, where "anybody can go and see the whole thing."

Hartman wondered if the resurgence of evangelism might provide an opportunity for abuse. Graham replied in the affirmative: "We could have the reappearance of some Elmer Gantrys, which could hurt all legitimate evangelists."

Hartman said: "Are you feeling any of that hurt?"

"Not yet, but we could, before it is all over."

His second appearance on "Good Morning, America" was in October, two weeks before his crusade in Cincinnati. The bad news this time was that the Minnesota Securities Division had protested BGEA's sale of unregistered annuities.

Graham said that a new state law had caused a mix-up. When his office heard about it, the sale was stopped. It would be straightened out.

ABC's Steve Bell, speaking from Washington on the same program, wondered why religious charities were so reluctant to reveal their finances. Graham explained that churches and church-affiliated organizations are not required by law to report to anyone. As for the Better Business Bureau, he called it "a wonderful organization," but explained that it had begun to offer reports on religious organizations only a few years ago. At the same time, it had set criteria for BBB approval that required so much paperwork and was so expensive (an independent audit by outside accountants, for instance) that only a handful of non-profit organizations felt they could afford to respond with the figures the BBB demanded. Naturally, the public did not know this, and when the BBB, in response to media questioning, reported that BGEA was not on their approved list, that made the headlines.

Among the much larger and more prominent organizations which also were *not* on the BBB's approved list was the United Jewish Appeal and the national Catholic Charities. "And I could go on with a long list," he said.

Finally, Bell asked, "Are we coming to a time when religious organizations are going to begin a turn toward total disclosure?"

Graham said, "I think they have to, Steve. The mood of the country has changed. . . . There are some charlatans coming along, and the public ought to be informed. . . ."

## Why Doesn't He Answer?

Having studied transcripts of Graham's televised remarks, I next turned to another tool of biographers, researchers, and journalists—the modern tape recorder. Discreetly used, it is an invaluable device. Mine picked up a host of voices as I canvassed stores, shopping centers, Sunday services, and street corners, injecting Graham's name into random conversations.

Over the years, I had noticed that the mention of Billy Graham seemed to elicit strong reactions. Either people liked him very much or disliked him intensely. As I conducted my one-man survey, that continued to be the case, but for the first time I became aware that each negative answer contained a specific cause for skepticism. And, almost nobody repeated the old catch phrase, "I don't agree with him, *but I think he's sincere.*"

To my astonishment, the man on the street seemed to harbor a wide variety of charges against the evangelist:

"With all that money piled up in Texas, he's got a nerve asking anybody for more."

"I've always been suspicious of those crowds coming forward on those TV shows. I hear half of them are paid shills—like he paid that Hollywood gangster named Mickey Cohen."

"He's gone soft on Catholicism, like holding that crusade at Notre Dame, and now he's turning Commie. Sure those reds came to hear him preach in Belgrade. Their bosses ordered them to. Freedom of religion, bunk!"

"I heard him the other night, and he's got a crust, telling me how to live. What's he know? He lives behind an electric fence and is guarded by trained dogs. Let him come out and get his hands dirty, and maybe I'll listen."

"If he's got nothing to hide, why doesn't he answer?"

This last query even came from the evangelist's longtime supporters. *Why doesn't he answer* became, ultimately, the issue that outweighed all others. Obviously, I had discovered a communications gap. Graham had answered his followers, by letter and radio and via David Hartman on "Good Morning, America." But these Americans had not heard. They were still mouthing the old rumors, as if they were gospel. What was equally obvious from their demeanor was that his apparent failure to answer was somehow equivalent to a plea of guilty, or perhaps indicated a pious contempt for common folk.

After surveying laymen and laywomen from several Bible Belt communities, I wondered if the anti-Graham rumors had altered the attitudes of Protestant ministers, particularly those who favored the idea of a Billy Graham crusade in their communities. A perfect example of this group was in Orlando, next door to my Florida home. For several years, an Orange County committee had been petitioning Graham to hold a crusade there. Coincidentally, a local editor had asked reporter Sue Hung to investigate the current sentiment of the area's clergy.

Her conclusion was reported in the *Orlando Sentinel Star* and testified that neither headlines about the "secret fund," nor any other tale about Graham, had tarnished his image. Everyone interviewed, she said, "reaffirmed their faith and continued support."

The Reverend Ernie Gross, president of the Orange County Council of Churches, said: "It made me feel bad that it happened. I did not see any immorality, but I saw poor management. I still support the crusade and his concept of his ministry."

The Reverend Jim Morsh told reporter Hung: "I see no misappropriation of funds, but sometimes some measure of accounting is advisable."

The Reverend O. Charles Horton stated: "Keep in mind, those funds are controlled by a board of businessmen, and their purposes . . . are documented and made known. To me, it was an error in judgment [not disclosing the fund or its purpose]. I certainly hope he [Graham] will hold a crusade here, and I will support it 100 percent.''

The hard core of Billy Graham backers apparently felt the same way. When editors asked Sterling Huston, director of crusades in North America, if criticism of the controversial WECEF fund had hurt crusade efforts, he replied, ''Absolutely not. We have nothing but understanding and support.''

Meanwhile the media were reporting some surprising and perhaps overdue developments. Religious charities had suddenly become worthy of front-page comment. The WECEF explosion had stimulated the Associated Press to undertake study of the field. It found that contributors had given all religious charities $12.84 billion in 1976. Most of this had come from individuals, and most of those charities had never given a single accounting to their donors.

But things were changing, and Billy Graham was one of those leading the way. Evangelical leaders had met in the office of Senator Mark Hatfield, to discuss a move by some politicians to legislate ''forced disclosure'' by all religious charities. Catholic bishops, long indifferent to requests for disclosure, had met earlier in Washington and adopted standards that enforced an annual financial audit.

World Vision, a Christian outreach organization, and the Save the Children Federation both asserted that they provided complete financial reports upon request.

Billy Graham stated that ''the mood of the country is moving in the direction of church-related groups providing financial information. And we'll gladly conform to it.'' The climate of public opinion was shifting, probably for the better, and Graham, along with many other religious leaders, was changing his attitude, too.

## The Nonconfrontation Policy

What was not changing, I learned through conversations with mutual friends, was Graham's policy of refusing to engage in controversies with his critics. Some called this reaction spineless. He called it biblical, citing the Sermon on the Mount, which put it clearly in the statement: ". . . Love your enemies and pray for those who persecute you" (Matthew 5:44 RSV). The Apostle Paul enlarged the sentiment to say: "Bless those who persecute you; bless and do not curse them" (Romans 12:14 RSV).

Later, describing Christian behavior, Paul said, ". . . When reviled, we bless; when persecuted, we endure; when slandered, we try to conciliate . . ." (1 Corinthians 4:12, 13 RSV).

Graham's model for his conciliating stance was a biblical character named Nehemiah, the restorer of the ruined city of Jerusalem and its governor more than 400 years before the birth of Jesus.

Assigned to build protective walls and gates, he made his plans and went to work. Several citizens complained that they were not consulted and that Nehemiah's plans were faulty. When they found Nehemiah at work on his walls, they formed a committee and demanded a confrontation. He said he was too busy. ". . . I am doing a great work, so that I cannot come down: why should the work cease . . . ?" (Nehemiah 6:3).

Five times, they challenged. Five times, he refused. Nehemiah would not leave his wall.

Graham says: "I've learned through the years not to reply to critics. Many of them want to fight and are hoping I will answer. If I'd replied, I would have bogged down in controversy years ago. In evangelism, we are simply too busy. This is God's work, and He will answer in His own time."

This policy of nonconfrontation is one Graham practices quietly and doggedly, often against the advice of friends. Frankly, I wondered if Graham's stance of righteous nonresistance was convincing enough to enable his ministry to endure the gathering storm.

Reviewing the catalogue of innuendoes and insinuations, I felt certain that his brief flurry of response had answered only a few charges. By now, the record of those charges was scattered around the world in libraries, magazine files, books, and newspaper morgues. Graham's eminence insured that he would be written about for decades. Soon other journalists would be digging up those unproven tales and basing their stories on them. Historians, when they use such materials, call them secondary sources. Biographers say that old clippings never die.

As yet, I did not know whether the charges were correct or false. If they were facts, they needed corroboration. If they were guesses, opinions, or outright lies, they should be corrected. Part of the answer was in my gut. I recalled the side of Graham which had caused one fellow minister and longtime friend to say. "I don't know how good a scrapper Billy would be in a fight, but I do know he can out-love any man I ever saw."

Was I too concerned, too agitated at the lack of a counterweight to all the anti-Graham verbiage in the media? Admittedly, his Nehemiah formula had worked in London in the 1950s and in New York in the 1960s.

## The Nehemiah Formula

In 1954, Graham and his wife and several aides were enroute to his first all-out British crusade. It was wintertime, and they were crossing the Atlantic, on their way to the English port of Southampton, when the blow fell. Hannen Swaffer, eminent London newsman, had received a copy of a BGEA calendar that was being used to publicize the crusade. One of its pages carried a printed statement that said, "There will always be an England, but will it always be the England we have known? Something tragic has happened . . . . When the war ended, a sense of frustration and disillusionment gripped England, and what Hitler's bombs could not do, Socialism with its accompanying evils shortly accomplished."

In 1954, socialism was England's dominant political doctrine. The word *Socialism*, as used on the BGEA calendar, Britons thought, could refer only to their current type of government. Newsman Swaffer cried, "It's a foul lie. Disown this ignorant nonsense." He demanded churchmen who were supporting the crusade, "Call Billy Graham to repentance before he has the effrontery to start converting us." His article in the *Daily Herald* was headlined BILLY, GO HOME. In London, a leader in Parliament talked of barring Graham from the British Isles.

Billy had never seen the calendar, and he radioed for an explanation. Then "I called Ruth and the others to my cabin, and we had two hours of prayer," Billy told me. "Before we docked at Southampton, a tug came alongside with twenty-five reporters and a dozen photographers. They were after my scalp, and we could do nothing but pray for wisdom. On the dock, we met another battalion of newsmen. Their first question was, 'Who invited you here, anyway?'

"Then we had a press conference," Graham recalls. "Bev Shea sang a fine old hymn. I talked and got in the first few thousand words. I answered every question as fully and frankly as possible. Through it all, I felt the greatest confidence I can remember that God would bless our meeting. Finally, Bev sang again, and everybody joined in. I tell you, that press conference almost turned into a revival."

The point is that Graham's response to a fire storm of criticism was prayer, courtesy, and his policy of refusing to fight back.

For him, it worked. It always had.

The final audience of that 1954 crusade, by the way, over-flowed London's largest soccer stadium. The platform was packed with dignitaries, dukes, generals, and bishops. And sit-ting beside Billy was the venerable Archbishop of Canterbury. That the mischief-making word in the calendar should have been *secularism* instead of *socialism* seemed irrelevant.

Later, the 1957 New York crusade blew up a different kind of storm. "The liberals thought I was too fundamental," Billy told me, "and the fundamentalists thought I was too liberal."

Both sides wanted to sponsor the crusade exclusively. At that time, liberal thinkers occupied the majority of high denomina-tional offices and Manhattan pulpits. Fundamentalists with ex-tremely different theological views refused to work with them. Finally, Billy announced that he would accept the sponsorship of the Protestant Council, a middle-of-the-road association in which both liberals and conservatives were active. The simmer-ing war between the extremists erupted in their religious jour-nals, but Graham refused to take sides. He had work to do.

In the end, the New York crusade became a triumph of evangelistic campaigning. As I wrote in my book, *God in the Garden*, "It ran longer than any other crusade. It attracted more people. It resulted in more converts."

One minister commented: "It's not important what anyone thinks of Billy Graham. What is important is what you can hear on the streets as men hum and whistle 'This is my story, this is my song, Praising my Savior all the day long.' "

But by 1977, the times had changed, and so had the nature of Graham's problems. To my knowledge, Ruth Graham was the first person to understand this. As she told me once, "I have known for years that certain things were going to change. The Bible tells about it. And when the change came, I've known that the devil would be too smart to make a martyr out of Bill. Instead, he would try to discredit his ministry. If Bill were to be assassinated, which would be so easy, that would make him a martyr. Instead, they will try character assassination. And that is exactly what is happening.''

What was happening in 1977, she was convinced, was that Satan was attacking the underpinnings of all the Graham ministries—indeed, of all evangelical ministries and of the Christian church itself.

If Billy could be brought down by an audacious assault on *his* financial integrity, so could all evangelists. Why, Graham was the man who had erased the old Elmer Gantry image by abolishing the infamous love offering on which so many ministers had fattened. It was Billy who had called his team together after an unsuccessful revival in California and demanded lists of every criticism they had heard, and who had incorporated their suggestions into a code that worked without fail through hundreds of crusades.

How incredible that the attacks of 1977–1978 should single out Billy Graham. As I have said, part of the answer was in my gut. But another part, perhaps the greater part, was in the cities that knew him best: in Montreat, where he lived; in Minneapolis, where his organization was headquartered; and in Cincinnati, where he was conducting his three-hundred-and-twentieth crusade.

## The Cincinnati Crusade

A crusade city takes on a special ambience at twilight. After dinner, in the blocks around the Cincinnati crusade arena, the crowd thickened as it swung along, everyone moving in the same direction, as if pulled by a gigantic magnet. Couples smiled and chatted as they stepped briskly down aging sidewalks near Riverfront Coliseum. For the first time in years, I saw families walking together and pedestrians carrying Bibles. The aura of comradery was almost luminous as the human streams converged at the final crossing before the huge arena.

Full of anticipation, I had arrived at the midpoint of the Tri-State crusade in October, planning only a quick look around—just enough to meet Graham's new personnel and to renew contacts with old friends. Most of all, I sought evidence of a "changed" Billy Graham, or a changed method of operation, or a changed theology—or anything else that would contribute to my mission.

Inside the Coliseum, Cliff Barrows was rehearsing a choir that filled the width of the building's far end. Its vocal harmonies were punctuated by the sound of shuffling feet, of Christian friends greeting one another, and of crying babies. The attendance that night was over 17,000.

My chair at the press table was not unlike the one I had first occupied more than two decades earlier. When Cliff turned from his music, donned his coat, and came to the lectern, I knew exactly what to expect. First, his affable announcement and introductions, then a celebrity guest (this night, it was a professional football player), and finally the famous voice of George Beverly Shea, setting the spiritual mood for Graham's sermon.

When Graham preached, I heard a familiar theme and saw a familiar style. Whatever change had taken place over the years was in the direction of a slower pace and fewer dramatics. But his blazing intensity and fervent sincerity were as potent as ever.

As expected, the response was an outpouring of people who had come to the arena full of confusion and hurt. Billy Graham told them: "I've never seen a person turn away from Jesus and be happy. I've never seen a person turn to Jesus and regret it. You are facing eternity; you are facing forever. You are not here by accident. I'm asking you to come home."

Inquirers filled the long aisles and flowed into a quiet throng in the bowl of the Coliseum. Some walked easily, some with difficulty. Counselors accompanied them, thumbing their Bibles, praying silently, ready when needed. A fragile little woman left a row on the upper level and began the steep descent. Hers was a long walk, a major undertaking. But she made it, all ninety-nine steps. "I had a need, and I knew Christ would meet my need," she said. She was eighty-five years old.

A youth left the choir section to make a decision. His path was level, but the passage was difficult for him, too. He had cerebral palsy. A seventeen-year-old high-school student clasped her fifteen-month-old baby to her breast, saying, "I've come to take Jesus as my Saviour."

When the service was over, I talked to old friends. They said the city had responded to the crusade with unexpected enthusiasm. A large majority of the churches had cooperated. Newspapers were treating the revival to daily front-page stories.

Christian morale was at the highest pitch anyone could remember. An example of this was the standing-room-only enrollment at the crusade's School of Evangelism. Over 1,400 ministers, from 78 denominations, had signed up for the week's schedule of day-and-night classes. Dr. Kenneth Chafin, dean of the school, exulted, "We'll be sending pastors back to 1,400 congregations with a new filling of the Holy Spirit."

Over two thousand homes were open daily to prayer groups. And three country boys, whose church was thirty-five miles from town, had added stars to their crowns by a feat that made local headlines. They had committed themselves to invite folk to the meetings and give away literature. But homes were far apart, and the boys were still too young to drive. So they hitched up old Dobbin and drove from farmhouse to farmhouse with Billy Graham literature in their buggy and a Billy Graham bumper sticker on their horse!

The best news I heard in Cincinnati was an announcement

brought to the crusade by George Wilson, a BGEA official. The
*Cincinnati Post* gave it this banner headline: GRAHAM AIDE SAYS
BOOKS ARE OPEN. The story began: "The Billy Graham
Evangelistic Association's financial affairs are now an open
book, and a minor flap in Minneapolis was resolved yesterday,
George Wilson, BGEA executive vice-president said here last
night."

Earlier that month, the BGEA board of directors, acting on
Graham's suggestion, had voted to release an annual report that
would cover the affairs of the BGEA and its affiliated organizations in a manner similar to the annual reports of publicly held
corporations. Each cent of income and every contribution would
be reported, and so would all expenditures. This was an important breakthrough. It would answer every intimation of malfea-
sance or misfeasance. To my knowledge, no other national
parachurch organization had gone this "second mile." The
statement would probably satisfy even the picky Better Business
Bureau.

As to the molehill that became a mountain in the Minnesota
statehouse, that baffling communications gap between BGEA
and the securities commissioner had been closed by filing a 1976
financial accounting. Reporting the story from Minneapolis, the
Associated Press revealed that BGEA's 1976 income had been
$28.7 million, while its expenditures had been $27.7 million.

In Cincinnati, a relaxed George Wilson told reporters: "We
got word today that they [the securities officials] are satisfied."

As the days in Cincinnati sped by, I began to feel a gnawing
regret at the distance between the evangelist and the people. His
platform had become so high. His voice was so magnified. Those
of us who had sat with him in small rooms were aware of his
warmth, wit, and transparent integrity, which did not show

through in public. Where was the Billy, I worried, who had been cast aside during his steep climb from Carolina farm boy to global crusader?

Talking with friends who had worked with him for a generation, I asked if this change was accidental or intentional. They had not noticed, they said. They had *better* notice, I replied.

Was there a remedy? I thought so. Somehow, the offstage Billy Graham should become better known. The glossy television image of the evangelist with an upraised Bible had turned plastic. I wanted Billy to rejoin the fumbling, hurting, imperfect human race. His Christmas specials were a step in that direction, I thought, but they were only a beginning.

Later, I wondered why I had gotten into such a futile discussion, for nobody, including myself, had an answer.

The final Saturday-evening service unveiled another change, this one for the better.

No collection was taken.

Graham told his audience: "We have met our crusade budget. So tonight, we'll dispense with a collection. But we hope you will go to church on Sunday and give there what you would have given here. Or send a check to one of your own charities. Every city in the world has its needy and its hungry. I'm told Cincinnati has its share. I'm going to ask that you help them."

His appeal had been prearranged with civic leaders who made up the crusade committee. The newspapers carried lists of approved charities and copies of the list were available at the Coliseum.

What was Graham's motive? Two claims have always bugged itinerant evangelists: first, the charge that they take a potful of money out of a community, and second, that they are obsessed with saving souls at the expense of serving suffering humanity. Knowing Graham, I am certain he would not have taken such an action without much prayer. Graham sending his audience out to give to its neighbors certainly must have discomfited many critics.

He was not using words, but deeds.

*Old Nehemiah and his wall*, I thought, *was a viable model, after all.*

As for the evangelist, I had not spoken to him directly, except for a brief hello. Over the years, I had learned that he gives himself utterly to the preparation of his crusade sermons. In our earliest contacts, he would often talk to me politely and then forget that we had even discussed a subject. Before preaching, his mind would be miles away. Afterwards, he would be damp with perspiration, often exhausted mentally and physically. So I stayed away, leaving his time free for local leaders and newsmen.

His next crusade would be in Las Vegas in late January 1978; surely as unlikely a sounding board for hallelujahs as might be found in this hemisphere. I promised myself to attend every service, to talk to his assistants, local pastors, and volunteer workers, and to those who came forward to profess their faith. I would try to squeeze them dry of the details of the nuts-and-bolts activities and the interpersonal relationships that undergird a crusade.

The phone rang as I packed my bags to leave Cincinnati. An official of BGEA, who was also an old friend, said: "We're holding our association's semiannual retreat in January, at Montego Bay in Jamaica. We rest and play and study the Bible. The staff and the team and the board of directors will be there. They're coming from all over the world. And Ruth and Billy, of course. Maybe you and your wife could join us."

I tried to hide my elation. "Thanks," I said. "I'll check our schedules and let you know."

# 3

# The Miracle of Montego Bay—1

*We took sweet counsel together, and walked unto the house of God in company.*

Psalms 55:14

Every two years, Billy Graham and his evangelical association pause in their meteoric reaching out for God, to draw deep and steadying breaths. I witnessed such a pause in January of 1978.

The year 1977 had been one of Graham's busiest. He had led crusades in Stockholm, in Manila, in Hungary, in India, and in the United States at South Bend, Asheville, and Cincinnati.

Major campaigns lay ahead in 1978: Las Vegas, Memphis, Toronto, Kansas City, Oslo, Stockholm, and a half-dozen crusades in Poland. Then there would be Singapore and Sydney, Australia.

All of these involved Billy's presence and preaching, but there is more to the Billy Graham Evangelistic Association than its leader. Its world-wide activities include offices in Kyoto, Berlin, Hong Kong, Singapore, and elsewhere. Team members are working on the continents of Africa, South America, Asia, Europe, and Australia. Their jobs are to see that the Gospel is preached by radio, television, films, in the local-language editions of *Decision* magazine and other BGEA publications, and by their own personal appearances.

Then, dotting the United States and the rest of the world are the foot soldiers of this vast army of crusaders: the men, women, and children who contribute their prayers and send in their contributions to pay for Graham's radio and TV time, print materials, movies, and to help finance crusades in Europe, Asia, Africa, and South America. Their name is legion, and their "caring and sharing," as Cliff Barrows puts it during crusade telecasts, provide the underpinnings for all else.

The quality of their loyalty has amazed Graham for years and evoked his deepest appreciation. Even when things were blackest, he said, with awed wonder: "The support that people have given us and the way they have rallied behind us this year has been truly amazing. We give God the glory and the praise and the honor."

Graham had issued a call to his scattered team in the late summer. It was needed and appreciated. Two full years had passed since their last consultation. Many of them were feeling that the mountains lying across their paths were higher and the trails upward more difficult to negotiate than ever. But a larger view would show that many BGEA workers had won significant victories over the last twenty-four months. Their reports would surface day by day, and all would be eager to share their joy with their brothers and sisters.

I was delighted that my wife and I were invited to attend this private conference. I believed that I knew, better than any outsider, what Billy Graham and his several hundred employees and his board of directors did with their time. But I also felt that it is not what you *do* that counts in the Christian equation: it is what you *are. Perhaps*, I told myself, *some insights would be forthcoming in Montego Bay.*

## Montego Bay

When we decided to accept his invitation to join his "family reunion," I was puzzled by why Billy had chosen such a site as the tropical island of Jamaica.

The choice was logical—even inspired—I learned. Graham had wanted a location in the Third World, yet one reasonably close to home. Geographically, Jamaica is located about midway between East Africa and South Korea, but it is close to the bulk of Graham's organization's members and those support workers stationed in Minneapolis.

It also offered a suitable meeting place in a giant Holiday Inn. William Walton, vice-chairman of the Holiday Inn corporation and a recent addition to the BGEA board of directors, made the inn available to Billy.

Jamaica is a warm place, too—or so Graham hoped—which might offer respite to some of those who had gone through the deep, deep winter of 1977–78. Altogether, it was a perfect setting. Team workers would feel that they were at a neutral crossroads, threatened neither by cultural shocks nor boredom.

As we debarked from the Air Jamaica plane that carried us from Miami to Montego Bay, I heard voices speaking English, German, Spanish, and French, and I saw faces of many nations. Later, I would meet their owners, for on that day all roads seemed to lead to Montego Bay.

A taxi of antique vintage bounced us along a curving coastal road between a frothy Caribbean Sea and undulant spines of flat-topped hills. A half-dozen miles away, we found the inn, immense and sprawling, a warren of cement boxes tumbled among groves of palm and frangipani. Inside, we saw familiar faces from many crusades and distant climes, smiling and remembering and welcoming us.

Billy and Ruth Graham had been among the earliest arrivals. They came directly from crusades in Manila and India, to gain a few days of rest as guests of their old friends, Johnny Cash and June Carter Cash, who own a hacienda in the highlands.

Other advance arrivals were members of the BGEA executive committee and its board of directors, who would help Billy with his long-range plans for future projects.

Two minor problems immediately complicated the evangelist's life. The first was a misunderstanding on the part of local Christians, who thought he had come to their island to conduct a crusade. Delegations of pastors and laymen visited the inn, to ask how they could get tickets for the bus loads of church members they were already organizing. With difficulty, Graham explained that this was a workshop open only to delegates—he called it a world missionary working session—and promised that one day he or Leighton Ford or Stephen Olford would come back to preach for the Jamaicans.

The second problem was the weather. It rained. January in Jamaica is supposed to be a time of clear skies and balmy breezes. It poured. Native Jamaicans said they had never seen such rain. Surely, God planned it that way, for the arriving delegations were thrown back from the beaches and the tennis courts, into committee and conference rooms, where they renewed old ties and lifted one another's spirits.

Crusaders are human, and they grow tired as the pressures of successive campaigns weigh on their shoulders. In temperate Jamaica, they could review their work, refresh their spirits, restore their strength, and recommit their hearts.

Billy had decided that this assembly would be unorganized, by previous standards—no outside speakers or distinguished guests. Instead, these warriors would enjoy a time of fellowship—like a family reunion—with the BGEA family and a few of their close friends.

### Why Are We Here?

Almost everybody knows Billy Graham, the evangelist of the spotlighted pulpit and the TV screen. Almost nobody knows Billy Graham, the pastor of the Billy Graham Evangelistic Association.

Every orator has a style which, I believe, is a combination of his essential personality plus certain learned skills. All of us are familiar with Graham's flashing eyes, soaring gestures, and machine-gun delivery. But he was a different man in Jamaica, a delightfully different man. In Montego Bay, he became a shepherd.

The first working session was held after dinner on the day of our arrival. The venue was a medium-size auditorium with a raised stage at one end. A piano and a lectern occupied the usual places. Wearing large-print badges, delegates streamed through doorways, found old friends, and coalesced into joyful clusters. Ruth and Billy Graham, Bev Shea, George Wilson, Leighton Ford, Cliff Barrows, Grady Wilson, T. W. Wilson, Walter Smyth, and several BGEA board members waited casually in front-row seats.

After the opening prayer and hymn, Billy went to the podium. His figure showed no trace of tiredness. His eyes were clear and warm. One sensed that this was meant to be a new beginning. His speaking style, when away from the pulpit, is a stimulating mix of personal anecdotes, observations, and musings.

"Why are we here?" he asked.

His answer rang out. "First of all, we're here for *fellowship*. This is not a Bible-study or Bible-teaching conference. Of course, there'll be some of that. But primarily it's a time when we get together every two years for fellowship. We don't get to see each other often enough!"

He looked out over his audience, seeing many unfamiliar

faces. Abruptly, he admitted that he knew far fewer than half of the people present, but he said he was going to get acquainted. "Because I'm going to be looking right down at your badge," he said, "trying to find out your name and match it with your face. And I hope you'll do the same with me."

His hand rose to his right lapel, groping for his own name tag, not finding it. "By the way," he blurted. "Where is *my* badge? My wife handed it to me, but I don't know what I did with it."

Immediately, we all felt at ease.

By why *were* we here?

He had mentioned fellowship, and he mentioned it again, saying, "Sometimes we feel isolated." He quoted the Apostle Paul, who had said, ". . . I . . . come unto you with joy by the will of God, and may with you be refreshed" (Romans 15:32).

"The second reason," he said, "is to hear reports and ideas. We're going to find out what has happened, and we're going to make plans for the next two years, if God gives us two more years.

"The third reason is to speak about a *new* vision," he said emphatically. "For the thrilling work of God goes on now in a way we never dreamed possible. A few years ago, we were one of the very few parachurch organizations with a world-wide ministry. Today, we're just one of many that God has raised up and is using, and thank God for every one of them. He has given *us* the ministry of radio, television, the printed page, and our crusades, *and I do not see any diminishing of that ministry whatsoever.*

"George Wilson told me, just a moment ago," Graham said, "that today—this Monday—brought in the largest amount of mail to our office in Minneapolis that we've ever had in one day in the history of our organization."

Billy turned to other matters. "I'm hoping this meeting will be an event to be remembered. We've talked about the 'Spirit of

Lausanne' which emerged from that great conference. I hope, when we leave here, we will talk about the 'Spirit of Jamaica': that *something* will happen that we cannot foresee and cannot plan and cannot organize."

Momentarily, he spoke of himself, allowing his private yearnings to show. He had mentioned a new vision, a new spirit, but his personal need was for one of man's oldest desires. "I come to you, after preaching this year in many parts of the world, with a hungry heart that is asking God to do something new and fresh in my life, and to fill me to overflowing for the ministry that lies just ahead."

*What a declaration*, I thought. *What a revelation of inner need and soul hunger.* He had said it simply, humbly, without striving for effect.

But now it was time for the real business of the evening. Balancing behind the podium like a diver preparing for a plunge, he said bluntly, "Always, at these meetings, I have given the opening address. This year, I've felt led to ask Leighton Ford. . . ."

This was a big surprise.

Leighton Ford is a phenomenon. Twenty-two years ago, he joined the team as an inexperienced associate evangelist. A Canadian and something of a boy orator, he quickly became a favorite in crusades among his countrymen. When he fell in love with and married Jean Graham, Billy's sister, he cemented his hold on the affections of the entire family. Since then, he has grown intellectually and administratively, until today he is known around the world as one of Protestantism's leading churchmen. When Graham retires, Ford will probably assume the leadership of the Billy Graham Evangelistic Association.

Graham's introduction was affectionate and laudatory, and his audience, as always, enjoyed the peek he first offered into his offstage life.

"Leighton came into my room this afternoon," he said. "He noticed the notes I'd been making for my own address tomorrow night, and he said, 'Well, this is interesting. You're speaking on the same subject that I've chosen for my talk tonight!' Then he read a little farther, and he said, 'Why, we're even using the same text.' "

Pausing, he looked directly at Leighton, half-smiling, half-challenging, then added, "So I'm waiting now with great anticipation to find out what he's going to say. Leighton, you come on up here. . . ."

### A Time of Privilege

Leighton Ford walked deliberately to the pulpit. He is dark haired, while Billy is graying. They are about the same height. Ford carries himself like a long-distance runner, his balance slightly forward. He had recently attended two important meetings: one was a Lausanne continuation committee, another was studying future evangelical concerns. If Protestantism has a bona fide "futurologist," Ford surely qualifies.

He began to talk clearly and deliberately, easing himself into the mind of his audience. Among us, someone had told me, there were over one hundred ministers. That night, Leighton Ford was not an evangelist. Instead, he was a minister to ministers and their wives and to every one of the BGEA associates.

I had expected a discourse on goals, or on finances, or on conversions. My carefully kept notes remind me that he talked exclusively about *us*—the Billy Graham Evangelistic Association.

"All of us are here tonight," he said, "to ask the Lord to speak to us in a special way."

Next, he asked every person within the sound of his voice to repeat four words silently but sincerely: "Lord, speak to me;

Lord, speak to me; Lord, speak to me."

It was a humbling beginning.

And then, cooly and methodically, he began to demolish areas of complacency in me (I speak only for myself), of which I had been unaware.

"There are no experts on the history of the twenty-first century," he said. "We can think about it, but we don't *know*." Technology and rapid communications may continue to carry the Gospel over the world, or they might make it necessary for "totalitarian systems to take over. . . ."

He had read the reports of many futurologists, he said, and some claimed that our spirits "are halting and there's no hope." Others say we can lick our problems, but they all agreed there is "no hope whatsoever, apart from a spiritual renewal."

He quoted W. W. Harmon, of the Stanford Research Institute, who said that, "our society is like an alcoholic just before he joins Alcoholics Anonymous. He knows that his problems are beyond him. He knows another technological fix is not going to do the job."

Swiftly, he shifted to a spirited presentation of conditions right now—of today—and why we were sitting in that hotel auditorium.

"The thing I would like to underline," he emphasized, hands slashing the air in a Graham-like gesture, "is that you and I have been called to this association with the privilege of ministering the Gospel at one of the greatest periods in the history of Christianity. I hope that we sense that tonight. *We are now at a time of fantastic privilege.*"

*Wow!* I thought. I had been thinking that the world was a sorry mess, beset by strikes, revolutions, terrorism, political assassinations—utterly beyond helping. Everybody said so, including (if you read between the lines) the *New York Times*, *Newsweek*, and *Time*. But not this young evangelist. He called today—tonight—a time of fantastic privilege.

Others were as surprised as I. One could almost hear Ford's declaration, heavy with portent, rumbling around in their minds.

And he was willing to prove his point. He had done his homework well. In 1776, only 7 percent of the citizens of the United States were church members.

By 1850, the figure was 20 percent.

By 1900, it was 36 percent.

By 1977, it was close to 60 percent.

And we talk about the good old days. What good old days? These days, Ford clearly implied, are the best of all.

## We Are a Church

It must be obvious, to anyone who understands or has worked with group dynamics that, for many people at Montego Bay, the image of their organization needed polishing and their roles in it needed reinforcement. Many of them had been isolated in distant countries for two years. Physically and emotionally, many were exhausted. The recent barrage of bad news, criticism, and controversy had fractured their morale. That Monday evening they were asking, "Who are we, anyhow? What is *my* role?"

Ford told them: "We are not a business, though we have to do business. We are not a corporation, in the usual sense, though we are incorporated. We are a church," he declared. "And if we ever forget that, we're finished!"

He waved his Bible like a banner, quoting from Matthew 24:14 (RSV): " 'And this gospel of the kingdom will be preached throughout the whole world, as a testimony to all nations; and then the end will come.' The end will not come until that task is done." His eyes blazed suddenly with fervor, "There is a task to be done, and until that task is done, this association will not be through with the call that God has given us.

"Renew your devotion to Christ," he cried. "Review the works you have done. Always ask, what is God's plan for us?"

Friends tell me that they have never thought of Billy Graham's organization as a church. I think they should.

Historically, there have been two forms of the church. One form of church is what you might call the congregation. Another form is the missionary or evangelistic order, which exists for a specific task. The BGEA exists for a specific task. It is a missionary, evangelistic order. BGEA is a specially called, missionary evangelistic order—like the Franciscans, like the Jesuits, like the Salvation Army, in its early days.

Ford's aim that night was not only to stress the unparalleled seasons ahead and the shattering of ancient obstacles to evangelizing. He also pointed out the obligation of this small army of workers to take advantage of every opening.

Mentioning the uncertainty that shrouds the future, he said he did not know if today's response to the Gospel was an ingathering, to prepare the church for great tribulations, or if it signalled a period when the church would be revived and reformed, to take the Gospel to the ends of the earth. "But I do know this," he declared. "That God has made those of us gathered here tonight *entitled* people, with opportunities and open doors such as there have never been before."

But opportunity has two edges. "If we begin to take for granted all the blessings, advantages, and privileges we have, if we become smug," he said, "and if we become spiritually supercool, saying, 'Gee, look what we're doing!'—if that's our attitude, then our entitlement is going to be taken away from us, and we'll miss this great open door that God has given us. That's what He's called us to think about this week."

Leighton Ford has been described as an intellectual, a word that carries a connotation of superiority, of looking down one's nose at the world. But his urging that audience toward an attitude of service was eloquent and touching.

He was talking about the privileges God has given His people when he asked, "Have you ever thought about the style in which God became man? How did He do it? How would you have planned Christmas, if you had been writing the scenario?"

This is how Ford would have planned it. "I'd have had Jesus born in Rome. I'd have had the trumpets blare. He would have been born in a palace. Caesar would have been His father. That's how I would have done it.

"That's not how God did it. When God sent us His Son, He was born in an obscure village. His mother was a peasant girl. His first visitors were shepherds, the lowliest of the low. When His parents came to dedicate Him, they didn't even have the price of two lambs. They had to give two pigeons, instead. That was all they had. That's how God did it."

And how did Christ handle His entitlement, His divinity? "He humbled Himself. He made Himself nothing," Ford said. "And God became man. And the Lord became the servant of all."

In the total silence of that auditorium, his words turned into long-lashed whips, seeking and flaying the last remnants of selfishness to which many of us clung. I can still hear them:

"Why did He come and die and suffer?

"He who was rich became poor, that He might make you and me rich, and give to you and me abundant life. He humbled Himself, not that we might escape suffering, but as a guarantee of suffering.

"Paul says your attitude should be that of Jesus Christ. Being like Jesus means a self-emptying. When I find Jesus Christ in my life, I find *myself*. He didn't say 'hate yourself' or 'despise yourself'; He said '*deny* yourself.' For we are servants, brothers and sisters, and when we stop seeing ourselves as servants of Christ, then we are in trouble."

Over and over during that week of moral chastening, Christ-like humility was urged on us by every association leader. It was a large pill to swallow. No other organization on the globe had such a famous or influential leader. No other organization had such talented people, or had been granted such favor by God's children, or had been given so many tools with which to reach out in His name to claim the world.

Ford finished his address by reminding us that John Wesley, founder of the Methodist Church, had left a prayer that he had used on a New Year's Eve long ago.

"I'm going to ask that we bow in prayer," Ford said. "I'm going to read this prayer, and I'm going to pause. And I ask you to think, in this silence, of how you can make this prayer your prayer, in whatever way God leads, as we close tonight.

"Let the Holy Spirit speak to you. Pray the prayer honestly, sincerely, as He helps you. Just silently, not out loud, but in your heart, saying what you really mean."

He began to read:

"Father, I am no longer my own but thine . . . . Put me to whatever thou wilt . . . . Rank me with whomever thou wilt . . . . Put me to doing. Put me to suffering . . . . Let me be employed for thee, exalted for thee, or brought low for thee . . . . Let me be full. Let me be empty . . . . Let me have all things. Let me have nothing . . . . And now thou art mine and I am thine . . . . So be it . . . . And let the covenant which we have made on earth be ratified in heaven."

I am no clairvoyant. I do not read minds. But I doubt if there was a single person at Montego Bay who, having heard that address, was not a better person because of it.

# 4

# The Miracle of Montego Bay—2

*Count it all joy, my brethren, when you meet various trials, for you know that the testing of your faith produces steadfastness. And let steadfastness have its full effect, that you may be perfect and complete, lacking in nothing.*

James 1:2–4 RSV

"A conference like this could change your life," my wife said.

"People don't change," I replied.

But they do. I saw it happen.

The rain arrived on the second day and hung on for the early sessions. It advanced from the west, embracing sea and land with a slanting wall of water that pounded the waves flat, carved gullies in the beach, and laid siege to every rooftop nail hole and hollow. One day, while conferees were eating lunch, an air-conditioning vent surrendered to the unseasonable pressure and crashed to the floor, followed by a rusty jet stream that might have come from a water cannon. Drenched and stricken, delegates from five continents scrambled for their lives.

I have not mentioned the baggage debacle. Scores of us arrived without luggage, without toothbrushes, hair curlers, or our carefully folded polyester, no-iron slacks or dresses. Three days is a long time to wait for such amenities.

Everyone's holiday in the sun became a good-natured coping

game. Schedules were hurriedly shuffled so that rainy after-noons, originally penciled in for anticipated rest and recreation, became working sessions. We looked forward to a sunny period, when an entire day might be dedicated to much-needed rest and relaxation.

As in any crowd situation, frustrations easily surfaced. One heard them spoken of in the crowded corridors and hallways and at coffee breaks. That first full day, my own nerve ends, sharp-ened by several months of exposure to anti-Graham propaganda, felt discordant vibrations from some of the campaigners.

We would meet and trade small talk, and then the frustration would spurt forth, in accents originating from Australia or Scan-dinavia, from Japan or the southern boondocks.

"We've sure been catching it lately."

"I know."

"They're calling us swindlers."

"Yes."

"Well, that's how the devil works. They didn't get anywhere criticizing our crusades—too many people saw them on TV. So now they're lying about Billy himself."

Sometimes I'd ask, "Who are *they?*"

Their answers were shrugs, a masking glaze of the eyes, and shoulders that slumped. Their answers were those of tired men and women who had traveled thousands of miles to recharge their batteries and were finding the power lines down.

Billy Graham addressed them the second night. All day they had listened to reports and introductions. His address had been scheduled to follow an afternoon of rest and sunshine. Instead, it followed a long morning session and a long afternoon session, in the clammy atmosphere of a tropical monsoon.

Graham's mission was clear-cut. This army was disheartened. The sweet smell of success had faded, for they had read an-tagonistic headlines in the secular and the religious press. Now, they hungered for reassurance and for whatever other rewards persuade men and women to exert themselves beyond the call of duty.

So far, the assemblage was a standard, industry-type situation. You have a product, and you have salesmen. Salesmen must believe in both their product and in themselves. So far, it was a perfect setup for the application of the "go-go" philosophy of increasing production. If you want a man to add to his productivity, give him the "Triple-R" treatment: Recognition, Responsibility, Reward. These three Rs have turned many a sputtering production line into a cornucopia of results. Big business sings its praises. That is what I expected from Billy Graham the second night in Jamaica.

But instead of following the route of traditional psychology, which holds that man's basic drive is to increase his pleasure and decrease his pain, he laid a course that followed Paul through Asia Minor. He discussed the seven churches to which the Apostle John was directed to write letters concerning their specific weaknesses.

Billy Graham began by telling us that a little voice had been speaking to him all across India, saying: "When you speak to the team, this is what you are to say."

He confessed to having one little problem—he had a cold. "Last Saturday," he said, "I could barely speak above a whisper. Now, the hoarseness is coming back." Nevertheless, he opened his Bible and read several passages from the first three chapters of the last book of the New Testament, Revelation. Within minutes, we were up to our eyes in mysteries, symbols, and metaphysics.


### Light Bearers to the World

I've talked to salesmen by the hundreds, trying to exhort and encourage. In my experience, never has anything except eyeball-to-eyeball confrontation obtained results. Though I was attending that conference as an observer, I wanted Graham to succeed in reinvigorating his army. I wanted those wonderful, friendly, patient, confused people to realize their importance and significance, and I wondered if this lesson from Revelation was the way to go.

Graham suddenly interrupted himself, saying, "I'm going to ask that we bow in prayer."

His supplication was exactly two sentences long: "We pray tonight, that the people assembled here will not be conscious of the preacher but that they may be conscious of the Lord Jesus Christ. We thank Thee for the revelation of Himself that we have just read, and we thank Thee for the messages to these churches, which are so relevant to us, as an organization and as individuals, tonight."

Resuming his discourse, he identified the new young churches that received letters. Young as they were, he said, the devil was already at work in them. In all churches, his strategy was the same. First he used persecution, harassment, and suffering. Then he caused intellectual confusion through false teachers, prophets, and cults. This was followed by moral delinquency, a consequence of accepting sub-Christian ethical standards.

The churches Billy Graham described were in Asia Minor. The churches his discourse called to my mind were in modern America. The strategies of the devil rarely change.

Abruptly, he outlined his own recent ministry and his crusades in Gothenberg, Notre Dame, and Manila. "Wherever we have been," he stated, "I have sensed these three strategies of the devil at work.

"And I believe that this study, of the message of our Lord to the seven churches, is designed to bring revival and purification to any church, parachurch organization, or individual who loves the Lord. . . ."

He returned to Revelation's symbolism of the lamp stands and

the stars. "Now, both stars and lamps diffuse light," he said.
"This means, to me, that the churches and the followers of
Christ are to be light bearers in the darkness of the world.

"Ye are the light of the world. . . . Let your light so shine
before men, that they may see your good works, and glorify your
Father which is in heaven" (Matthew 5:14, 16).

His eyes embraced row upon row of listeners, and he said
slowly, "The question I would ask at this time is: Are *you* bearing the light, the reflected glory of the Lord Jesus Christ, in your
life, in your family, in your ministry?"

I began to relax, feeling more at ease, trying to put myself into
the shoes of his foot soldiers. If I was supposed to be a light
bearer—if that is what those stars and candlesticks in Revelation
meant—perhaps I could better identify my strengths and weaknesses, as well as those of the Billy Graham Evangelistic Association.

The first church he discussed was at Ephesus. Its error,
Graham said, was in abandoning its first love. What was its first
love? "I think it was primarily their love for the souls of men,"
he said. He talked about an Ephesian congregation that had lost
its original enthusiasm for telling the story of salvation to its
neighbors.

He was talking about the Ephesians, but he was also talking to
Christians everywhere. In particular, he was talking to every
man and woman who drew a paycheck from the treasury of
BGEA. Hang on to your first love, he warned. Never lose your
zest for being soul savers.

He told of an incident on the plane that had brought him and
Ruth Graham to Jamaica. A stewardess had delivered a note,
asking if she could speak to them. He said yes.

"She came and knelt down, and tears started streaming down
her face. She said, 'I'm crying because I'm so happy. Yesterday,
I found Jesus Christ as my Saviour. I've studied the religions of

the world, and I bought a Bible and became convinced that Jesus was the only one who could meet the needs of my heart and soul. Yesterday, I accepted Him all by myself. For you to be on my plane today confirms my decision.'

"She was an evangelist right there, for people all around were listening," he cried. "If we lose that first love for souls, Jesus said He would remove His power from us."

He paused, letting the thought penetrate. "And I'm asking myself this week," he continued searchingly, "will we, in this little conference, hear the voice of the Lord?

"No organization, neither BGEA nor any other, has a permanent place in the world. Christ said, 'Renew the works you used to do, or I'll take my power from you.'

"What does that say to us today?"

Having made this point, he turned to the condition of the other churches.

The church at Smyrna was being persecuted, and its people were suffering.

The church at Pergamos had compromised its beliefs.

The church at Thyatira had compromised its morals.

The church at Sardis was threatened by spiritual deadness.

The church at Philadelphia was passive.

The church at Laodicea was complacent.

And it was clear that every one of those churches presented a pattern of an affliction that could also corrupt the Billy Graham Evangelistic Association. We humans all suffer, grow cold and stale, lose our enthusiasm, become complacent and passive. The parallel was inescapable.

The only sound in that great hall was the soft shuffling of many feet as I listened, revising my estimate of the suitability of Revelation as a spiritual stimulant.

As Graham dissected those early churches, certain items emerged that must be mentioned. For example, as he expounded on the suffering of those Smyrnian churchmen, I began to wonder if he might be talking to himself.

Or about himself.

"It was a dangerous thing to be a Christian in Smyrna," he said. "They were a poor people. . . . And then there was slander. Tongues were wagging busily. False rumors were circulating.

## A Spiritual Battle

"When some of those things came out this summer, which some of you have read, I talked to my son at the university," he reminisced. "He said, 'Dad, you shouldn't even think about it. You know where these lies are coming from, don't you?'

"I asked, 'What do you mean?'

"He said, 'Well, who's the father of lies?'

" 'The devil,' I said.

" 'So that's where they're coming from,' he told me. 'You're in a spiritual battle.'

"Jesus said, 'Fear none of those things which thou shalt suffer.'

"I am a coward," Graham stated abruptly, wondering if he could stand up against modern torture. "Would I deny my Lord?" he questioned. "I've almost asked the Lord to preserve me from that trial. Yet, if that's God's will for me, that's what I want. Yet"—a thoughtful pause—"I don't want it."

His puzzled eyes searched his Bible, seeking renewed strength. "Blessed are ye, when men shall revile you, and persecute you, and say all manner of evil against you falsely, for my sake," he read triumphantly. "Rejoice, and be exceeding glad; for great is your reward in heaven. . . ."

I was thinking of the hurt that must have clutched his heart after reading those newspaper headlines which challenged his character and his integrity the previous June.

"What about your own heart?" he asked us. "Is God taking you through some testing period now?"

The other cities of Asia Minor followed, in a swift sequence of analogies. His certainty and authority resonated like the ringing of a bell.

"The church at Sardis," Graham said, "was an empty shell, a spiritual graveyard. Could it be that the Billy Graham Association will someday become a gigantic deception?

"What would Jesus say to us tonight, if He were here?"

He told of crisscrossing America and Europe, of seeing great churches, universities, and seminaries, and of seeing the boards and the bureaus, and the hundreds of cathedrals that once had the purpose of honoring God. Now, many of them are dead, empty—their power gone.

"The lamp stand has been removed," he said. "And maybe, in recent years, God has been raising up all these parachurch organizations to say something to the churches, because the work that we [BGEA] do could be done by the church.

"And that's the reason we've worked with the church from the very beginning. We've joined hands with the church to try to strengthen and help the church. We've been a failure in many ways. We've looked for every method possible to conserve [our converts].

"But God told the church at Sardis to repent, or He would remove His power."

His sixth church was Philadelphia. It represented the opportunities that lay open to evangelism. "There's a door opened that no man can shut," he said. "This Gospel must be preached into all of the world, then shall the end come.

"You know," he said, "I believe that right now the Gospel is being preached in all the world."

The church at Laodicea was complacent. It was also rich,

powerful, and pompous. Those qualities were not enough.
Graham quoted Zechariah: ". . . Not by might, nor by power,
but by my spirit. . . ."

"We have money and computers and gadgets, and almost everything in the church or in our association could be done au-
tomatically. We can send it up to George Wilson [executive
vice-president in Minneapolis] and get it done by automation,"
he said, "but it would be like the dry bones of Ezekiel."

Graham's voice had weakened under the stress of his long
address, but his seven churches had been projected, examined,
and prescribed for.

"We need the breath of God and the presence and power of
the Holy Spirit," he said. "I believe the Holy Spirit is moving
throughout the world, and we must be in step with Him.

"Let the listener hear what the Spirit says," he concluded.

I walked back to my room, digesting the message and ponder-
ing its impact. Graham's points were impressive. The response
to them, I felt, was lackadaisical. I wondered why.

The day had been long.

Many still suffered from jet lag.

We Americans have never learned the art of public self-
examination.

Perhaps I had expected too much.

That night, I reread the first three chapters of Revelation. The
voice "like a trumpet," which had given instructions to John for
the correction of the churches, had provided an amazing pattern
for the curing of modern waywardness. Graham had used it well,
but I had missed it. The "one like a Son of man," who dictated
to John, had first *praised* those erring churches, citing their
splendid but flawed virtues before naming their transgressions.

"I have a few things against you," Graham had told his workers, including himself in his faultfinding. That night I found myself wondering why he had not spoken more about the associa-

tion's assets, about its people, who were both gifted and holy.

My notebook contains an entry for that evening that reads: "I have now heard from the big guns of BGEA for one day and two nights. Their summons to holiness and discipleship is direct and without compromise. I am impatient to hear from the foot soldiers. Graham's ministry, once limited to preaching, now circles the world. This motel is full of colorful and courageous globetrotters. I need to hear from them."

Next day, I did.

### Incandescent Men and Women

George Wilson, who is BGEA's executive vice-president, once told me, "God is able to do exceedingly abundant, above all that we see or think, for any cause that glorifies Him and is supported by prayer."

My journey to Jamaica provided an exceedingly abundant demonstration. Evidence came from the lips of speaker after speaker—in snippets of information, inspiration, anecdotage, and wisdom.

Wilson, who has been described as looking more like a tycoon of industry than an evangelist, chose to talk to us about the national media blitz against BGEA's alleged financial secrecy. He explained in detail how every misunderstanding had been clarified and settled, including the Minnesota Securities Commission snafu, the Better Business Bureau flap, and the national press's misreading of the purpose of WECEF in buying North Carolina mountain land for a Bible school.

He said the board of directors of BGEA had already voted to publish an annual financial report, prepared by certified public accountants, of the kind issued annually by such corporations as Exxon, General Motors, and IBM. The report would reveal the income and expenditures of BGEA and all of its related ministries. (The 1977 report was issued in the summer of 1978.)

"I saw a bumper sticker the other day," he concluded. "It said, 'America ain't perfect, but we ain't done yet.'

"We've made mistekes in BGEA, and we're going to make more, but *we ain't done yet.* God still has a job for us to do."

The association had a new president. Introducing him, Billy Graham first explained how BGEA is governed. It has a board, consisting of approximately twenty-five members, which meets two or three times a year. It has an executive committee of seven, which usually meets every two months.

Both groups had met in Jamaica the weekend before I arrived. Allan Emery, Jr., was elected president of the board. George Bennett, former treasurer of Harvard University, was elected treasurer.

"I have been praying," Billy said, "that the Lord would send someone to be president of our association. I have been praying I'd be relieved of the responsibility, so I could give more time to preaching and writing, because I feel called of God to continue this crusade evangelism . . . .

"Allan Emery, we believe, was sent of God . . . ."

Allan Emery's theme was that you only could know a person when you knew what he longed for, so he spoke of some of the members of the BGEA executive committee in those terms. To me, they had always been faceless businessmen. Afterwards, they were important and vital humans, with significant ambitions—people to whom one could relate. I was agreeably surprised to learn that the executive committee included some of America's most respected industrialists.

Allan Emery spoke on other subjects, too, but what he said of his associates on the BGEA board made a deep impression. His final words were typical: "I believe there's no greater honor in this life than that of taking up the role of a servant, as our Lord did. Our responsibility is that of support and encouragement . . . . Count on us to be available to you, to pray for you, and to support you in every way we can, until Jesus comes. Amen."

Throughout each day, speakers seemed to alternate between thought and action. "How do we look at ourselves?" Leighton Ford had asked. Hudson Amerding, president of Wheaton College, echoed that thought, demanding that we look at ourselves as slaves of Jesus Christ.

Early in the week, Billy introduced Howard Jones, the first black person to join the team. "It made quite a stir among Christians," he said. "But Howard had the courage to come and be a loner for a while. And we have come to love him, to know him, to travel with him, to live with him. I don't think we have more effective witnesses for Christ than Howard and Wanda Jones."

Then, showing the extent to which this program was unplanned, he said, "I'm going to ask Howard to give us a report and speak on whatever the Lord has laid on his heart to say to us."

Jones's first comment was a personal reaction: "I want to say I believe I could leave for home tomorrow with a new vision of Jesus Christ, and a new sense of dedication to the ministry to which God has called me."

He told next of an incident in his personal ministry. He had been invited to a locker-room meeting with the Cleveland baseball team. One of their members was first baseman Andre Thornton, a Christian. Shortly after their conversation, Thornton and his wife and two children were driving on a turnpike. They ran into a blizzard and hit ice. Their van overturned, and Mrs. Thornton and a baby daughter were killed. Thornton and his five-year-old son lived. Jones read the news and called the ball player.

"Brother, I need your prayers," Thornton told him. "I need some counsel from the Word."

Jones paused thoughtfully. "You know, the Lord has taught me a lesson. Please understand what I'm trying to say. Sometimes, we preachers get too concerned with the crowds. And sometimes God has to show us that there are *individuals* that are hurting—people who have needs—people who are in grief and sorrow. So these past weeks, I've been ministering to this dear brother, and I want you to pray for him.''

The recurring theme of the week in Jamaica was emphasized in some small or large way every day. Dr. John W. Williams, a black member of the board of BGEA, did it in a large way. His address was about the all-sufficient power of God's grace.

Dr. Williams is pastor of the Saint Stephen Baptist church of Kansas City, vice-president of the National Association for the Advancement of Colored People, and chairman of the Billy Graham crusade in Kansas City in 1978. He is a powerful man, a shaker and a mover, a man whose words can thunder.

Years ago, John Williams was a rising young evangelist with a great future, with plenty to boast about. God gave him a thorn in his flesh.

He lost his voice.

A tonsil operation failed to help. A second operation on his vocal cords made matters worse. ''My voice went away to nothing,'' he said. ''I cried and I prayed night and day, asking God to restore me, but nothing happened.

''I said, 'You called me to preach, God. Please help me now.' '' And God did help him, enabling Williams ''to do a greater work with a broken-down voice than I'd been able to do before.''

But he prayed to God harder than ever. ''One Sunday, in Corpus Christi, Texas,'' he told us, ''I was speaking, and when it looked like I was about to be carried away, my voice suddenly came back to me.

''I want to tell you it was a joy for God to use me again. And that's when I found out what God's grace means. I thought I already knew, but I found out then what it *really* means.

''God always has a higher remedy.''

Finally, he told of the Indian boy who wanted to be a brave. A requirement was for him to spend a night alone in the forest. Time after time he put it off, but finally he decided to do it. So he walked into the dark forest, hearing the roars and screams of wild animals. His skin crinkled with fear, and he crouched behind a tree, sobbing out his terror. As dawn broke, he heard the snapping of a twig behind him, and he spun around, his heart leaping. He saw his father there, with an arrow in his bow. In relief, he shouted, "Father, what are you doing here? How long have you been here?"

His parent said, "I've been here all through the night, son. I was watching over you."

Williams reached out his arms until they seemed to embrace every member of that BGEA gathering. "I want to tell you something," he said. "Out in the forest of life, God's grace is watching over us. Do what He says, and every time you look around, He'll be there."

As if spurred by a sudden thought, he ordered us—*ordered* us—to reach out and touch somebody and say, simply, "God is here."

And every man and woman in that audience obeyed, leaning forward to a person in the row ahead, turning to the person behind, or reaching out to people on both sides. Some of us did it swiftly, some eagerly, some shyly, some hopefully. All of us did it.

And the soft sound that filled that auditorium was like the crashing of surf on an endless beach, even a surf that spoke with secret tongues, saying, "God is here. . . . *Here* . . . . HERE . . . ."

### Going Where the People Are

A condition for which I was not prepared—one of which I had not even been aware—was the extraordinary global outreach and commitment of the Billy Graham organization. If I had not gone to Jamaica, I probably would never have known of it.

In a nutshell, one can safely say that the sun never sets on the Graham ministry. Nor does an hour ever pass, I am told, without someone, somewhere, listening to his messages through radio, television, motion picture, a team member, or Billy Graham himself.

The responsibility is awesome.

BGEA international offices are situated in Buenos Aires, Sydney, Winnipeg, London, Paris, Frankfurt, Hong Kong, Tokyo, Mexico City, and Madrid. Each office is incorporated and directed by concerned local people. They raise funds, direct the publishing of *Decision* magazine, show and produce films, and cooperate in international crusades. Each office is autonomous and keeps its own books, but the American BGEA has organized it, partially subsidizes it, and takes no revenue in return. The financial goal of each office is, of course, to become fiscally independent.

Sam Jones, a vigorous young Christian, told us of the activities of the Billy Graham office in Hong Kong. A major activity is the distribution of *Decision* magazine to subscribers in twenty-one Asiatic countries and to distribution centers in ten other countries. This *Decision* is a special edition, edited for the area served.

The Hong Kong office handles movies, too. *The Hiding Place* enabled it to make an important breakthrough. At first, no theater owner would book it. Finally, one exhibitor took a chance. In one week, almost 25,000 people saw the movie. After expenses, it turned a profit of $7,000.

"The border to China is totally closed," Jones said in this 1978 message. "But a day is coming when it must open. And when the walls come tumbling down, we must be ready to go in. Our work in Hong Kong is very strategic.

"Even now, we know people in China who are actively engaged in church work. We cannot mention their names, but we manage to get certain articles to them from time to time, to help them in their work. Please pray for this ministry.

"The church all over China is very active. This is happening all over Asia. They work in small groups and cells. Six months ago, I went to North Borneo, and a missionary asked me if I would like to go to church. That Sunday, he took me to four different churches. One met in a factory, one in a bookstore, one in a church basement. All were secret churches. This was North Borneo, but it is also happening in Rangoon, Jakarta, and other places. Secret Christians are meeting secretly. They need your prayers."

And I thought of the great churches of America, many of them half-empty on Sunday and totally empty during the week, whose members have shifted to Sunday golf, or watching football, or sunbathing, or camping. Humanistic ideas have persuaded so many of us that we can worship God adequately in His woods and waters, that church has become an anachronism. I think not. Fellowship with other Christians is as essential today as it was when Paul established his first church.

Ken McVety is Graham's man in Tokyo. He told us that Japan is a nation "of full hands and empty hearts, rich, but without God." His all-Japanese office hums with activity. One monthly chore is the publication of *Ketsudan No Toki,* which means *Decision* magazine, with every word printed in Japanese. He told us about an extraordinary Japan-produced evangelistic motion picture called *Shiokari Pass,* which pastors and missionaries call the best means ever for reaching non-Christians. Significantly, its exhibition in theaters turned a profit of $150,000, which was used for other evangelistic work.

My space, my time, and my talents are inadequate to describe the many miracles about which we heard from the association's front-line fighters. Every continent, and many countries of the free world, has its separate board of directors, staff, and programs. All seek to preach the Gospel in whatever way is compatible with the laws and culture of their community.

India offers a striking example.

Dr. Abdul Akbar Haqq first joined Billy Graham over two decades ago. Since then he has worked mostly in that subcontinent, with its 600 million people, its 550,000 villages, and its 2,000 towns and cities.

Christianity is as old in India as it is in Rome. Mahatma Gandhi's policy of nonviolence was borrowed from Jesus. When India was partitioned and a million refugees were butchered, her Christian churches helped both Muslim and Hindu sides. Dr. Haqq was one of the helpers.

"We were not afraid. We were drunk with the Spirit of God," he told us. "Millions of Hindus, Sikhs, and Muslims are alive today because of the work of Christians. They'll never forget the strange man [Jesus] who could inspire persons to give their lives serving mankind.

"I want you all to know," he exclaimed suddenly, "that Billy Graham and the Billy Graham Association are carrying evangelism right into the Third World. This is not being done by anyone else. And it takes some doing. You must be nervous each time you stand up to preach. But we must go back and then go back again, because harvesting time has come."

Signs of another harvesttime were also visible in South America. Norman Inoska is one of three BGEA ambassadors who serve South Americans. He and his wife have been missionaries for twenty years. He told us of preaching in Peru at a church which had grown from a membership of exactly one person to over twelve hundred in just two years.

"We spoke a year ago in a Roman Catholic church in the city of Bogota," he said. "Many of the town's first families were there. At our invitation, over two hundred and fifty persons came forward. This is unprecedented."

He told of showing a BGEA film *The Restless Ones* to eight hundred students at a girls' school. Exactly one-half, four hundred young women, confessed their acceptance of Jesus Christ as Saviour at the film's conclusion.

John Dillon, director of associate crusades, reported on the last seven years of his ministry.

In seven years, the nine associate evangelists had gone everywhere. Each was accompanied by a team of BGEA musicians and crusade coordinators. Often, music teams went ahead to prepare the way. Congregations and choirs were organized.

"During these years," Dillon said, "they have spoken in more than four hundred and fifty cities, to over eleven million persons."

I read a list of their revivals, a list as long as my arm, naming big and little cities: Anchorage, Alaska; Enid, Oklahoma; Leamington, Ontario; Calicut, India; Salida, Colombia; Papua, New Guinea; Agana, Guam; Zion, Illinois; Cebu, Philippines; Umtali, Rhodesia; Swaziland, Africa; Thessaloniki, Greece; Grand Cayman, British West Indies; Burnie, Tasmania—and on into every quarter of the world.

Ralph Bell is an associate evangelist, a Canadian, and a black athlete who could have made it big in professional baseball or football, if he had not chosen to become a minister.

He landed at Guadalcanal in 1977 after Barry Berryman, BGEA's man in Australia, had brought island religious leaders together for the first time in memory. Guitarist Jimmy Mamou was his song leader.

Their first meeting was attended by one-third of the island's entire population. "That night, after I'd gone to bed," Bell said, "policemen knocked on my door. They'd been in uniform and on duty, handling the crowd. Now they wanted to give their lives to Christ."

The crusade moved to the island of Malaita, and though the

towns were smaller, the response was larger. Some inquirers
traveled over the sea for three days in open canoes. Others
tramped along mountain trails for seventy-two hours. Many
brought tape recorders so they could carry Bell's message back
to their villages.

"I'll always be grateful to BGEA," Bell told us, "for giving
me this opportunity to minister."

To be honest, I was astonished at the extent of this amazingly
ubiquitous ministry. Despite my long association with Graham's
major crusades, I had heard little about the associate
evangelists. Yet, Graham's associates had preached to 11 million
people. Surely, if newsmen want to expose Graham's "secret"
operations, they should mention the thousands of sermons delivered to eager audiences in those 450-plus communities.

But this record is just a beginning, Dillon explained. Hundreds
of single-church crusades are crying to be activated, a field that
is virtually untouched. How to do it best is a question being
explored by planners.

As in every Billy Graham crusade, each minicrusade community establishes its own budget, raises its own funds, pays its
bills, and reports to the public. Neither Billy nor any of his
associates accepts a love offering or a honorarium from any
speaking engagement. Musical teams and crusade specialists receive only their living expenses while in a crusade community.

Billy Graham frequently asserts that his ministries have met
with success not because he is a better preacher than those who
have preceded him, but because he has taken advantage of
technological advances in order to reach larger audiences.

Leighton Ford's address to us had stressed the use of the tools
that God had placed in BGEA hands and the innovative techniques that their men and women used to take the Gospel to
once-distant people. The missonary opportunity in South
America illustrates the point.

Chuck Ward, international TV coordinator, told us: "I remember many years ago, when my wife and I arrived in Venezuela as missionaries, and I was sent to the headwaters of the Amazon. My assignment was to help some primitive congregations in those river areas.

"It took about six days to get there. I went a short distance by airplane, then walked many miles. Next I rode in an ancient jalopy, and finally I traveled for four days in a dugout canoe, poling up the river.

"On the day I got there, I came down with hepatitis. And all this was to reach twenty or thirty people in that congregation, who were meeting in a palm-thatched hut. What a tremendous effort, and what a cost.

"In contrast, a month ago I sat down with one of our television men, and he told me he had just saturated the great nation of Brazil with the Gospel message through the TV personality of Billy Graham. We received thirty thousand letters in response to that one telecast."

Numbers do not tell the whole story, but I could not fail to calculate the difference in the effort expended and the audience reached. Since 1972, when Graham's international television ministry began, his BGEA team has broadcast the Gospel in ten languages in over fifty countries.

Basically, the problem of evangelism never changes. Always, it is how to reach non-Christians. Twenty years ago, people were inaccessible because of distance and lack of transportation. Today, they are inaccessible because of their new way of living. The forest's green jungle has turned into the gray jungle of concrete apartments.

"These great blocks of buildings are rising around the world," Chuck Ward said. "Many of them have electronically controlled doors and guards, which make it almost impossible for a person to reach these people."

But television is one tool that can be used. It penetrates the concrete jungle. "Rio is practically all apartment buildings," Ward said. "So is the heart of São Paulo. Many of those thirty thousand letters were from those cities."

Something else had happened in the Billy Graham ministry— something very big, which provided a thread that wove its way through almost every report and conversation to which I listened.

They called this happening "the little film." Its name was *The Hiding Place*.

Produced in 1974 and released in 1975 by World Wide Pictures, which is Graham's motion picture arm, *The Hiding Place* immediately attracted favorable attention. It dramatized Corrie ten Boom's book about her family's heroic fight to save hundreds of refugee Jews by hiding them in a secret room in their Haarlem attic during the Nazi occupation of Holland.

Sherwood Wirt, former editor of *Decision* magazine, saw *The Hiding Place* and wrote: "Ravensbruck is humanity's crucifixion, for there Betsie [Corrie's sister] dies along with 96,000 other women victims. . . . But the Resurrection is there also, for at the end Corrie is miraculously set free to enter upon a new life and ministry in the name of Jesus Christ."

Over two million copies of Miss ten Boom's gripping story were in print when the movie was made. Because it relentlessly depicted the barbaric behavior of Nazi troops in occupied Holland, some critics said that it would open old wounds. Its premier showing in Hollywood, in fact, was stink bombed by parties suspected to be American Nazis.

But in 1977, the film took off.

This extraordinary film has been translated into Spanish, Italian, French, and even Korean. It is being shown on college campuses, in prisons, in nursing homes, and in convalescent centers. In Australia, it is paving the way for Graham's 1979

Sydney crusade, and has been used to raise enough money to build a men's convalescent home.

Equally important is the psychological reaction of Graham's entire organization to the world's reception of this evangelistic tool. For many, it pumped new life into their missions. A Norwegian film representative, for instance, told us: "In 1976, I was so worn out physically and economically that I considered giving up this work. And then *The Hiding Place* happened. As a result, a door has been opened to evangelistic films, and I have even been begged by cinema proprietors to obtain more of them."

"Once we received a lot of criticism for using film to proclaim the Gospel, but the feeling gradually subsided," Graham once told me. "We cannot sit back and wait for the unchurched to come to us. We must go out to where they are. They are going to movies and theaters. And so must we, bearing a message. This was the method and plan of Christ."

But those break-through experiences were of the past. What of tomorrow? We heard discussions of proposed crusades in Las Vegas, Louisville, and Kansas City, and of journeys to Poland and Australia. A young Billy Graham and his team had visited "down under" in 1959 for a memorable series of meetings. Grady Wilson, an associate evangelist and one of Graham's closest friends, had written home, saying: "When Billy gave the invitation, people began streaming down the aisles. More than 3,000 came forward. Finally, Billy threw up his hands and said: 'Stop, ladies and gentlemen. There's no more room. If you want to give your lives to Christ, go home and drop me a letter, and we will send you literature.' "

Graham would be returning in 1979 for a crusade in Sydney. Barry Berryman, chief of the Australian office and crusade coordinator, told us of elaborate preparations: "We have a vision to build our Sydney crusade into an evangelistic thrust that will reach beyond our city limits to the countryside and to other states. Would you please pray for us?" he begged.

### Priestly Service

I had come to Montego Bay to renew my acquaintance with Billy Graham and the workers in his association. They were an extraordinary crew, which included such diverse personalities as Bible scholars, secretaries, jungle pilots, missionaries, TV technicians, and business executives.

The week had passed swiftly, satiating my eyes and ears. I had enjoyed marvelous fellowship, even though I was an outsider. Complete openness had been the rule. But I knew I had to probe much deeper than physical amenities and coffee-table chatter.

So what did the week's lectures tell me about the source of Graham's power? What had that to do with such modern intricacies of evangelism as currency exchange, UHF broadcasting, and chronic jet lag?

During the Montego Bay meeting, Kenneth Kantzer, the new editor of *Christianity Today*, added another seminal thought that, for me and many others, seemed to fill that dim auditorium like a great sunburst.

"We tend to be action oriented," he said. "We get things done. We like people who set out to do things and do them. But you know, Scripture reminds us that it is more important to *be* than it is to *do*," he said. "Our number-one concern is not what shall we *do*, but *what kind of person am I?* Do I love God? Does my heart overflow with a Godlike love for my fellow human beings?"

Kantzer's words came drumming across the rows of listeners as steadily as a rock beat, while his eyes pinned us all to our pasts. "This alone is what we are to hunt for," he declared. "Here lies the difference between biblical evangelism and scalp hunting. In one case, our supreme motive is another trophy—to dangle another scalp, spiritually speaking, from our belts. In the other case, we love God so supremely, and we love our fellow humans so desperately, that we cannot help but share with them the most wonderful thing we have ever known.

"I have only one life to live. I don't want to do the wrong thing with it. I want God to select my tasks by reaching down into my life. I want Him to lead me to do really worthwhile things, and to give me the gifts I need to do them."

He was speaking for all of us, as much as for himself.

"There's no other way," he added, "that I can be sure I'm spending my years on this planet doing the things that are most needed for Christ and for His kingdom."

I thought he had finished, but suddenly his long fingers closed in a symbolic gesture and squeezed us all into one single flesh, into one purposive force called the Billy Graham ministry. "It is interesting that God has not commanded us to have a gift," he concluded. "Rather, He has commanded us to serve and minister to each other, and He will *give* us the gifts we need. And then we can minister to our brothers and sisters in Jesus Christ and to the needy world out beyond. Amen."

As he turned from the lectern, a wind stirred in hundreds of throats, many people stood, and I heard the voices of men and women saying, "May it be so."

On the final Friday of the session, the crowd's adrenal glands must have been flowing like a millrace. The weather was superb. The sun beamed on us, and people beamed on one another. Christian laughter rounds out everything, and so the day ended, as always, with a prayer of thanksgiving, and then came the announcement that the final gathering would be a Saturday-morning communion service.

"Prepare your hearts," Billy Graham requested, suggesting that we pack our bags early, so there would be time for soul-searching. It was a wise injunction.

By nine o'clock on Saturday morning, every auditorium seat was occupied. Holiday clothing was replaced by tourist garb, tropical prints by double knits. The lobby below was jammed wall-to-wall with luggage. Soon, it would be winging to destinations across the seven seas.

The speaker was to be Roy Gustafson, an associate evangelist and friend of Graham since they were young Bible students at the Florida Bible Institute in Tampa. Gustafson had also conducted more than eighty groups of pilgrims through the Holy Land and taught Bible classes around the world. Introducing him, Graham said, "In the Middle East, the Jews think of Roy as a rabbi. The Arabs think of him as a joyous Christian. But nobody knows more than he does about conditions in that tortured part of the world."

His message fitted into this unstructured conference like a misplaced piece into a jigsaw puzzle. It made the whole intelligible. He talked about growing in grace, being born again, and priesthood.

He made it clear to us that this Saturday meeting was unique. We had assembled on other mornings as evangelists, pastors, secretaries, set-up men, and so forth.

"Today, we are here to worship," he said. "We're here as a family of priests. Listen. When we were born into Christ's family, we became part of a holy priesthood."

At the end of this address, Roy told of a Jamaican youth who had come forward at a plantation revival meeting. The boy could not read or write, but he wanted to know more about Jesus. So they told him. Then he asked to be baptized, and they baptized him.

"Finally, he came to the Lord's Table, as we're going to come to it this morning," Gustafson said. "He'd never been a worshiper before. Down here, they always stand when they pray, and when his turn came, he folded his hands together and looked up, and he said, 'O God, You is so sweet for giving me Jesus.' He repeated that three times, and then he sat down.

"That young fellow didn't know it, but *he* was a holy priest. He was a holy priest, and he was offering something to God—just those few words."

Victor Nelson, a senior member of the Graham team, moved to a chair behind a makeshift communion table.

"Victor is going to lead us," Gustafson said. "He won't officiate. Only *One* can officiate at this table, and He is present in our midst—our Lord Jesus Himself. Let's see if we can find something this morning that we can offer to Him that He'll be satisfied with."

So that plain, untidy upper room in a crowded Jamaican inn became a holy temple for a time, as priests served other priests, and we all broke bread together and sipped our hallowed wine from paper cups.

Following the sun westward, our plane raced toward Miami. Already we travelers were in another world. Some of us were pilgrims, some were survivors of an expensive vacation, others were ambassadors of commerce. Regardless, each of us was boxed in by invisible walls of self-concern. We fiddled nervously with briefcases, scribbled notes to ourselves, and attacked our personal projects.

My personal project was an examination of the secret mind of Billy Graham. Or, putting it another way, I was searching for the roots of his integrity. In short, was he a saint or a sinner?

After a week in Jamaica, what had I learned?

James Bond would not have been impressed by my investigative efforts. I had sat in conferences and committee meetings and seminars devoted almost exclusively to evangelical homilies. I had allowed myself to be warmed (and disarmed?) by brotherly love. The Bible calls it *agape,* which is a Greek word with the technical meaning of "love feast." Jamaica had been a love feast for every person I had met—of that I was certain.

So I was flying home from Montego Bay with empty hands. Empty-handed, yes. Empty-hearted, no. I had learned a new word, which prescribed a unique way of life. That word and that way of life had permeated every thought and every action of the scores of people with whom I had talked and walked and dined—yes, and prayed—all that week.

The word is *discipleship,* which means to walk in the footsteps of Jesus Christ.

Billy Graham's next crusade was just over the horizon, in the notorious pleasure dome called Las Vegas, Nevada. For eight feverish days, that crusade would be the focus of all that Graham and his people believed in, all that he stood for.

As our Whisperjet touched down in a blaze of sunset, I knew what I had to do.

I would follow, as closely as I dared, in the footsteps of those who followed in His footsteps. It would be an exciting journey.

# 5

# The Kamikaze Crusade

*Behold, I send you forth as sheep in the midst of wolves: be ye therefore wise as serpents, and harmless as doves.*

Matthew 10:16

The best way to approach Las Vegas is via a night flight.

As your plane crosses the mountains that form the saucer that is Las Vegas valley, you peer through the window into a soot-black pit. The plane circles and descends, and suddenly you are aware of a distant, glowing spot of color, like a ruby tossed onto a black blanket.

Coming closer, you see flame-colored tentacles shooting out from the faraway jewel, tracing city patterns that seem to float in a midnight fog. When the wind is right, your glide path parallels the incandescent roadway known around the world as the Strip. Its glow tells you that people are down there—working, playing, sleeping—but your senses are already numbed by a spectacle unlike any other on earth.

Gigantic electrical displays take shape below, spelling out familiar symbols of pomp and pleasure, then vanish. Caesar's Palace, the Sands, the M.G.M. Grand—their emanations bathe the faces of fellow travelers.

In the center of its dead desert, Las Vegas alone is alive, sucking into its rainbow flames such moths as dare its dangers.

The pilot's intercom crackles. "We are approaching the Las Vegas airport," he says. "Please fasten your seat belts."

Fasten your seat belts, indeed. For this is the world's greatest playground, the world's capital of entertainment. Here are hotels built like palaces, each lobby embracing jungles of slot machines, dice tables, and roulette wheels. Here live reputed criminal overlords. Here are the fabled holdings of the deceased Howard Hughes.

In sum, here is what millions of gamblers call Sin City, U.S.A. Its temples are furnished with every imaginable comfort, plus the accoutrements and hype of American eat-drink-and-get-lucky culture. Its priests are pimps and pitmen.

Las Vegas—precious jewel, fulminating sewer—or launching pad for a religious awakening that might sweep the world.

Public awareness of the Greater Las Vegas crusade began when, along every road leading into the city—the Tonopah highway, running from Reno; Interstate 15, shooting across from Los Angeles; Highway 15, from Salt Lake City; and Highway 93, from Kingman, Arizona—huge thirty-sheet billboards announced that evangelist Billy Graham was coming to town.

Although I had known Billy Graham for years and had learned to trust his prayer-based decisions, I wondered if maybe this time he had taken on too much. Here, if anywhere, was Satan's stronghold.

Why Las Vegas? Why, when in a single month his Minneapolis headquarters receives as many as 700 requests for crusades? Why, with only the support of a small and scattered band of Las Vegas churches, and after the Year of the Locust had already beset him, had he not canceled?

A successful crusade needs foot soldiers, who must be borrowed from hundreds of participating churches. The Billy Graham crusade in Anaheim, California, is an example. An army of 175,000 people was recruited there, to distribute literature by knocking on the doors of every home they could reach. Some 4,000 Bible-group leaders were trained, and 2,000 ushers were recruited. Householders opened their homes—4,600 of them—to weekly prayer meetings. Legions of choristers and counselors were assembled.

Here in Las Vegas, the churches, so many of them, were poor; they were weak; they were demoralized in the face of an enemy so much more numerous and powerful.

When he counted, Larry Turner, Graham's representative in Las Vegas, found he could depend on only 115 churches—a handful, compared to other cities. Three out of four of these had fewer than 200 members.

In the words of the Reverend Ken Forshee, pastor of the First Christian Church and a living example of what old-timers called "a great man of God," the situation was desperate.

"Our church size is small," he said. "The image of the church is small. The images of the churchman and the pastor are small. Because of those small images, the pastor finds himself relegated to a small role in the community, and to thinking of himself as having small responsibilities. To be blunt, three-quarters of our pastors have to moonlight to make ends meet."

I met another pastor who told me the same story. He wore a clerical collar, but he carried a pair of shears in his pocket. "I cut quite a lot of hair on the side," he said.

So why Las Vegas?

"Our problem is how best to invest our time," Graham once told me. "For every invitation we accept, we turn down scores. I usually consult Cliff Barrows, Grady Wilson, T. W. Wilson, and Walter Smyth before making a final commitment. Although some cities press us almost to the limit, we have learned that when we look to God for guidance as to the city or the university campus we are to visit, we rarely make a mistake."

Las Vegas was a city that had pressed hard. Ken Forshee reported that his first overture to BGEA elicited the gloomy statement: "It's not clear to us yet that we should come."

"Well, it's clear to me," Forshee retorted. "It's been clear for some time."

Impoverished, scorned as they were, this faithful band of Christians reminded me of the struggling churches that had spread around the Mediterranean and carried the Gospel to the Roman world.

The process of creating a crusade organization was blueprinted years ago by the BGEA. Today, it varies only to cope with local conditions. Its origins run back through the careers of earlier evangelists, who also possessed charisma and the faith that moves mountains.

Larry Turner compares a crusade to an iceberg. "The days and nights when Billy preaches are the tip. The bulk of the work is hidden—forty-five percent happens before the crusade and forty-five percent happens after."

He added, "We first organize our committees: prayer, finance, counseling, delegations, music, follow-up. We prepare the ground next."

Preparing the ground in Las Vegas involved pastors and laymen driving interminable distances under a blistering sun to meet with groups at every crossroads they could find. In summer heat, they crossed the desert into Utah, Arizona, and California.

"We let out a lot of line," Turner recalls. One pastor, Mel Stewart, drove fifteen hundred miles in three days, just going to ministers' meetings.

Then there are the committees. Nothing is more important than the prayer committee. Fervent prayer is the secret weapon of every Graham crusade. Billy discovered long ago that the prayer life of Jesus Christ provides an example unexplored by most Christians. Indeed, he found that many church members simply do not know how to pray.

But, after a crusade, they do. Today, the Graham preparation team includes men and women who form prayer groups for both sexes. In Las Vegas, hundreds of home-prayer meetings blossomed quickly. Eventually, 580 homes were open to prayer.

In December, Lydia Smith, of the team, organized the first women's prayer rally. Her month-long tour of churches and homes, praying with lonely couples and bustling clubs, guiding their energies toward the week of meetings, led to a gratifying attendance of one thousand women.

Millie Dienert, of Philadelphia, was the principal speaker. A graceful, attractive woman, she becomes a giant behind the lectern. Her addresses have inspired hundreds of thousands of women, on every continent. Years ago, she volunteered to assist Billy Graham, offering her many talents gratis. Since then, Mrs. Dienert has traveled as many air miles, I suppose, as any person on earth, to lead women of all races in glorifying and praising God. Her visit to Las Vegas, many reported, was a turning point in their prayer lives.

In the early church, earnest prayer was the only motive force available to Christians who sought to enlarge their fellowship. Today, prayer remains the principal fuel that drives every Graham crusade, but close behind, in this electronic age, is the technology of communications.

A crusade must be advertised. Early evangelists were slow to utilize business techniques, but not Billy Graham. In fact, his now-celebrated 1949 crusade in Los Angeles, which served as his launching pad, almost died aborning because its financial committee had originally refused to spend more than $5,000 for radio and newspaper ads. Billy insisted on $25,000. The money became available, and the rest is history.

In Las Vegas, the advertising committee bought a double showing of the country's biggest billboards. Graham's famous face, in full color and ten feet tall, bracketed every highway. The competition was considerable. Even larger signs proclaimed the presence of Sammy Davis, Jr., Frank Sinatra, and "Coming soon, Muhammad Ali."

Advertising technicians have a language of their own. A favorite word is *penetration,* which means the degree to which a community is aware of the team's campaign. Billboards achieve a certain degree of penetration—so do newspaper advertisements, and so do press stories and TV interviews. In Las Vegas, the crusade committee employed two additional techniques. One was threshold visitation—ringing doorbells. The other was telephone visitation—ringing phone bells. But some families in this "town without clocks" were never home. They were the thousands employed on night shifts. Ordinarily, a visitation committee would divide a city into segments and methodically visit every house, leaving invitations and literature. Here, the time was too short, and too many doorbells went unanswered.

Jack Cousins recalled the Chicago crusade of 1971. During the preparation, snow and rain had filled the streets with slush. Volunteers were reluctant to work. An approach via telephone was tried. Two veteran workers, Hubert and Rachel Mitchell of Los Angeles, were invited to penetrate Chicago, and they did. Now, they penetrated Las Vegas.

A bank of phones was set up in a church, and volunteers were trained. Soon, thousands of startled Las Vegans heard a friendly voice inviting them to listen to Billy. Every invitation concluded with a word of prayer for the receiver of the call.

Rachel Mitchell told me, "I made over one thousand calls myself, and it is amazing that I encountered only a half-dozen or so who reacted unfavorably. Over six hundred promised that they would attend. Many prolonged our conversation and prayer time to discuss their own spiritual problems."

Every church within one hundred miles was invited to send a bus load of pilgrims to each crusade service. Called "Operation

Andrew," the plan required that half the seats be reserved for non-Christians. Special blocks of tickets were reserved for each delegation.

Young people make up a large segment of a crusade audience. Usually they are reached through campus organizations. Not in Las Vegas. There was no Young Life, no Youth for Christ, no Campus Crusade. Team member Lowell Jackson visited the board of education. Eventually, vigorous rallies were held in seventeen schools.

At one of them, Ralph Bell, an effective BGEA evangelist, was the speaker. Concluding his address, he could not resist extending an invitation to accept Jesus Christ. Eighty-eight high schoolers accepted.

Seeking new wrinkles in the practice of evangelism, I heard of "nurture groups," and asked, "What does a nurture group do?"

"It fosters the growth of immature Christians," a group member told me.

How do you turn a novice into a veteran, a boy into a man, a convert into a Paul or Silas? The nurture groups made that objective their business. I learned to call them the Green Berets of evangelism. By adding this program, Graham tries to guarantee that any person who comes forward will have friends to whom he can turn in time of trouble.

Another program insures that those who come forward will find a warm and reassuring friend immediately—a counselor. Counselor training is intensive. It lasts for weeks, sessions are often held at sunrise, and the training requires personal sacrifice. Charles Riggs and Jack Cousins, of the team, have instructed crusade counselors around the world. They came to Las Vegas four months early.

An astonishing thing happened when they announced their training classes. Twelve hundred men, women, and youths enrolled, and over one thousand graduated. The churches responded, too. They discovered new strengths in their fellowship. In actions, Christian workers became bold.

Larry Turner described the gathering of holy momentum: "As they began to meet together, they started to sense their strength. Interchurch meetings doubled their self-confidence. Training classes gave them scriptural knowledge they had never possessed. Before we knew it, they were volunteering for every job in sight.

"We had to limit the number participating in the choir, for instance. We had run out of seats."

### A Sense of Foreboding

An outsider living in town would have reckoned that Las Vegas, the secular city, was still untouched.

Except for the heat within the Christian community, the Strip remained chilly. Jut-jawed individuals expressed candid antagonism.

"Graham's got to be against gambling," a casino owner said. "He'll kill my business."

Another said, "I know about evangelists. They come to town for a few weeks, get people all worked up, and then go home with a bagful of loot."

The facts are that a crusade pulls visitors into a town and helps business (though perhaps not that of gamblers). Graham never "works up" his audience. And neither he nor his team takes money home for their personal bank accounts. They are paid annual salaries by BGEA. During a crusade, they receive expense money from the local crusade committee.

This lack of understanding about finances is an international phenomenon. Apparently the Elmer Gantry image is embedded in the minds of people everywhere. I have encountered it in Europe, Africa, and Asia.

Eventually, the blazing sincerity of Billy Graham silences the scoffers whenever he preaches, but for a time in mid-January of 1978, a sense of foreboding drew a shadow over his plans for Las Vegas.

T. W. Wilson, a boyhood friend who is Graham's executive assistant, told me of Billy's anxiety. "He felt that he did not really understand the people there," Wilson said. "He needed to know more about what they were up against and what he would be up against. One day he said, 'We've got to go early.'"

So Graham and Wilson landed, unannounced, four days ahead of schedule, at McCarran Airport outside of Las Vegas. Immediately they launched a series of on-the-spot meetings with Larry Turner, the Reverend Ken Forshee, and other local ministers and team members who had brought this unlikely project so far so fast.

Billy asked for the blunt truth. He got it, particularly from Jim Reid, the no-nonsense "Chaplain of the Strip," and pastor of the Koinonia Church:

"Satan is here," Reid said. "He does not want a crusade in Las Vegas."

Taking note of all he saw and all he heard, Billy Graham took counsel with his advisors and retired to pray and prepare.

Monday, the countdown began with the customary precrusade press conference. As a former newspaper reporter, I have frequently watched the first encounters of Billy Graham and the local press. How would he be treated in Las Vegas? No one knew.

Graham, who felt that he had been burned by some of the searing headlines that followed the *Charlotte Observer* stories, must have been apprehensive as he approached his first contact with the reporters of Las Vegas.

He entered the conference room unannounced, wearing a gray pinstripe suit and a red vest. After shaking hands all around, he asked for questions. Several reporters wanted to know if he would gamble while in Las Vegas.

"I do not intend to stand in front of a slot machine and put in money. There are several reasons. First, I don't think I could win anything," he said, drawing a laugh. "Second, if people saw me there, I would be setting a very poor example, for while a thing in itself might not be a sin, my example might cause other people to stumble."

Suddenly, he began to talk theology: "But the greatest gamble of all," he said, "is when a man gambles with his soul." Pencils scribbled and reporters pressed their microphones closer.

"What about the Mormons?" a reporter asked.

Graham knew that the Mormon church had refused to support the crusade. He did not hesitate. "I do not accept the teachings of the Mormon church, but Mormon bishops tell me that they have never heard me preach anything on television that they did not believe." He added, "Some of my best friends are Mormons, and many support us."

Another reporter asked if he accepted the Mormon church as one of America's great denominations.

He replied, seriously: "I do not think of any denomination. I believe that everyone in the world who has accepted Christ as his Lord and Saviour is a member of the body of Christ, which is called the church of Christ."

Each Graham press conference sheds a new ray or so of light on his inner feelings. A reporter reminded him of a recent poll that had named him America's most influential religious leader. "In your wildest dreams," he asked, "did you ever think that you would become a world figure? And if you had it to do over again, are there things you would modify?"

The evangelist replied: "The thing that I would modify the most is that I would study more and preach less."

His plans for the future?

He will stay with his vocation. He had been tempted many times to stray into other activities, to walk in every demonstration imaginable, and to run for high political office. "But I think God has led me to stay with the Bible. People talk about my retirement. I'm not going to retire."

Did he believe in visitors from outer space? He said the earth had received visitors from outer space long ago. The Bible calls them angels. "I believe in angels," he stated. "But I don't find anything in the Bible about UFOs."

Are we approaching the end of our age?

His answer was another lesson in theology. Certain signs are falling into place. The end of the age does not mean the end of civilization or of the earth. It is the end of a period in which man is working with God through the Holy Spirit. When Christ comes back, it will mean the end of evil, he explained. Christ is going to reign as the true Messiah, and the earth will become a wonderful Utopia.

The countdown continued Monday evening, with a reception sponsored by the team to honor the Las Vegas committees. Billy and Ruth were also guests. At first, those Las Vegans, who had seen Hollywood's brightest talents come and go, did not know what to make of these evangelistic stars. Then, quickly, they surrendered to the atmosphere of iced punch, cookies, and brotherly love. It was a memorable evening.

Tuesday began with a sunrise prayer breakfast. Graham was a guest of honor and the principal speaker. Walking along the Strip, I saw the morning sky above Caesar's Palace crisscrossed by vapor trails from the military jets at Nellis Air Base. The esplanade before the Palace was a tangle of cars. Smartly garbed couples were hurrying into the lobby. An attendant muttered, "Now I've seen everything. A traffic jam at sunrise."

The queue of ticket holders wound from the showroom, where breakfast would be served, through an obstacle course of slot machines, down a corridor between boutiques and tourist-trap shops, and vanished around corners. This was an *event*.

As I looked about for the usual press table, a voice called my name. Walter Smyth, an old friend from BGEA, was beckoning. I accepted his invitation and slid into an empty chair.

"Welcome," said a familiar voice tinged with a Carolina accent. It was Mrs. Billy Graham. By chance, I had landed at the team table, with Billy's calm and charming wife as a breakfast companion.

Graham's message was perhaps the finest address I have heard him deliver. Its focal point was the possibility that this crusade in Las Vegas could become the spark that would light the fires of an awakening. Suddenly, I understood why he had selected Las Vegas for what some had called a kamikaze crusade. Against all logic, it might ignite a flame of revival that could be fanned into a religious awakening for all America.

"A Nevada of people that belong to God could set a spiritual fire that might sweep the East, the North, and the South," he declared.

An awakening has profound spiritual meaning for evangelists, but is little understood by laymen. In essence, it is a revival that feeds on itself, redoubling its heat and movement like a prairie fire, until its flames burn the sin out of vast numbers of people. Awakenings have occurred in America in 1734, 1783, and 1849.

A new awakening is the dream of every young evangelist. In 1949, before a crusade, the young Billy had said, "I want to see God sweep in, because if Los Angeles could have a great revival, the ramifications and repercussions could sweep across the entire world."

And here in Las Vegas, in 1978, he was again talking of an awakening, of a fire in the Nevada desert. I thought about it deeply, wondering if any lesser dream could sustain his God-intoxicated campaigns.

In all the months that have followed that morning, I have found no better answer to the riddle. How greatly that dream was needed, and how deeply it was appreciated in Las Vegas, I would learn on the crusade's opening day. The occasion was a team breakfast.

A team breakfast is a special occasion, akin to a military staff's final briefing on the morn of a critical attack. It is also a spiritual service station, offering fuel and lubrication for overheated crusade workers. The breakfast was held in a conventional conference room in the Landmark Hotel. The ration was coffee and a roll. The only conference furniture was a lectern—not a bar chart or projector was in sight. Waiting team members and local committee members sat around several large, circular tables. I found a seat, grateful for this chance to become acquainted with the team's younger generation.

Precisely on time, Billy and Ruth joined us.

I shall mention only highlights of the session, but I hope they will convey the wonder and mystery of that unique gathering. It began when Larry Turner went to the lectern.

Turner explained the problem of Las Vegas, a boom town without roots, an all-night town, with 50,000 waitresses, entertainers, bellboys, and casino workers who could not be reached by conventional means.

He described the various meetings held by crusade workers the night before, as a sort of crusade dress rehearsal. Afterwards, he said, he had met small groups chatting excitedly into the wee hours, reluctant to go home, still buoyed by the experience of joining hands with groups from other churches.

Ken Forshee was next. Everyone knew Ken. He was tall, spare, articulate, and his words rang with faith and sincerity. He thanked Billy Graham for bringing his team to Las Vegas. "Every person is a jewel. They've claimed our hearts," he said.

Next came Jim Reid, the bluff "Chaplain of the Strip," whose church stands within shouting distance of Caesar's Palace, the M.G.M. Grand, the Dunes, and the Flamingo Hilton. He pulled no punches.

"Everything is money here," he told the team. "Unless you're making it big, you're nothing. Every value is based on money. Las Vegas has always been a money machine. Since computers came in, it's worse than ever. People have become ciphers with which to make more money. That's the only objective. The dollar is king."

He presented another challenge. "Anything goes here—total hedonism. Prostitution is wide open. There's a large gay community, maybe eighty percent of the boys who work in the choruses and a smaller percentage of the girls.

"There's great emptiness here, so cults abound—every kind including Scientology and Moonies. Many show people are messed up with Tarot cards, parapsychology, and reincarnation. Demonism is big. The church of Satan is very active, and some of its members are high up in the community. It's a sign of the basic emptiness in their lives."

He seemed abruptly to decide that his vinegary explosion might be too much for the team. His smile swept the room.

"But you have dazzled me in coming to Las Vegas," he said. "And I think this crusade may cause a reaction that will make the recent raid on Entebbe look like a country picnic."

When Billy Graham walked to the lectern, the room became utterly quiet. I recalled another meeting when he had felt especially threatened by Satan. The All-Britain crusade of 1967 was beginning—a campaign that tied together ten giant TV screens in various British cities with the twenty-thousand-seat auditorium in London called Earl's Court. It represented eleven crusades in one, yet it was a single, gigantic crusade. Nothing like it had ever been attempted.

That first night in London, many seats were empty. Electronic gremlins got into every TV cable between London and the provinces. Smoking newspaper headlines roundly criticized Billy's publicity, his refusal to condemn Vietnam, his refusal to debate theology, his lack of a solution to offer the Middle East. That night, as on this opening day in 1978, he stood on the brink of what might have become a tragic failure.

In Las Vegas, he told those pastors: "We don't come with neat panaceas. I am not an expert on religion. The only thing that I am certain of is my own relationship with God—and the knowledge that my sins are forgiven."

He regretted the gadgetry of evangelism. "It's like Saul's armor when little David went out to meet Goliath. If this crusade is a success, it will be because the Spirit of God has breathed upon these physical gadgets and has blessed them."

He reasserted his mission: "We have come to proclaim the simple, clear, saving Gospel of Jesus Christ. Let men debate our methods, let them attack our personalities, let them rebuke our simple message. But so long as the Gospel is preached and people's lives are changed, and they go out into society to live the Christian life, what the critics say about us does not matter."

Then, quietly, he reminded us of Matthew's description of Jesus sending His disciples out to heal and teach, saying, "I am sending you out as sheep among wolves. Be wary as serpents and harmless as doves."

He said: "We need to consider this in our personal lives. We are watched here. We are watched here more than any other place in the world. What an opportunity we are given to *live* what we believe. So let's live our faith in Jesus Christ."

Larry Turner closed the meeting with a simple declaration: "Remember that this is no Sin City. Many fine people are living here."

Billy suggested that all of us should pray for the opening crusade service, so men and women at each table clasped hands to their right and left in closed circles of prayer. Then they bowed their heads and opened their hearts, so that a half-dozen voices rose simultaneously from a half-dozen tables, the words mingling and blending until the human ear could make no sense of the sounds.

But not one person in that group doubted that God was listening and that He would sort it all out.

# 6

# Las Vegas: A City Reborn

*I heard a reporter ask Graham: "Who won? You or the devil?"*

*Billy replied: "There'll never be a final victory until Jesus returns. Only then will the victory be complete."*

One of Satan's favorite devices is to lull one into a false sense of security. In Las Vegas, on the afternoon of Wednesday, February 1, 1978, I suspected I was being lulled.

Obviously, each member of the Billy Graham team was a talented and dedicated worker. Each also was a charmer, capable, as someone said, "of charming the skin off a snake." Reviewing their stories about the period of preparation for the crusade, I perceived that they had done their work well. Each phase of evangelistic activity had developed and expanded according to a tested formula. No member of the local committee had found the team intolerant or overbearing. The fruits of the Jamaican get-together in January were being demonstrated by the warm regard which each member of the group held for every other member.

I had to remind myself that my self-elected task for the next week was to examine the fundamentals of Billy Graham's public ministry. After much thought, I had decided to look for *changes*. I knew his old style and his old sermon content, from frequent exposure. Now I would look for changes that might be symptoms of an allegedly *different* Billy Graham. I would look for signs of insincerity, of the abandonment of the faith of his fathers and his own early ministry.

He had stood before a skeptical 1957 audience of clergymen in London and vowed, *"I am a churchman."* But two decades had passed. Was he still convinced that the church, despite its shortcomings, was the best instrument for changing people, and thus changing society? Other concerns were held by various friends.

What were his current intentions? To extend his ministry to other continents? To reap a greater harvest of inquirers for America to see on his televised services? To erect a marble-and-glass monument to himself, akin to the presidential museums of Johnson, Kennedy, Eisenhower, and Truman? All these had been rumored.

Then there was his message.

The previous winter, *McCall's* had published an interview which quoted him as saying, "I don't play God anymore." What could that appalling quote signify? Many who read it thought that it might mean he was no longer certain of his biblical moorings. If he no longer played God, what did he play? By hard listening and hard thinking, I concluded, I might find out.

Just before the first crusade service of the week, TV station KORK telecast a thirty-minute special called "A conversation with Billy Graham." Their interviewer, Kathie Milone, presented a relaxed evangelist and an assortment of views. I listened, mildly surprised, wondering at the perfect timing. Was this a coincidence, or the work of what critics have called Graham's "high-powered, super-slick public-relations team?" Certainly, it was a perfect lead-in for the initial service.

**Milone:**  Is there a new morality today?
**Graham:**  No. It's the same old immorality.

**Milone:** Are more young people bound for hell and damnation? It seems to be getting worse.

**Graham:** We have a new generation of young people. [He cited a Gallup poll of 346,000 high schoolers. A large majority was against drugs, and 70 percent was against sexual permissiveness.]

**Milone:** Would you equate the occult with the devil?

**Graham:** I'd equate it with man's search for God.

**Milone:** How would you define sin?

**Graham:** Sin is the breaking of God's law, the breaking of the moral commandments. There are about one hundred and twenty-two Greek words translated as *sin* in the Bible. The most prominent ones mean that one has missed the mark—that we missed God's requirements for holiness and righteousness.

**Milone:** Is gambling sinful?

**Graham:** Almost everything we do is gambling, but the greatest gamble of all is when we gamble our souls in our relationship with God. When a person rejects Christ, that's a big gamble. Suppose there's an eternity or a heaven and a hell. The believer gains in this life by knowing the peace and joy Christ gives, but he also gains in eternity. If there is no heaven or hell, he's had heaven in his heart.

**Milone:** Is the crusade a big money-making business?

**Graham:** It doesn't make any money at all. In fact, it's going to cost money. If there is any overage, it will go to some social need.

### Wednesday, February 1—Opening Night

The daylight hours passed quickly. Las Vegans picked up their *Valley Times*, and read one of the friendliest imaginable editorials. "Billy Graham—we'll bet on him anytime," the newspaper said. They added that he was far more than an evangelist; he was

a world statesman . . . . a man at ease with the leaders of nations . . . . one who commands worldwide attention in the
press . . . . is listed regularly as one of the ten most admired
men in the world.

"Lunching with a handful of Las Vegans the other day, he was
relaxed and gracious—and very candid in private conversation,"
the editorial continued. "There's not a trace of the phoney in
him. He's genuine.

"He has not come to put Las Vegas down or to condemn us.
. . . But he sees room for improvement, as we all do. . . . He
said a 'spiritual awakening' could begin here that would make us
a 'super-state'. . . . We may not take the pledge. But we
wouldn't miss him for the world. . . . No matter what your
faith, take your family, take your friends."

Assuredly, that did not sound like the description of a martyr
in the midst of a swarm of locusts.

The Landmark Hotel, which was our headquarters, was a tow-
ering architectural toadstool across the way from the Convention Center. At twilight, a tidal wave of cars, coaches, and buses
spilled into the center's gigantic parking lot. Volunteers with
lighted batons split the torrent into metallic rivers that honked
and beeped their way to a halt in rainbow ranks covering the
space of a dozen football fields.

At the center's door, we were greeted by a smiling usher who
handed us a buff-colored sheet called the "Crusade News."

I asked, "What's this for?"

He replied, "The hymns for tonight are on the back. Inside,
you'll find some important announcements."

The first night's guest singers would be Norma Zimmer, of the
Lawrence Welk TV show, and Johnny Cash, both longtime
friends of Graham, both stars in their own right. Two of the
hymns, I noted, were "Blessed Assurance" and "Leaning on
the Everlasting Arms." A memory floated up of the opening

service in London, in 1966. Unless I was mistaken, both songs had been sung by those stalwart Britishers on the first night of their crusade two decades ago. Somehow, it was comforting.

Inside, the "Crusade News" announced a special meeting for women only. "The purpose will be to discuss ways of continuing our ministry of prayer," it stated. "Millie Dienert will present the message."

My wife said, "The women here are lucky. There's no speaker on earth I'd rather hear than Millie."

Another announcement reported a radio broadcast called "New Life for You," that would run for four weeks after the crusade's finale. Its announced times were 3:30 A.M. (an unprecedented hour, surely), 3:45 P.M., and 7:30 P.M. The program would provide a rallying place, I knew, for the hearts of those who had accepted Christ.

Another page gave Graham's answers to three often-asked questions. The first letter writer admitted having a feeling that God did not really exist, which caused her to fall into a depression so serious that she became ill. The second complained of the hypocrisy in many churches and asked, "Can't I become a Christian without joining a church?" The third argued that the best sermons and sacred music were on radio and TV, so why attend a church and "hear a much inferior sermon and amateur music?"

Graham's foursquare answers accepted no excuses. The Bible says that God does exist. Believe it. Turn to the Gospel of John and "ask God to show you, through its pages, that He exists and that He loves you." As for attending church: "First, settle matters between yourself and God. Trust Christ alone for your salvation. When you have made your peace with God . . . . become associated with some church." As for substituting a TV program, he said: "The church is the only institution organized by Christ. Christians have always required a loving relationship with such fellowships.'' He praised the benefits of baptism into the church, fellowship at the communion table, and mutual prayer. ''So support your own church and pray that radio and TV services may reach those as yet untouched by the Gospel.''

We saw that thousands of people were already in their seats, though the service was not scheduled to start for another forty minutes. At one end of the building, the immense choir— certainly the largest in Las Vegas history—sat in banked rows. The platform with the evangelist's automated pulpit rose between the choir and the open space where inquirers would assemble. Now it was empty, except for two dead TV cameras standing on straddled legs.

Beyond, beginning with the first rows, a host of seated people formed a flat plain of wall-to-wall humanity, their bright gowns and faces giving the center the appearance of a prairie abloom with wild flowers.

We found seats at the press table, with reporters and communications technicians from around the world. TV crews from Germany, France, and Sweden were shooting documentaries. Later, while the evangelist preached, their whispered conferences would become an excited babble, as their cameramen darted about like broken-field runners. I could remember other press tables, in New Orleans and Nashville, when I had been almost the only newsperson present.

I have always regretted that the TV presentation of a Billy Graham meeting never has time to present the holy hubbub of preparation. Before the meeting, Cliff Barrows calls his army of choristers to a practice. Coatless, he paces the platform, arms uplifted or spread wide, while his voice leads, coaches, exhorts, and inspires. The air vibrates as phrases are repeated and harmonies are perfected.

Readers who are regular viewers of Graham's crusade telecasts are accustomed to a fairly standard format. What they miss is the preparatory confusion, the astonishing number of small children scrambling around in search of seats, amateur photographers advancing to the platform for a quick flash shot, the camaraderie of friends waving to each other, and the inevitable lost child.

Tedd Smith, brilliant composer and crusade organist for many years, was at the keyboard of his grand piano, to the left (from the audience's side) of the pulpit. Between him and the forward rail was a spotlighted space large enough for a soloist or a small group. The arrangement was new. The beloved Ethel Waters, Myrtle Hall, and George Beverly Shea had always used the pulpit mike, but singers of small stature, like Norma Zimmer and tiny Kim Wickes and winsome Evie Tornquist, seemed lost behind the big box.

On the opposite side of the platform, a huge organ console was manned by organist John Innes. He was a newcomer since I had last written about crusade music, but I soon discovered that he was good. Both instruments were equipped with mike pickups that amplified and flung their sound into the huge spaces of the center. Two small figures—men with tools flapping against their hips—appeared to be untangling wires and tightening connections. Similar activity is common to movie and television sets before the cameras roll, and that is what most evangelistic platforms have become today—studios.

This night, George Beverly Shea, leaning against the evangelist's lectern, rehearsed "How Great Thou Art" against the background of a thousand voices. His trial run was a bonus for us early arrivals.

A small group of men and women suddenly emerged from a screened doorway behind the platform and climbed the steps at each end, to take their places in padded chairs behind the pulpit. Several of them wore clerical collars. They were committee members, local pastors, the mayor of Las Vegas, the governor of

Nevada, and—though we did not see him arrive—a smiling Billy Graham.

I have felt a sense of anticipation in many audiences around the world. One such audience was a group of war correspondents during World War II, when we awaited confirmation by General Dwight Eisenhower that our Allied armies had finally crossed the Rhine and were racing to victory in the heartland of Nazi Germany. But I had never felt anything like the electricity that now stirred the air of this huge auditorium.

## . . . Not to Condemn . . .

Suddenly, the long-awaited moment was at hand. Cliff Barrows was at the lectern. Smiling, he said, "Good evening, ladies and gentlemen. Welcome to the crusade of Greater San Diego."

*San Diego?*

Stunned silence ensued, followed by a good-natured thunderclap of laughter that shook the rafters. Unaware of what he had said, Cliff stood still, his smile a frozen parody. Then someone called, "Man, this is Las Vegas." Barrows's grin widened, becoming an admission of his own fallibility.

The Reverend Ken Forshee, who had worked so hard at preparing the crusade, was brought to the lectern and presented to the audience. His heart was so full that his words poured forth in a joyous stream. "This is the moment we've been waiting for," he said, "for God has called us all together."

Other committee members were on the platform, and some were in the audience. Forshee said that everyone who had given so much should be on the platform, too, but the stage was far too small. To accommodate all who deserved thanks would require at least five thousand seats. "Indeed, this whole room ought to be a platform," he added, "and *everyone* a guest of honor."

Billy Graham was next. As he reached the pulpit, I was startled by a sound that began softly and then mounted, until it filled

the room. Every person in the hall, except for two dozen or so
who sat in wheelchairs, had risen. Their welcome to the
evangelist lasted for many minutes and faded only as he began to
speak.

"Last night," he said, "my wife and I came over here and sat
in those rear seats." His arm indicated a distant row. "The choir
was assembling for its last rehearsal, and I looked across this
vast hall and said to myself, 'I doubt that it will ever be filled.'
And tonight they've taken down that back wall, and the crowd
has gone way beyond what we expected. In fact, the audience
here tonight exceeds the audiences of the opening nights in many
of our crusades across the United States. How little faith I
had. . . ."

The clatter of clapping drowned out his words.

He told of receiving his first impression of Nevada from a
novel written by Zane Grey. Its hero was named Nevada. "So
it's a thrill to see thousands of Christians here tonight. This is a
tremendous thing, and it will be an encouragement to Christians
throughout the world when they hear about you Christians here
in Las Vegas."

This was vintage Graham, expressing a personal affection for
his audience, praising its witness, stroking its self-esteem. After
many years of watching and listening, I am convinced that, even
if only a baker's dozen turned out some night to hear him preach,
he would still find a way to express his gratitude.

An opening-night crowd is different from all others: It has
formed its opinions of the evangelist from his "Hour of Decision" broadcasts and his TV appearances. But there is much
more to Billy Graham than the man with the Bible, the pointing
finger, and his proclamation of the good news. This informal
moment is important to both sides. Frequently, humor creates a
bridge.

So Graham told a story about an old prospector who came out

of the mountains to a small Nevada town and met a drunken cowboy in front of a saloon. The cowboy was firing two six-shooters in all directions. Facing the prospector, he demanded, "Old man, do you know how to dance?"

"No, I don't."

"Maybe you'd better learn."

Hot lead kicked up the dust, and the old man began to dance.

Soon, the cowboy's guns were empty. The prospector reached into his saddlebag and pulled out a sawed-off shotgun. Aiming it at the cowboy's head, he asked, "Son, have you ever kissed a mule?"

The cowboy looked at the shotgun. He looked at the spot where the critter's tail was attached to his body, and he got the message.

"No, I've never kissed a mule," he said, "but I've always wanted to."

After the laughter, Graham made his point, saying: "We've never held a crusade before in Las Vegas, *but we've always wanted to.* And we're here not to entertain or put on a show. We've come to proclaim the Gospel of Jesus Christ. And if nothing else happens beyond this many people coming together and standing up and singing "Blessed Assurance," that in itself could have a tremendous impact on this community. And I believe this is only the beginning."

Swiftly, he introduced Johnny Cash: "Now I want you to meet a man who loves the Lord. One of my closest friends, Johnny Cash."

Two children carrying cameras leaped from their front-row seats and dashed forward to take pictures. So did others, drawn like steel filings to the magnetic man in black. Finally, they formed a human crescent before Cash, while their flashbulbs winked like fireflies. The same thing happened every night.

Crusade meetings usually include a spot in which a well-known personality gives a testimony of his Christian experience. The Las Vegas meetings would rely mostly on Johnny Cash. I wish my written words could convey his sincerity. This opening night, he was ill, but had defied the advice of Billy and Ruth Graham and his own physician, in order to attend. God's show must go on, too. So Johnny was there.

He thanked Billy for "letting June [his wife] and me come for all five nights."

Several books have described the fall and rise of Johnny Cash. In outline, it is the familiar saga of the talented but undisciplined youth, who hits the primrose path, makes the drug scene, spends time in a prison or a psychiatric ward, and finally begins the long climb back with the help of someone who loves him.

June Carter Cash believed in Johnny and in the promises of Jesus that God would answer prayer. Each night during that crusade, they were together on the platform. Johnny would give his testimony of what had happened to him, and then they would sing. Always, he had words of hope and of gratitude for the miracle that had saved him.

His message was always different, yet always the same. On opening night, he said: "I just want everybody to know that I'm a Christian." A generation earlier, such a bold declaration might have kept a box-office star out of nightclubs for the remainder of his life. He added: "I've learned a great lesson in this little bout with the flu. When you can't give your best for the Master, He sure can make you feel good just to give what little you have to give."

Always, he mentioned the need for change. "You can't change your life yourself, but Jesus Christ can. He has the power, if we just allow Him to live in us. Let Him take over, and we don't have to worry. You can't do anything He won't forgive. He'll not only forgive, but He'll forget your sins, like He did for me."

God invites everybody, he said that night, "Addicts, drunk-

ards, prostitutes, whatever—if they come to Him just like they
are. I know. I was from the dregs—and He changed me.''

He told us about a blackjack dealer in town. "He didn't make
a decision for Christ because he didn't think he could live it in
the job he had. But you know, that might be trying to do God's
thinking for Him, 'cause I believe the Lord would love to have a
Christian blackjack dealer in this town.

"Why, right now, in our hotel," he added, "there are nine
bellboys who've recently been converted. They have a prayer
meeting every day. God doesn't ask you to change your work.
He didn't tell me to stop being an entertainer. The thing is,
there's a calling to be a Christian wherever I go, to witness to
Him. And I thank God for the opportunity to do so."

June Carter Cash usually added a few words, and then they
sang such favorites as "Why Me, Lord," "Precious Memories,"
and "Rock of Ages."

While the choir and the audience sang together, I reviewed the
purpose of my presence. It was so easy to relax and bask in the
ambience of such trusting hearts.

My motives were a mixed bag. From the beginning, I had been
convinced that the attacks on Graham were Satan-inspired. But I
was also prepared to be critical for good and sufficient cause.
Evangelism, a gift of God, is a precious responsibility, which
few men have been able to carry. Graham seemed to be one of
those men. To vilify an evangelist is one thing; to vilify
*evangelism* is to dishonor God.

So I would watch and listen.

The evangelist sat quietly on the platform, among his guests
and associates. Security guards were at each stairway. Graham's
eyes were closed, and his chin rested on his right hand in an
attitude of prayer. I found myself wondering: *Is that a pose?*

Realizing that I had never before doubted the implication of
any attitude, I looked about, at the nearest faces. Were they

wondering about Billy, too? How many others, as they watched this service later on TV, might wonder?

The rumble of George Beverly Shea's bass voice drew me back to the present. He was at the lectern; a veteran campaigner for Christ. He was singing the same hymn with which he had opened the successful London crusade of 1966.

Billy had not moved. Since his very early days, he had depended on Bev to set the spiritual mood. A thousand times, he must have sat like that, soaking up the words and music while his own thoughts shaped themselves into fragments of prayer that asked for support and guidance.

I doubt if TV viewers can sense the spiritual harmony that exists between these two remarkable men. Born nine years before Graham, Bev Shea has sung in almost every crusade since his appearance on Billy's initial radio program, "Songs in the Night," over Chicago's radio station WCFL.

Unlike guest singers, he never uses the microphone beside Tedd Smith's grand piano. He sings at Graham's own lectern, as an evangelist of song. Sometimes he asks Billy to name a selection, but their work has endured so long, and their empathy is so complete, that once he learns the theme of Billy's sermon, he comes up with exactly the right music. And then his famous voice, like gentle thunder, prepares the audience.

Long ago, I had learned Graham's way of leading his hearers into his message. A request for prayer comes first, then a stream-of-consciousness outflow in preparation for the Gospel. "My message will not be long tonight; not as long as they once were," he said. He asked for silence. He hoped that all those who knew how to pray would be in prayer, "for there are many people here tonight because God has brought them here. They are searching, questing for answers to the problems of their lives."

When Graham began, his voice was low-keyed. Every syllable

indicated that he was relaxed, confident, and definitely in charge—which was all right with that Las Vegas audience.

"I want you to turn with me to the third chapter of John," he said. "The third chapter of the Gospel of John. Now, will you join me in prayer?

"Our Father and our God," he said suddenly but reverently. "I pray that this night the people will not be conscious of the speaker but will be conscious only of our Lord Jesus Christ—who is the power of God unto salvation—and that He will transform them this night by His power. For we ask it in His name. Amen."

The acoustics in the huge hall were a puzzle. Nearby loudspeakers emitted a whirlwind of echoes. Later, I learned that hundreds had trouble understanding the message. Tomorrow, the decibels would be under better control.

Graham named a favorite text, as he does invariably at the start of every sermon. It was John 3:16. I read along in my King James Bible: "For God so loved the world, that he gave his only begotten Son, that whosoever believeth in him should not perish, but have everlasting life."

He said: "It's all wrapped up in those twenty-five words. That's all you need to know, to have your life changed forever."

He read the next verse: "For God sent not his Son into the world to condemn the world; but that the world through him might be saved."

He laid his Bible aside. "I did not come to Las Vegas to condemn Las Vegas," he declared. "We came to preach the good news that God wants to love you, that God wants to forgive you, and that God can change your life through Jesus Christ."

Turn-of-the-century preachers used threats of hell to scare sinners. That was the style when Billy first began to preach. Subsequent study broadened his understanding of the biblical message. Almost as long as I can remember, his method has been to make a positive presentation of the love of God. That would be his theme for this entire crusade.

On the second night, he spoke to an audience of young people about the rich young man who asked Jesus what he had to do to inherit eternal life. Jesus said he should surrender himself and all his possessions—whatever was most precious to him—to God. No halfway measures. Do it like the Spaniard, Cortez, who landed in South America centuries ago and burned his ships on the beach, so there remained no other way to go but forward. But the young man who came to see Jesus had great possessions, and he turned away from Jesus, never to be heard from again.

On Friday, the theme was the same, but his illustration was the blind man named Bartimaeus, who had given up hope of regaining his sight. One day, he heard that Jesus was passing by, and he cried aloud, "Help me. . . . help me, Master." And the Lord responded. Graham spoke of Las Vegas and how it was responding to support this crusade. "Jesus of Nazareth is passing by," he said. "The Scripture says the blind man followed Jesus. I'm going to ask that *you* follow Jesus."

On Saturday, he illustrated God's love by telling of the prodigal son. While the youth went to the city and revelled in sin, he said, the father waited at home. When the son, broken in spirit and in purse, timidly returned to his family, the father was so delighted that he killed a fatted calf and gave his son a robe and a ring. With arms flung wide, his eyes probing the audience for others who had strayed, Graham cried, "God has been looking down the road for you for a long, long time!"

Sunday would be a daunting day for the team, as well as for the local committee. The final service would signal an ending and a fresh beginning. Would the fine weather hold? Would the spirit of love and cooperation among churchmen endure? Would the budget of $230,000 be met?

A Billy Graham crusade is much more than meets the eye of a

comfortable television viewer. For instance, there is the support given by newspapers. Las Vegas publishers were generous. Thursday morning, readers of the *Review-Journal*, the state's largest paper, read a gigantic headline atop page one which said, 13,000 OVERWHELM GRAHAM CRUSADE. Later, it reported, GRAHAM CRUSADE AGAIN PLAYS TO SRO.

Sunday's sermon was longer and more complex, because Graham followed the biblical account of Paul's discourse on Mars Hill in Athens. Athens was a city given to idols, so much so that it had even built an idol to an unknown god. "We have our idols, too: money, cars, pleasures, sex. Of all sins," Graham declared, "God hates idolatry the worst."

Paul's audience consisted of four groups. Some were Epicureans, who sought more pleasures. Others were Stoics, whose brains were galaxies of circling thoughts that swung through endless orbits. And the gossipers were there, lips dripping with rumor and tattle.

Finally, there were the rare ones, the seekers after truth.

"And that characterizes millions of Americans right now," Graham said. "They want truth."

Turning to Paul's message on Mars Hill, Graham translated it for Las Vegans. In Greece or Nevada, we are all of one blood. The Bible has no place for racial prejudice.

Best of all, God is close at hand. The Athenians thought He was a long way off and not really interested. Wrong, said Paul. He's close. He loves you!

"That's the message I want to leave ringing in your ears." Graham's arms swept upward, embracing the hall. "Let's say it all together. God loves you. God loves you."

The shouted sound filled the hall, rolling above the ranks of listening Las Vegans like crashing surf. *God loves you. God loves you . . . .*

There was more, but I hardly listened.

God loves you, he had said. But you must repent, for you will be judged on an appointed day, and many will be thrown into a lake of fire.

Many Athenians [Las Vegans] laughed at the notion. Some delayed, putting off their decision. . . . A few believed.

"Paul had preached the Word, and that's what we've done. . . . Do you know Christ? . . . This is our last day . . . ."

Creeping gently as a summer breeze came the sweetness of "Almost Persuaded," as its sound embraced that temple. Soon, the aisles began to fill.

This is not the place to tell of the hundreds who responded, or of the counselors who furthered their understanding of the Gospel, or of the corps of workers who mailed out their names, addresses, and phone numbers so that some churchman could clasp hands and lead them into a Christian community. My mission was to find answers. Through the sermons of this pressure-cooker campaign, Graham had answered.

In no manner that I could discern had he changed his faith.

Two other *action* sermons added their testimony to this observation. The first was a special service for the "show-biz" people of the Las Vegas Strip. Later, *Decision* magazine told about it:

It was three o'clock Saturday morning. The last show on the Strip had ended at 2:30.

More than one thousand card dealers, keno runners, bartenders, dancers, restaurant workers and featured entertainers gathered in the Las Vegas Convention Center. They were there for a special evangelistic service . . . .

Opening the Scriptures, Billy Graham spoke directly to the need to be born again. When the invitation was given to receive Jesus Christ, hands were raised. Then, after everyone else was dismissed, those who had raised their hands stayed to talk with counselors about Jesus.

### The Phil Donahue Interview

The second "happening" was the Phil Donahue interview with Billy Graham. Overnight, carpenters turned the choir's end of the convention hall into a sound studio. Thursday afternoon, choir members—as a reward for faithful service—got first choice of the seats.

I attended for two reasons. I knew that Donahue had to ask questions about WECEF and its "secret" millions, about bribing Mickey Cohen, and perhaps about other innuendoes in current books. Graham's acceptance of Donahue's guest spot was a daring, and even dangerous, gambit, some thought. Under the tattoo of Phil's questions, how could Billy maintain his role as a modern Nehemiah?

Well, he did and he didn't.

The debonair Donahue took the hand mike as soon as Billy and Ruth arrived at the back of the platform and complimented the audience, the city, and his guest. Energy and sophistication were in his every gesture, in every turn of his carefully layered and graying hair. As a starter, he tried to persuade Graham to admit that this sand-swept metropolis was America's Sin City. Graham replied that maybe things were a little more garish than usual, but that Las Vegas was a mixture of good and bad, like every other city in the world.

But wasn't gambling a sin?

The Bible said little about gambling. But if it is based on greed, then it is a sin. Anything that is based on greed is sinful—even watching television.

Here was an encounter between giants, it soon became clear, with the evangelist topping the entertainer on more than a few points.

"Let's pretend that I'm at your crusade," Phil said.

"Let's not pretend," said Graham. "How about coming?"

The audience shouted, "Yeah!"

Phil tried to compliment his guest. "Why, you're the Johnny Carson of evangelism," he said.

"I'd rather think of myself as the Phil Donahue of evangelism."

"Are you praying for him [Johnny]?"

"I sure am," Graham said. "And I've seen some of your shows that needed praying for, too."

For a long moment, laughter stopped the program cold.

Discussing the universe, Graham advanced the idea that, though other worlds in the universe might be populated, ours was the only one where men had sinned against God. Phil interrupted to say: "Now wait a minute. If you're right, I wish I'd been born out *there*. Then I wouldn't be anxious and worried about all this. . . ."

Billy reminded him: "Well, if you're worried and anxious, what you need is to be born again."

*That* was evangelizing! That was evangelizing by reaching out to an audience he could never have touched on his own. Before the taping was over, I had ticked off additional points he had made:

> God visited this planet in the person of Jesus Christ.
>
> Christ is coming back.
>
> He will return and set up a perfect kingdom, without sin or death.
>
> You are chosen. Everyone is chosen, because God loves the whole world.
>
> A Christian has the Holy Spirit living within him, who produces the fruit of the Spirit, which is love.
>
> You must produce this fruit [love] because, no matter how insignificant you may be, you are witnessing, and somebody is watching you and being affected by you.
>
> Christian leaders have to set an example.

Eventually, Donahue turned to more controversial questions. He asked what Graham does with all the money he makes. Graham said he made a million dollars on the book *Angels*, but gave it all to Wheaton College, his alma mater. His salary is paid by the Billy Graham Evangelistic Association and is $39,500 per year (surely the most publicized salary in America). "I do not get one dime for appearing in Las Vegas."

A woman in the audience said she had watched him since she was a little girl. She'd heard that his message had changed.

The words of his reply were unequivocal, factual, temperate. "My basic message *has not* changed: the message of the fact that the Bible is the authoritative Word of God; the fact that Jesus was virgin born; the fact that Christ died for our sins on the cross; the fact that Jesus Christ rose from the dead; the fact that He's coming again; and the fact that you need to repent to receive Him as your Saviour."

He could have been reciting the Apostles' Creed, a statement of faith dated less than five hundred years after the death of Jesus.

Equally blunt was Graham's reply to Phil's query about the charge that he had offered Mickey Cohen, the Jewish gangster, $10,000 to attend the Madison Square Garden crusade of 1957 and be converted to Christianity. He said: "We and none of my associates have ever offered or paid one cent for any person, at any time in the history of my ministry, to come forward."

Then Phil switched to politics, asking: "Were you part of a meeting to choose Richard Nixon's vice-president?"

"That's partially true. I went up to congratulate him on being nominated, because I'd been asked to lead a prayer [at the convention]. He said, 'Come on in. We're going to have a discussion about the vice-president. It's a historical thing, and you may want to observe it.' So I was taken into the room. Now, he had meetings all night. I just went to the first meeting, and it lasted maybe thirty minutes."

But was it ethical for a religious leader to be so closely identified with politics? Watergate was in every mind as Phil put the next question:

"Should one of the leading churchmen of the world be making that kind of recommendation [naming a vice-president], given the wording of the First Amendment?"

Graham had been the intimate of more presidents than any churchman in our history. What could he say? Grinning like a small boy who has been "stood in a corner," he said: "My wife agrees entirely with you. She thinks that all my advice should be spiritual and moral and not political, and I think she's right."

A wave of applause hit the mikes, and decibel needles jumped. Graham had touched a nerve.

Toward the end of the hour, Ruth Graham joined her husband. Phil questioned her about her grandchildren (twelve of them, going on fourteen); about being liberated (the truly liberated woman is one who has been liberated by Jesus Christ); and if she ever fought with her husband.

"No."

"You don't fight?"

"Oh, I disagree with him, but I'm very careful not to do it with curlers in my hair."

Had it ever been serious enough for her to consider divorce?

"No! I've never thought of divorce, in all these thirty-five years of married life," she said. "But I did think of murder a few times."

Amid laughter, Phil brought the program to a graceful conclusion.

I had been royally entertained, but had I learned little or learned much? Regardless, I felt I had just heard the best sermon of Graham's crusade, and that was a heartening bonus.

## Seeds in the Wind

The going-home crowd after a crusade service is unlike any other. Football crowds divide into winners and losers, intent on hurrying to some oasis. A circus crowd coagulates into families and plods toward some sanctuary, trailing balloons and children. The Las Vegas crowd lingered. Their voices were low when they spoke, as if speaking might shatter the ambience that surrounded them. Their faces shone. They walked quietly. When they reached the parking lot and started their car motors, they moved off slowly.

I asked a teenage girl: "What did you get out of the crusade?" "Oh, so much," she said.

A young mother replied: "I could never put it into words, but it was wonderful."

A white-haired woman, walking alone, had stopped to rest on her cane. She replied: "I found some friends."

A common thought still bound them together. This crusade had been something special. But now it was over, and they had to return to the real world that waited for them across Paradise Avenue, down the Tonopah Highway, or up Route 15 to Salt Lake City.

Back at the center, inquirers and counselors were paired, age for age and sex for sex, and their heads were close as they spoke of a commitment to Christ. Here and there, a twosome became a threesome as a clergyman-advisor answered a signal from a counselor who needed help. The latter had been trained intensively for six weeks prior to the crusade; the ministers had spent their lives in Bible study. Between them, they sought to answer the questions asked by every babe in Christ.

On the platform, Cliff Barrows and George Beverly Shea were saying good-byes and signing autographs. Down a corridor, Billy Graham was changing his soggy clothing. The Graham style of preaching requires an athlete's stamina and is infused with vehement conviction. He once wrote: "In a crusade, all I can think about is preaching. Morning, noon, and night, I am thinking about sermons. I forget my own personal affairs and everything."

I had learned not to speak to him about any important matters after a service. His mind would be too occupied to remember it. Tonight, that strain had ended. His mind was free, and his heart was singing. "I doubt that anyone can share the feeling of sheer relief, joy, abandonment, and exhilaration that comes at the end of a major crusade," he has explained. For weeks, he carried a heavy load. Now the pressures are lifted, and now one can relax.

Ahead of us, at the team office in the Landmark Hotel, I knew that the process of departure was accelerating. The office suite would be buzzing with phone calls, queries about airplane flight times, and swift farewells. Some of the team had packed their suitcases before breakfast, gone to an assigned church and sung, soloed, or preached a sermon, returned to the center for the final crusade service, and now had planes to catch.

Larry Turner was off to Sweden, to prepare the ground for a crusade scheduled for the autumn of 1978.

Bev Shea would go home to Western Springs, Illinois, to rest his voice. He and Johnny Cash had developed an ailment called "Las Vegas throat," caused by the dry atmosphere in that town.

Cliff Barrows would hurry to Memphis to address a conference of church leaders—a vital step in preparing for that impending crusade in May.

Walter Smyth, vice-president for international crusades, would fly behind the iron curtain to open new doors for Christian evangelism.

Lydia Smith, whose specialty was organizing prayer groups, would hurry to Toronto to help with the June Canadian crusade.

Tom Phillips, borrowed from the Memphis task force, would return to his work there.

Lowell Jackson, specialist with youth, would dash to Memphis to organize the city's teenagers.

Akbar Haqq would fly to India, then to Timor in Indonesia, thence to Salonica, Greece, for preaching engagements, and finally return to India, to conduct a unique All-India Institute on Evangelism.

George Wilson, BGEA's executive vice-president, would spend the next three days in his Minneapolis headquarters, then go to Chicago for one board meeting, thence to Honolulu, to sit with the board of the BGEA radio station that serves the Hawaiian Islands.

Bill Brown, in charge of World Wide Films, BGEA's prizewinning picture-producing affiliate, would return to the studios in Los Angeles.

Roger Palms, editor of *Decision* magazine, would fly to Los Angeles on a writing assignment.

Sterling Huston, national director of crusades, would go to Memphis to check their facilities—including special rooms for the clerical staff, the team room, Graham's conference room, hotel reservations, transportation, and such—for the next crusade.

Fred Dienert and Walter Bennett, partners in the Walter Bennett advertising agency, which supervises the making of the television tapes of Graham's crusades, would also inspect the Memphis auditorium and make arrangements for their cameras and crews.

Don Bailey, BGEA's patient expert on communications and Graham's press secretary, would remain close to his boss's side, to help with press conferences, interviews, and statements, and to handle the endless stream of long-distance queries that originate in newspaper offices around the world.

Finally, Billy and Ruth Graham would fly to Los Angeles to appear briefly on the ''Merv Griffin Show.'' Then they would fly to Dallas, where he would receive an Abraham Lincoln Award from the Southern Baptists. After that, they would take a plane to Mexico (he slept the first forty-eight hours there), where he would finish the book he had been writing on the Holy Spirit.

Jack Cousins and other team members would remain in Las Vegas for several months, to help local pastors and congregations master the follow-up techniques for incorporating new converts into their Christian fellowships.

Other team members were already at work, plowing the ground for a Kansas City harvest in August.

Evangelists, it must be clear, are the jet set of Christianity. They jet around the world, returning home for abbreviated get-acquainted holidays with their families, and then fly on to their next assignments. Some of the team are ministers, some laymen. All are men and women of great talent and ability. They could have made it big in a business or profession. Instead, they chose the anonymity of the Lord.

They are a very special breed.

With all Billy Graham's command of technology, what had his crusade accomplished in Las Vegas? Las Vegas was still the same city, but his visit had stiffened the spines of its Christians. Its ministers had learned how to work together. The crusade had reinvigorated all the churches. It had added members to many churches. God had made the headlines and TV newscasts for the first time in local history. Christians were walking with a new and holy boldness.

I heard a reporter ask Graham: ''Who won? You or the devil?''

Graham replied: ''There'll never be a final victory until Jesus returns. Only then will the victory be complete.''

But even a partial victory in this year of the locusts was significant to them. A visiting group of young people from Salt Lake City had rented a bus and driven across the desert to the crusade. I met them on the afternoon of their arrival, when I visited a church and found them lying, wall to wall, on sleeping bags and quilts in the recreation hall—boys down one side, girls down the other.

After the Sunday service, I saw them board their bus for the returning trip to Utah. They had slept on that hard wood floor for two nights, but their eyes were the brightest I'd ever seen. They had been a standard Operation Andrew mixture—one Christian to one nonbeliever—when they arrived. I wondered what they were now.

They would ride home, grow up, move around, and be scattered like seeds in the wind. Some of them would settle on rocky ground and some on fallow. Some would be choked by weeds, but some would sprout and bloom.

The Utah bus joined a lengthening queue of pickups, vans, and touring cars. Soon, the outbound lanes would be crowded with homing pilgrims. We dodged our way across Paradise Road and turned into the Landmark, our home for a week, and were engulfed by the bedlam of voices, clanking slot machines, and the solid beat of a brass combo.

A faded dowager stood on spiked heels before a bank of "bandits," mindlessly dropping quarters into one slot after another. A keno runner, wearing a high-rise bra and fake-wet hip huggers, slithered through the crowd carrying a pile of greenbacks on a keno tray. A theatrical type, his shirt unbuttoned to his navel and chino pants glued to his body, circled like a panther about a trio of coeds.

Church was out, and we had come home to hell.

# 7

# The Mickey Cohen Caper

*Phil Donahue:* *One of the allegations is that your association offered to pay Mickey Cohen ten thousand dollars to
show up at one of your crusades at Madison Square Garden
and come forward and commit himself to Christ.*

*Billy Graham:* *We and none of my associates have ever
offered or paid one cent for any person at any time in the
history of my ministry to come forward . . . .*

From a Donahue
telecast taped in
Las Vegas, February 2, 1978

Enough is enough.

My pilgrimage had taken me through the Billy Graham headquarters in Minneapolis. Neither its people nor its policies had
changed all that much since my visits a decade earlier.

In Jamaica, I had eavesdropped on BGEA workers—from
superstars to acolytes—and found them as humanly vulnerable
as they were dedicated.

In Las Vegas, I had witnessed a daring raid by Spirit-filled
commandos, which had rocked and jarred that apostate community to its neon-lighted heels. Again, the evangelizing tactics I
had witnessed were the same as those about which I had written
for years. Neither their thrust, theme, nor results varied in any
significant way from Graham's earlier inspired use of electronic
media to sow the seeds of the Word.

So I was driven to the conclusion that the association itself
had not changed.

But America had changed.

The nation had watched the upward climb of Billy Graham
with mingled emotions. At first, the press had called him a "hot
gospeller" and a "Barrymore in Gabardine." The kid evangelist
who had infuriated President Harry Truman by praying on the
White House lawn had survived, to become a sought-after White
House visitor. And the American people had gotten in the habit
of voting him—year after year—one of the nation's most admired citizens.

In short, with a quarter-century of single-minded advocacy of
the Christian way of life, Graham had gained unprecedented
esteem and acceptance. But he had also gained unprecedented
visibility, which made him a target.

The Watergate boggle had made him unusually vulnerable. It
had changed the public's attitude toward leaders in every walk of
life, with the exception of sports heroes. Billy Graham had become one of America's most conspicuous dart boards.

And because of that fact, I was in Las Vegas, which was only a
hop, skip, and jump from the old stamping ground of Mickey
Cohen, the Hollywood mobster who had risen from his grave,
through the medium of printer's ink, to harass the evangelist
who had been his friend.

Somewhere across the state line, I was sure, I could find
documents or witnesses useful to my quest. So I began to
explore one of the most abusive and derogatory charges of which
an evangelist can be accused. It appeared as the opening chapter
of a book published late in 1977.

The author asserted that Billy Graham, on the threshold of
national acclaim, needed a convert of "headline-grabbing proportions . . . an anti-Christ, to be dramatically converted at
stage center," so he hired a shill, mobster Mickey Cohen, from
Los Angeles.

The author claimed that Cohen agreed to a phoney conversion

for the sum of $10,000 "direct from the Billy Graham treasure chest."

He asserted that Cohen, according to the agreement, went to New York and attended a 1957 service at Madison Square Garden, where "two dozen photographers and reporters were tipped and ready . . . waiting for Mickey to hit the sawdust trail." He added that Cohen, when the invitation was given, double-crossed Graham; that he had "taken the payoff money and run."

The author asserted that he obtained the above facts from Cohen during a 1976 visit to him in a Los Angeles hospital, where Cohen was dying of cancer of the stomach. The interview, the author claimed, was taped and witnessed.

Quoting Mickey's last words, he claimed that the ex-gangster said: "The ten-thousand-dollar payoff is the —— truth. Billy knows it, I know it, and now *you* know it."

An interesting story. I spent six months running it down, checking enough of it to satisfy my hunger for the truth.

### The 1949 Invitation

The story starts with an amazing little mobster named Mickey Cohen, whose heyday coincided with Billy Graham's 1949 arrival in Los Angeles.

Mickey was a New Jersey punk and strong-arm man who went west and turned himself into an authentic Al Capone-style gangster. When Bugsy Siegel, Los Angeles's top hood, was blasted to kingdom come by parties unknown, Cohen out-murdered and out-brawled all rivals, until he became the undisputed top honcho of the film capital. Rumor said that he handled over $600,000 daily in his gambling enterprises.

His peak income was estimated at twelve thousand dollars a day. He lived high, bought three suits at a time, and threw them away when they got wrinkled. He had fifteen hundred pairs of sox. He was full of phobias. He would not open a door until he had placed a tissue around the knob. He would answer a phone only after wrapping the receiver in a tissue. If a guest left a single stray hair on Cohen's washbasin, Mickey's day was ruined. He could not stand body odor and spent forty dollars a week on an expensive cologne. He grabbed every check in sight when he dined at famous restaurants, which he did almost nightly.

He also made a deal with a newspaper editor, whereby he would feed the editor tips on the city's gangs and their capers in exchange for favorable treatment in news stories. Old-timers believe it was that arrangement which led to Cohen being designated not as Cohen the killer, the mobster, the hood, but as "Mickey Cohen, the well-known gambler."

The "well-known gambler" first met Graham in 1949, when Billy and his team had just survived the longest dry spell of their evangelistic career; a period climaxed by a crusade that had fizzled and flopped in Altoona, Pennsylvania. They were determined not to fail in Los Angeles. At this turning point in their careers, the winds of success were beginning to blow. Scarcely out of their twenties, the team was attracting Hollywood stars and business tycoons to their tented services.

One night, Jim Vaus dropped into the Los Angeles crusade tent with his wife—with no worry whatever about a ticket to heaven—and found himself challenged by Graham's message. "It was on the eve of what was to have been the biggest heist of my life," Vaus told me later.

Turning over a new leaf, he quit working for Cohen as a wiretapper, and prepared himself for a ministry of his own. In the years since, he has used his electronic magic to woo thousands of young men from the devil's camp into the straight world of decency and faith.

Jim Vaus himself, if not Exhibit *A* in Graham's succour list of lost souls, was surely Exhibit *B*, for he was a gone-wrong preacher's son, a gone-wrong air force officer, and a gone-wrong electronics expert. He had won Mickey's heart by slithering under his house, despite a sputtering fuse, and disarming a bomb that could have blown them both to bits.

With his own 1949 conversion, Vaus began making amends with vigor. He visited the district attorney and promised to pay back every person he had defrauded. With equal fervor, he worried about the soul of his former boss, Los Angeles's number-one bad boy, Mickey Cohen. One night—one fateful night—he felt certain enough of his campaign to enlist Mickey on the Lord's side that he told Billy: "Mickey says he'd like for you to come out to his house. I think he'll listen to you."

I can imagine Billy Graham's thoughts at that moment. Possessing the faith that nothing accidental ever happens to a child of the kingdom, Billy had already seen abundant evidence of the Lord's blessing. Stuart Hamblin, a western radio star and sportsman, had already come forward, to the clattering of typewriters and the clacking of gossip columnists.

Graham must have thought Cohen's invitation was the will of God. If only *that* lost soul could be rescued—with thousands of ghetto kids making idols of his likes—what a triumph that would be for the Lord. As he and Cliff Barrows and Jim Vaus drove through the dark streets of Brentwood, I imagine Graham could hear distant trumpets.

No doubt about it; in 1949, Mickey was tops. No matter that his reputation as the town's number-one bad boy was largely self-generated—a product of his yen for personal publicity. At that point, he was the undisputed boss of the biggest nonsyndicate bookie business west of Chicago.

He had won his perch on the catbird seat by using muscle, and he would hold it by using muscle. Several times, bombings and shootings engineered by rivals had resulted in the deaths of his closest associates.

Wounded and scarred of face, Cohen survived ten attacks. Two bodyguards died of gang bullets. His lawyer lost half his face to a shotgun blast. His accountant, due to testify about Mickey's income, dropped dead of a "heart attack." A partner who had moved back to New York committed suicide. Police record the lawlessness of their clients on a document called a "make sheet." Mickey's police make sheet was four and one-half pages long. So he traveled with bodyguards, kept his home under electronic surveillance (designed by Jim Vaus), and ordered a bulletproof car.

Paradoxically, he insisted on living up to his reputation as "Mr. First Nighter," appeared on TV shows, and ran a money-raising jubilee for Israeli relief. He was a strange and complex man, playing a strange and complex role. By his own lights, he was good and moral. His proudest boast was that he had "never killed anybody that, by our way of life, didn't deserve it."

Perhaps the truth about his secret self was glimpsed in this remark by a local citizen, who said: "Why do we put up with him? He is a pipsqueak and a myth. He has done a snow job on the local columnists. He has deliberately courted headlines to build his own name. . . . Even the Eastern mobsters have been taken in by the Cohen headlines."

### The Meeting, 1949

That nocturnal meeting in Mickey's Brentwood home must have been memorable. The house stood at 513 Moreno Avenue, and had cost $150,000. Mickey had redecorated and rebuilt its interior, paying $48,000 more.

Billy told me about it in late 1963, when I was editing his memoirs for *McCall's* magazine. Jim Vaus told me the story again in 1966, when I interviewed him. And Mickey told it in his own words to his biographer, John Peer Nugent, in the early 1970s.

Graham recalled: "I remember having a little feeling of uncertainty and hesitation, and yet inside me there was a boldness and courage, because I knew that I was going to witness to a famous man in the name of Jesus Christ.

"Mickey came to the door, and I was surprised to see how short he was [five feet, five inches]. He was very friendly . . . . and he looked at me with those big, brown, curious eyes of his. I doubt if he had ever talked to a preacher, and certainly never to an evangelist, before."

Cohen recalled a similar uneasiness. "I was a little bit uncomfortable in the hands of all those church people," he said.

What did they talk about?

Graham's memo to me says: "I explained the Gospel to Mickey, from A to Z, as simply, as forthrightly, and as best I could, praying subconsciously all the time that God would help me find the right words."

How did Mickey react? "Mickey told me something about his own life, especially about the charitable organizations he had contributed to, and the good things he had done. He told me that, while he had another religious belief, he respected me and that he certainly respected what Jim Vaus had done. Before we left, we had prayer."

The next day, the story of that meeting was headlined in the Los Angeles papers, and Graham learned something about the mobster that others already knew well. Whatever Mickey Cohen did, newsworthy or not, he reported it to the papers.

"The publicity made me sick," Graham told me. "I felt that a wonderful opportunity to witness for Christ might be spoiled. From that day on, I began to pray seriously and hard for Cohen's conversion."

## The "Saving" of Mickey Cohen

Both careers picked up speed. Billy was starting his climb toward international evangelism. Mickey was heading for prison. In 1951, Cohen was arrested, tried, and sentenced to five years. The indictment was for income-tax evasion, but the real rap included every crime of violence you could name. Rumor said that Mickey had salted away $1 million before the trial.

Before Cohen was bused off to McNeil Island prison, Billy counseled and prayed with him at the Los Angeles county jail. According to Mickey, "His visit electrified the whole building the minute he hit the place." Quoting Mickey again: "The first thing he said to me was, 'Mick, you've tried everything else. Why don't you try Christianity?' "

After the visit, Billy told the press: "Cohen is worth saving."

Cohen said: "Maybe he's got something."

When Mickey emerged from prison after three and one-half years of good behavior, no brass band met him. No key to the city was proffered. Instead, he was told to get lost. The handwriting on the walls of Los Angeles was clear: Mickey's reign was over. The $1 million treasure he had stashed away turned out to be a hoax. As a 14-carat hood, the muscleman had "lost his juice." Nevertheless, he bounced back to the same old life-style. Developing a new hustle, he managed to stay alive by borrowing, grafting, freeloading, and trading on his old image.

Mickey also contrived to keep himself in luxury. He did this through the deft recruitment of old friends and dear hearts into a group of lenders informally called the "Save Mickey From Poverty" club. Jim Vaus was one of its first members.

Vaus was not a sucker, as much as a loyal friend. I recently contacted him after finding a transcript of our years-ago interviews in my file room. Over the phone, he told me that Mickey had come to him following his release from McNeil Island prison, and that he had "helped him with rent on his apartment, buying groceries for his pantry, and loaning him a car.

"I never thought of repayment," Vaus said. "He was at loose ends, and I was the one who suggested that he write a book. I thought that at least that would be something to keep him occupied and away from the old mob.

"I even gave him the run of my office, and he used to come in every morning and dictate to my secretary. Somewhere in my files, if I could find it, there's a copy of what he wrote."

About this time, a colorful character named W. C. Jones entered the picture. A reformed gambler and alcoholic, Jones had become a dedicated "born-againer." He was one of the prosperous businessmen who had invited Graham and his team to stage their 1949 crusade in the City of Angels. Sitting on the platform most nights, he had gotten to know the more unusual converts. One of these was Jim Vaus.

So it was inevitable that Jones should hear of Vaus's earnest campaign to save Mickey's soul. After a while, he asked for an introduction. Thereafter, the salvation of Mickey became his high-priority project.

Thus Jones, in his eagerness to finish the job that Graham had started and Vaus had nursed along with kindness and cash, fell into Mickey's orbit and became a prize pushover following Cohen's release from prison.

Between borrowing money and listening to homilies on Christian living, Mickey felt a yearning that had visited his conscience much of late. He yearned to be loved. Now that the syndicate had no further use for him, he was a bad boy who wanted to be thought good. Psychologists would call him a split personality. For a while after his release from McNeil prison, he had happily accompanied Cal Meador, his probation officer, to camps for delinquent boys, warning them that crime did not pay. Time and again, he turned up at rallies conducted by the Volunteers of America. Earlier, he had proudly raised $350,000 for destitute Jews settling in newborn Israel. His usual tip for a shave or haircut was a $20 bill.

So he listened—closely, I believe—to the earnest importunings of Billy's friend, W. C. Jones, until they reached a climax. That was the day, I believe, on which Cohen and Jones went to Cohen's apartment for a counseling and prayer session that lasted for five hours and which ended, Jones always believed, in Mickey accepting Jesus Christ as Lord and Saviour. Later— much later—Mickey denied that he had ever contemplated abandoning Jewry. For the time being, however, Jones was convinced he had led another lost sheep back to the fold.

In the light of future events, it could be that he had misunderstood. It is also possible that Mickey, for reasons hidden in his warped psyche, had later lied.

### The First Trip to New York

The fine art of evangelizing, as understood by Jones and Vaus at that time, undoubtedly included, as it does now, several essential steps. The first required an inquirer (Mickey) to accept by faith the divinity of Jesus Christ as the Son of God. Second, evangelism attempted to give each inquirer a rudimentary understanding of evangelical doctrines, sometimes known as "the faith of our fathers." Finally, it required that the inquirer should make his submission to the Lord before the eyes of men— publicly.

Let us assume that Jones had made the initial breakthrough. In evangelistic jargon, he had "led Mickey to the Lord." But that was only the beginning. A new babe in Christ requires nourishment, and neither Jones nor Vaus felt qualified to administer the Gospel pablum required by so hardened a sinner as their new charge. Only one man could perform that function to Mickey's satisfaction. They would contact Billy Graham, who was in New York, and get his consent to a meeting. There must have been hurried phone calls, arrangements about time and place, and considerable rejoicing.

Jones and Vaus paid the tab. The transcript of Mickey's subsequent tax evasion case (Number 17503, U.S. Court of Appeals, Ninth Circuit, Los Angeles) records that Vaus spent $400 for a plane ticket and Jones paid $507 for accommodations, which included $66 for candy. Another $135 flew from Jones's purse to Mickey's sticky fingers for spending money. The hotel was the exclusive Waldorf-Astoria. The repentant Cohen insisted on being reborn first class.

What happened in New York? My files hold a United Press clipping which says that "Mickey Cohen, former West Coast gambling czar, flew here yesterday for a private prayer meeting with evangelist Billy Graham." It says nothing about a conversion.

Graham must have answered all of Mickey's questions, as he had done for thousands of other inquirers, but he would surely also insist that Mickey carry out the scriptural injunction requiring a *public* confession.

A public confession? Perhaps W. C. Jones or Vaus, who were strong churchmen in their own communities, could arrange for Cohen to come forward at one of their churches. Or perhaps Mickey would rather return to the Garden next month, when the New York crusade would be in session.

Mickey's mind must have lighted up at that prospect. If anyone doubts it, a view of his pile of oversize, blue, leather-bound scrapbooks, with their huge glassine envelopes full of photos and stories of Mick's real and imagined escapades, would surely be a convincer. Or if one doubts that his ego demanded such a spotlight, a visit to his apartment—where every possession bore his

initials in printing, engraving, embroidery, or wood carving—
would do the same.

When reporters hunted down Graham for his version of the
rendezvous, they found him in Buffalo, New York. He was not
happy to see them. "Surely a man ought to be able to seek
spiritual counsel without having his search publicized," he said.
"My job is to try to win every person to Christ; especially persons who would have influence for Christ in our society."

To summarize the events of Mickey Cohen's "conversion":

- Mickey Cohen did go to New York to see Billy Graham, but
  not to go forward at a crusade meeting, because the crusade
  would not start for another three weeks. Instead, they met at
  the Waldorf-Astoria hotel.
- Cohen did not hire himself out as a shill, but was apparently
  converted, according to W. C. Jones's statement, during a
  three-hour session of prayer and counseling with Graham.
- Cohen did not travel on money provided by the Billy
  Graham organization, but on money contributed by two old
  friends: Jim Vaus, who had once been his employee, and
  W. C. Jones, who had met Cohen through Vaus after the
  1949 crusade.

### The Second Trip to New York

I have no trouble in believing that every word of the above is
true, but it is certainly not the whole story.

Because, only a few weeks later, Mickey Cohen returned to
New York to attend a service at the Graham crusade. Who paid
for this second trip? According to the *Saturday Evening Post*,
"Mickey was invited to appear on the Mike Wallace television
show. Intoxicated by the heady wine of national publicity and
further soothed by some $1,800 in non-taxable expense money,

Mickey flew east and sat in the Wallace hot seat on May 19th.''

On May twenty-first, he showed up at Graham's crusade. Why? Many members of the Graham team have asked that question. Did he intend to go forward? Or was his motive a simple, egocentric obsession to squeeze from every occasion the maximum production of Mickey Cohen press notices? Had he lived on publicity for so long that now he was hooked? I believe he was a torn and unhappy man. On one hand, he craved the serenity and joy offered by Christianity. On the other, he was intoxicated by his vision of being a little Caesar.

The brief interval between trips had certainly been punctuated by periods of unease among the faithful. Elated by his session with Billy Graham, Mickey must have delighted in regaling his old California cronies with anecdotes from the Waldorf rendezvous. In fact, those old cronies were already a matter of disagreement between Mickey and W. C. Jones. Ex-cons, racketeers, and hoods of proven competence, their influence on Mickey was passionately deplored by Jones.

At one point, an aggravated Mickey had bluntly told Jones, ''If my convertin' is gonna mean I've gotta give up all my pals, let's call the whole thing off.''

All his life, Mickey had been a troublemaker. It must have occurred to more than one team member that his going forward at a crusade meeting might turn into a mob-inspired donnybrook. Why else was he traveling with bodyguards? It also presented a nice, unprecedented question. When a hoodlum goes forward to the altar, do his bodyguards go, too?

The omens were not good. One team member was assigned to meet Mickey at the airport. He missed him. Other team members reported that the press had been mysteriously alerted to Mickey's prospective attendance. A special force of photographers had been sent to the Garden to cover this final moment of Mickey's long wrestling match with the devil.

True to his word, Mickey showed up at the Garden as promised, slick shaven, cologne scented, and wearing an unwrinkled suit. Like an invading general, he led an army of photographers straight to Graham's dressing room. His bodyguards walked a half-pace behind. Ushers stopped the photographers, but Mickey found Ruth and bussed her solidly (she told me recently) and then explained it was picture-taking time.

Peremptorily, he called for Billy. Ruth explained that press coverage was hardly an appropriate accompaniment for such a solemn moment. Mickey was stunned. His volatile temper began to sparkle and sputter. His bodyguards flexed their muscles and argued, with mercenary zeal, that their boss was a big man, who made his own rules.

But not here. Billy went to his place on the platform. The service was beginning. Mickey was escorted to a loge reserved for special guests. Ruth, with daughters Ann and Gigi, found chairs a few feet away, in the first ground-level row.

Billy remembered that evening. "Mickey had informed all the newspapers that he was going to be there, and I tried to avoid seeing him," Billy says. "I did not have any pictures taken with him. I did not allow it. So he stood in front of Madison Square Garden and had his picture taken under the marquee."

Ruth goes further. She was in the first row. Mickey was in a loge behind. During the service, Ruth saw a photographer creeping in and focusing his camera. The photo he planned would show the mobster looming behind the front-row figures of Graham's wife and children.

As the photographer set himself to shoot, Ruth surprised herself by leaning forward and thrusting her hymnbook before the camera lens.

"If we had been trying to get publicity," she told me recently, "there would never have been a book over that shutter."

My research into the episode unfortunately does not include

the subject of Billy's sermon that night. Whatever it was, if Mickey was the target, it missed. When Billy gave the invitation, the little gangster never moved a muscle, never gave a single hint of body language that would reveal his inner emotions.

After the benediction, Cohen and his bodyguards were captured by photographers. "How about those pictures, Mick?" they said. "Let's get Graham." Slowly, Mickey led them to the front of Madison Square Garden and posed there under the marquee that bore Billy's name. He was a strutting, vain, disappointed, and, in some ways, a pitiable little man.

So there you have it—a straight-forward account of an effort by Christians to turn a mobster into a believer. But the attempt failed, and ordinarily that would have been that.

## The 1961 Cohen Trial

What follows demonstrates the damage that a resourceful devil can do, given a few simple ingredients. First, we follow Mickey back to Hollywood, where his star was on the rise. Thanks to an appearance on a Mike Wallace telecast, he was a news item. Thanks to his personal acquaintance with Billy Graham, America's most magnetic public figure, Cohen possessed a fund of small talk and intimate anecdotes that made him a welcome visitor along Hollywood's party circuit.

The situation was perfect for the exploitation of his still-incomplete life story, which was the only item in his bag of tricks having cash value. So gossip about his visit with Billy became a door opener and a preface to a series of "touches."

In time, Mickey's truth and his inventions became one and the same. Borrowing money at an extraordinary rate said to be about $100,000 a year, he beat a pathway through Tinseltown, while living a life that legal papers subsequently described as "without visible means of support."

The strain of creative exaggeration must have been great for the unlettered Mickey as he went from door to door, from restaurant to saloon, but he was up to it. "What's a guy to do?" he once complained to a pal. "The mob won't let me operate here. If I open up in the territory of some friendly sheriff, the Los Angeles cops will follow me. I got no chance to make an honest living." So he hustled, and eventually crossed the path of a famous TV and movie star named Red Skelton.

Mickey's first phone call to Red said, "I've got onto something that's good for both of us." Shortly thereafter, he appeared at Skelton's house, movie script under his arm. As usual, the name of Billy Graham came up, and Mickey volunteered the information that the evangelist had paid him $15,000 just to sit in his audience in New York. And he would have gotten $25,000 if he had gone forward and converted to Christianity. In fact, "This here script was copied for me by Billy Graham's secretary," he said.

"It's a great story, with a great part for you," Mickey added, watching his quarry. "In fact, I've come out here to offer you the chance to play me—to play the leading role of Mickey Cohen."

Red was amused. He was six-foot-two, with red hair. Mickey was short, pudgy, black haired. Red said, "Well, thanks, but I can't see you as a tall redheaded fellow."

"Well, it was just a shot in the dark," the hustler said, and proceeded with his real business, which was to try to touch his "friend" for a few thousand to tide him over. Ben Hecht was coming to town to finish his script, Cohen said, and that would turn it into a million-dollar property.

"No dice," Red concluded.

Mickey had a way with him, a directness and ingeniousness, that plastered a patina of truthfulness over his most outrageous demands. Between 1957 and 1960, Mickey's borrowings continued at a dizzy pace. Eventually, agents of the Internal Revenue Service became so interested that they infiltrated his turf and compiled a list of hundreds of Mickey's contributors. The donations ranged from a few dollars to $50,000 per touch.

Inevitably, Uncle Sam took a dim view of Mickey's loans, calling them income. A grand jury indicted him in 1960. His trial began in May of 1961, in a federal court under the gavel of Judge H. H. Boldt, who was imported to the Los Angeles bench to offset the razzle-dazzle atmosphere of a genuine celebrity extravaganza. The issue was: Had Mickey evaded taxes?

After a month of testimony and a parade of such famous names as Red Skelton and Jerry Lewis, the court decided that indeed he had evaded paying taxes, and sentenced him to fifteen years in Alcatraz.

Among the early witnesses was actor Red Skelton. The prosecution's lawyers asked him what he knew about the source of Mickey's income. Remembering Mickey's boasts about being paid by Graham to sit in his audience, Skelton told the court of Cohen's claim.

A blizzard of headlines swept across the nation, announcing the news that:

COHEN PAID $15,000 BY BILLY GRAHAM TO SIT AT REVIVAL, COMEDIAN DECLARES

BILLY GRAHAM PAID GAMBLER "TO ATTEND," SKELTON SAYS

COHEN SAYS BILLY GRAHAM PAID HIM $15,000 TO ATTEND REVIVAL.

One day later, in smaller type, deep in the back pages, earnest searchers might have found Graham's response, saying: GRAHAM DENIES HE TRIED TO BUY COHEN CONVERSION.

To pin Mickey more tightly to the mat, government attorneys had corralled a battalion of witnesses who had loaned him money. One by one, they told their sworn stories of loans that were never repaid. W. C. Jones, publicly itemizing his own contributions before and after the mobster's junkets to Manhattan, proudly asserted: "I considered it a privilege to attempt to turn this human deficit into a community asset." The adventure had cost him only $5,000, Jones said. Mickey swore it had cost him several times that.

Another witness was a Mrs. Eleanor Churchin, described by reporters as a press agent. Her story duplicated Skelton's hearsay testimony. Mickey had informed her that the amount he really got from Graham was closer to $10,000, she claimed. Again, headline writers rolled the juicy scandal across their pages.

Fortunately, Jim Vaus was in the wings. Scheduled to testify about his own Cohen contributions, he was amazed when he heard her statement, because he knew that she knew it was not true. Granted, Vaus and Jones had helped Mickey with sizable sums, but none of their money had come from Billy or from the BGEA. During the lunch break, Vaus cornered Cohen and demanded a showdown.

"I knew that Billy had never made any payment of any kind to Mickey," he told me recently. "I told him and his lawyer that I knew Mrs. Churchin's testimony was false and that I was going on the stand to tell the truth. I asked him, in a very nonthreatening and friendly way, to speak to Mrs. Churchin and tell her that she would be well-advised to go to the judge and tell him she'd perjured herself."

Next day, she did.

Not many papers carried her recantation. So the truth, as usual, never caught up with the lie. An account carried by the *Pensacola News Journal* for June 11, 1961, was typical. It said:

"A woman witness at the trial of Mickey Cohen has admitted . . . that she made up the story that evangelist Billy Graham had offered Cohen $10,000 to become converted to Christianity. It was a gimmick to publicize Cohen in the interest of a proposed book and a movie of his life, said Mrs. Eleanor Churchin, the witness."

The report appeared also in the prestigious journal, *Christianity Today*, on June 5, 1961. The article identified Mrs. Churchin as a press agent who had invented the bribe story as "a publicity stunt for a book on Cohen's life that she wanted to write."

## Alcatraz and Pardon Appeals

Sentenced to prison for fifteen years, Mickey went first to Alcatraz and then to the federal penitentiary in Atlanta. Within a year of the transfer, a fellow convict leaped on him from behind and tried to beat out his brains with a lead pipe.

When he healed, Cohen was crippled for life. A move to a federal stockade in Springfield, Missouri, which had special treatment facilities, produced some improvement, but not much. With the passing of time, it became evident that Cohen would never again be a menace to society, so relatives and friends combined forces to seek a compassionate parole. The project's spark plug was Harry, Mickey's brother. Suffering from ulcers and high blood pressure himself, he wrote innumerable letters and made tireless speeches on Mickey's behalf.

Jim Vaus also became one of those who petitioned for clemency. So did Billy Graham, in a letter addressed to the authorities that said: "I have known Mickey Cohen ever since 1949 . . . . I am fully aware of his past record. But as he has been crippled for life by the beating he received at the hands of another inmate in the Atlanta penitentiary, I believe that both justice and mercy would be served by giving him a medical parole."

Harry Cohen, seeking a forum for his plea, was invited to

appear on a Los Angeles telecast conducted by Joe Pyne. Pyne permitted Harry to deliver his pitch describing Mickey's pitiable state and asking listeners to address requests for mercy to the proper authorities.

Suddenly, the name of Billy Graham fell from Pyne's lips. He asked Harry about the $10,000 his brother had received from the evangelist to turn Christian. Harry was unprepared. Explaining that he had lived in Chicago during those crusade days, he said he had no real knowledge of the matter. Pyne persisted, asserting that there must have been talk in the family, gossip among the sisters and brothers, about the prospect of Mickey changing his faith. The record showed that Cohen had made a trip to New York and conferred with the evangelist. Did Billy Graham pay for his ticket? Did Billy pay for his suite at the Waldorf-Astoria?

Harry tried to sidestep, but stumbled. "Well," he responded, "if Mickey made a trip like that, the money had to come from somebody who wanted to see him real bad, didn't it?" The impression left was an unintended but damning indictment of Billy Graham. Ordinarily, that would have been the end of it, but Pyne also conducted a daily radio talk show. The radio program's format invited listeners to call in and ask questions. So for three days, listeners called Pyne and said, Wasn't it a shame? How in the world could a fine man like Graham get messed up with a crook like Cohen?

### Cohen's Denial

During Mickey's long convalescence, Graham had doggedly nursed the hope that the little felon, who once had been so close to rebirth, would feel the call again. In talks with Dr. L. Nelson Bell, his father-in-law, Graham had communicated this dream. From time to time, flurries of letters had been exchanged between Montreat and Springfield, most of them written by the persuasive doctor. At least once, Dr. and Mrs. Bell had visited and counseled Mickey in his Springfield prison cell. For years, the Cohen name was high on the Graham family's prayer list.

"We have all their letters in our vault," Ruth Graham told me one day. I was invited to examine those letters. Mickey had written from the prison in Missouri, and he had discussed the $10,000 payment tale in meticulous detail.

When I comprehended his amazing declarations to the Bells, with each envelope proclaiming the evidence of origin, I knew I had found the truth. Uprooted from the old Graham storage vault, every letter between Mickey and Billy (and copies of letters between Mickey and Jim Vaus and between Mickey and his brother, Harry) stands foursquare against the allegation that Graham made a payoff.

Cohen's letter of apology to the Grahams, which was penned on large sheets of white hospital stationery in a firm, childish scrawl, faced the issue squarely. It began with a special salutation: "My Very Dear Billy and Ruth." It continued with the assertion that his brother's ad lib remarks were beyond understanding. He had written to Harry that there was not "one iota of truth to the story." Not even "one semblance" of truth.

Cohen was writing, he confessed humbly, "in shame and sorrow." If there was anything he could do to stop "this completely untruthful, ugly rumor," he was at their beck and call. He described the tale as a "silly, uncalled for, untrue statement," that Harry would never repeat.

Mickey received his pardon from the government in 1974. Returning to his family and friends in Los Angeles, he tried to pick up the pieces of his life, but cancer had invaded him and drained away much of his strength. Despite great pain, he did succeed in completing one of his life's ambitions, the writing of an autobiography. He carried the book with him wherever he went—hard evidence at last of his claim that Mickey Cohen was a very special person. To his credit, the little man never stopped trying.

Cohen was a very special person. Significantly, his book made no claim whatever that Billy Graham had ever offered him money or paid him to attend a crusade. Instead, he protested almost too much that he had been born a Jew and had never considered the action of being anything else.

I have a feeling that the old, abrasive Mickey had mellowed. His contact with the Grahams, with the Bells, with Jim Vaus, even with the proselytizing W. C. Jones, must have changed some of his perceptions and insights. Aside from his family, they were the ones who had remained most faithful. "Rest assured that we continue to remember you," Billy had written Cohen in his last letter.

Mickey was one of a kind, easily misinterpreted. Billy had seen that he was worth saving. Of course he was. When Christ died, He was atoning for Cohen's sins as much as for any man's. I believe that Mickey sensed this fact, for he had been informed of it during the briefings of both the Grahams and the Bells.

In the anguish that followed his brother's TV misstep, Cohen had to be honest, grateful, and—at long last—truly humble. Perhaps the tortured, enfeebled man had then experienced the only "turning about" of which he was capable. Writing to Billy and Ruth, his letter closed with a reference to the good old days. He said: "If anybody had questioned Billy's integrity, they would have had me to fight. And the same still goes today, I can assure you, even though I am a cripple." Those were Mickey's last written words on or about the payoff. I believe he meant them.

Myer Harris Cohen died of cancer in a California hospital on July 29, 1976. His estate was left to old friends and members of his family. It amounted to $3,000.

# 8

# The Twenty-Three-Million-Dollar Flap

*Having the legal right to say nothing, Graham chose to reveal his financial affairs to an unprecedented degree.*

We come now to a riddle wrapped in a mystery concealed in an enigma, to paraphrase Winston Churchill's *bon mot* of World War II.

It concerns one of the most thorough financial investigations to which any evangelist has ever been subjected, as well as one of the most astonishing flip-flops in contemporary journalism.

That flip-flop included the publication of a newsmongering attack on Graham's integrity that, whether intended or not, spooked his followers from coast to coast and could have delivered the *coup de grace* to his longest-held—and perhaps his most important—dream.

In brief, that dream was the evangelist's bequest to posterity. It evolved naturally from his remarkable career and would provide its capstone. It required the establishment of two unique institutions.

The first would be a center and library for the postgraduate study of global evangelism, tuned to this electronic, computerized age.

The second would be a Bible school, set deep in a forest habitat, suitable for contemplation and self-enrichment through intensive study of the Scriptures. With neither classes, examinations, nor grades, it would offer an anchorage in which new Christians might become steady in their faith during whatever term they could attend. For older Christians, it would provide a refuge from the storms of life while providing daily instruction in the Word of God.

Graham realized that building these two unprecedented institutions in his remaining years would not be easy. Nor could it be done under the auspices of the Billy Graham Evangelistic Association, with its intense evangelistic orientation. So, in 1970, he and his team and his advisors measured his expanding influence and potential income and devised a vehicle first called the Billy Graham Philanthropic Trust. After several name changes, it became known as the World Evangelism and Christian Education Fund (WECEF).

Nor was it so wild a dream. Religious groups, throughout America's brief history, had followed a similar formula, establishing training institutions for their own leaders. Harvard, Yale, Dartmouth, and Oberlin come quickly to mind.

Graham's method was to establish a special fund. Its announced purposes were:

- To hold and invest estate bequests, trusts, and similar contributions, and other designated gifts that could be used for these purposes, and to build a training center devoted to the work of world evangelism.
- To turn some of the resources of the fund toward the development of a laymen's Bible training center.
- To assist other Christian organizations working in the fields of evangelism and related areas of Christian education and communications.
- To assist needy students, particularly those from the Third World, to obtain training in evangelism.

Those goals were typical of America at its unselfish best. How ironical that such goals, such deeply rooted Christian and humane ideals, should be distorted into a smear. For a smear is what the *Charlotte Observer*'s story started. Call it a misunderstanding, if you will, but it resulted in a smear. I have named it "the WECEF flap."

### The February 1977 Article

In the beginning, the *Observer*'s interest was warmly benign. In 1976, reporter Mary Bishop asked Graham for an interview, in order to write a story about him and his family. He granted the request readily and met several times with her. He assumed that her profile would be much like many others published during his lifetime. As time passed, however, other interviews were sought and granted. Obviously, the story's focus was extending beyond the Graham family.

On February 6, 1977, the *Observer*—its masthead declaring it to be "the foremost paper in the Carolinas"—began publication of a four-part series of articles about the evangelist. To no one's surprise, it was exhaustively researched, and it summarized every facet of the life story of a local boy who made good.

Pages upon pages of panegyrical prose were headed by such laudatory headlines as: HE SITS WITH PRESIDENTS AND EMPERORS, HE'S ADVISER TO THE MIGHTY, HE SELLS HIS FAITH, and FOR MANY HE'S HALLOWED GROUND.

In her concluding installment, Mary Bishop commented: "In a disillusioning world, Billy Graham is the only untarnished hero left to many—a lasting example of clean living, self-discipline, and good citizenship."

Another staff writer, Robert Hodierne, wrote an accompanying financial piece for the series' opener that was headlined: GRAHAM'S BUSINESS: HOW IT GREW. Hodierne described the evangelist's decision to go on the air in 1950, which led him eventually into the media of television, motion pictures, books, magazines, and overseas missions. By 1976, he said, BGEA's income was approximately $26 million.

In view of subsequent developments, Hodierne made two comments that are interesting. "Unlike some nationally known religious leaders," he said, "Graham's group has shunned displays of wealth. For instance, the fanciest of the BGEA's 18 cars is a 1976 Mercury station wagon. Graham evidently has no taste for fancy cars. He and his wife own a Jeep and a Volvo."

He added: "And unlike many other well-known evangelists, Graham's organization and Graham himself have avoided even the hint of scandal."

Overall, the February series was as friendly and reassuring a profile about a celebrity as I have ever read. Mary Bishop obviously admired Ruth and Billy and their modest, down-to-earth, life-style. Hodierne appeared to admire the business efficiency of George Wilson, BGEA's astute executive vice-president, and only fussed a little at his reluctance to bare financial details.

I feel certain that both Billy and Ruth were pleased, and Billy visited the *Observer*'s office to thank editor David Lawrence for a story, to quote the paper's publisher, that was "accurate and fair."

### June, 1977

On Thursday, June 23, 1977, the *Asheville Citizen* and the *Asheville Times,* one morning and one evening newspaper, ran the story of WECEF's purchase of North Carolina mountain acres for a Bible institute. Both of the Asheville stories reported that a Graham-related organization, known as the World Evangelism and Christian Education Fund, had paid a total of $2.5 million for the acreage. The *Asheville Citizen* even reported that the fund had "assets of around $20 million," and "liabilities in the neighborhood of $15 million." Their authority was Billy Graham.

The day before the articles appeared, on Wednesday, June 22, 1977, Billy received a phone call saying that the *Charlotte Observer* wanted a quick interview. Two reporters—Mary Bishop and Robert Hodierne—known to Graham through their highly laudatory series published by the *Observer* a few months earlier, had more questions to ask. They involved some ethical questions that "we do not take lightly," the voice said.

"Then come over tomorrow. We'll meet you at the office."

How Graham's mind must have spun as he tried to think through to the kernel of that call. What more could they want? He recalled an earlier conference in Charlotte with an *Observer* group that included those same reporters and their publisher. With some misgivings, he remembered that their questions repeatedly had probed the financial aspect of the Billy Graham Evangelistic Association.

In preparation for the *Observer*'s interview, Graham first called Allan Emery, who had attended the Charlotte conference so many months earlier.

Sensing that this might be no ordinary confrontation, Emery said, "I'm coming down."

Graham then called several friends among the newspaper publishers he knew well. He told them frankly that he was baffled at the *Observer*'s insistence that an ethical question was involved. "In their view," he wondered aloud, "what have I done wrong? Am I obligated to answer every question they ask? What is happening to my personal privacy?"

The publishers told him that he had no obligation to disclose anything that he did not want to disclose. One friend, an important owner of newspapers, said, "I can't even figure out what the problem is, because if you want to withhold information, that's your business."

Billy talked with Ruth, his wife, about the impending visit. Ordinarily, he preferred meeting media representatives in the comfortable conference room in the Assembly Drive office building.

"Let's have them come up to the house," she suggested. "If we don't, they might think we're hiding something. And I'd like them to see exactly how we live."

T. W. Wilson met the reporters at the office on Thursday, June 23 and drove them up the narrow, serpentine road. The day was temperate, and Ruth had arranged a circle of chairs on their shady, country-style porch. In line with Graham's new policy of recording his interviews, a tested tape machine hummed in discreet readiness.

At first, there was small talk and uneasy laughter. Billy, the courteous host, finally asked, "What can we do for you?"

Bob Hodierne said, "Tell us about this land."

"The whole story is in the Asheville paper this morning, and it is accurate."

The land in question was a tract of about 1100 acres, known locally as Porter's Cove. For the last ten years, a favorite sport in Buncombe County had been guessing who owned what land: Billy Graham, Jackie Gleason, Arthur Godfrey, the Arabs, the Japanese. So, finally, the what-does-Billy-own game was ending.

Hodierne said, "The Porter's Cove property is certainly a gorgeous piece of land."

"That's what we thought," Graham responded.

The reporter knew the land and had brought aerial photographs of it. Moreover, he knew all about its background, having spent hours tracing every turn and twist of the negotiations that finally resulted in its title going to the World Evangelism and Christian Education Fund. But now he had a complaint. His investigation had aroused some suspicions.

Hodierne began setting the scene. "The reason we're here,"

he said, and then explained that the *Observer* was trying to present an accurate picture of Graham's ministry. He had flown to Minneapolis to talk to George Wilson, BGEA's executive vice-president. They had discussed the various ministries of the BGEA, the management of each, and its financial contribution to the whole. He had been told that BGEA owned only the land on which its offices were located, and that the association did not hold stocks or bonds.

"So it came as quite a surprise to me," Hodierne said, "to find WECEF holding 2,600 acres—give or take a hundred acres—of prime development land in Buncombe County. And I don't understand why Mr. Wilson—and in subsequent discussion, with the rest of you gentlemen, why you—didn't mention this other arm of the Billy Graham ministry."

There it was. The first card was on the table. Hodierne was saying that Billy Graham and his people had lied. Why?

"I personally had assumed," Graham responded, "with all the interviews that you had with everybody, that you knew all these things, especially since WECEF files a 990 form [with the Internal Revenue Service] and it's a public record."

"These things" to which Billy referred were the trust named WECEF and its holdings of land and stocks and bonds. What he did not yet perceive, I believe, is that Hodierne believed with all his heart that WECEF was a part of, and a subsidiary to, BGEA.

What Hodierne did not understand—and never would—was that WECEF was an entirely separate corporation from BGEA in the minds of everyone connected with either organization. In the mental processes of both managements, and in all their day-to-day operations, each was an entity separate from the other.

So the interview started with the reporter asserting a misconception of that relationship. Despite the repeated statements of Graham and Emery, who was soon to become the president of BGEA, Hodierne continued to proclaim that mistaken idea throughout the WECEF flap. His basic error was further compounded by his misjudgment of the integrity of the men he faced, and by a bias that prevented him from accepting their replies as truth.

Hodierne's first concern was to force an admission that WECEF was in fact a BGEA subsidiary. Here are fragments from some of those taped exchanges.

"Most of the money for WECEF comes from BGEA. . . ." Hodierne stated.

"*Through* BGEA," Graham corrected.

"There's a terrific overlap of the boards of directors. Directors who are on both boards 'are the real inner circle.' "

Graham explained that originally WECEF had been set up as a money-*raising* trust. Its directors were appointed with no reference to BGEA. Later, when its function changed, and when BGEA became its principal source of funds, legal counsel advised BGEA to appoint the trust's board.

Emery added that BGEA could not really exert control, because WECEF was run by an operating committee of eight persons, and only two of them were associated with BGEA.

"But you certainly could cause it to wither on the vine. . . ." Bob argued. "I think we're really splitting hairs. I don't think there is any doubt that WECEF is the charitable arm, the foundation arm, of the Billy Graham ministry."

Graham said, "I wish you'd asked us at that meeting [in Charlotte], because we would have answered you directly."

"We were pretty direct," Bob challenged. "As a matter of fact, a couple of things came up . . . and one of them dealt with the ownership of stocks and bonds. . . . The question was, did you all *own* any stocks and bonds, and we were taken by the answer, which was no."

"BGEA *doesn't* own any stocks or bonds," Graham said.

"BGEA certainly doesn't, but WECEF does."

"Again, we're talking about two separate corporations," explained Billy.

The same subject came up later, and Emery said that it was wholly accurate to say that BGEA owned no stocks and bonds.

"But we weren't doing a story on BGEA," Bob argued. "We were doing a story on the Billy Graham ministry."

Billy interrupted again, "Mary [Bishop] never told me that. When she first came here, she never told me that there was going to be a long, involved, and in-depth story. I thought it was just a story that was going to appear on the church page. That was my impression. I didn't give her very much time. If I'd known what it was going to be, I'd have given her days."

One last effort to help Hodierne understand came when Graham stressed the uniqueness of WECEF. "I think you misunderstand about how we started," he explained. "We started with the idea that BGEA would never be giving money. WECEF was organized to raise money and to give it to needy people and organizations. At BGEA, we are constantly asked for help.

"I don't know of any other parachurch organization in America that has given away the money that we have given away all over the world."

Graham then explained in detail how BGEA had helped to train several hundred students from many nations, particularly young people from undeveloped countries.

"And we changed the name ultimately [to WECEF] on the basis that we wanted the name always to carry what it was. Get it away from Billy Graham. Get it away from my control. My day is coming soon. I've lived the better part of my life."

He related how the idea of WECEF had been received enthusiastically by contributors. "We had one man," he said, "who got all excited about our program of a trust where nobody [who worked for it] would get a dime and every dollar would go for the purpose called for in the charter. The man said, 'I don't know of another organization in the world like this. I'll give you a million dollars.' "

Then Graham explained the financing of WECEF: grants from estates, trusts, special collections, and fund-raisers in various cities. "We wanted only to evangelize, and the BGEA was our tool," he said. "So the trust became our philanthropy. Operated by dedicated money managers, it could do a much better job than BGEA could in the field of philanthropy, because it was administered by an executive committee which chose beneficiaries with full awareness of their Christian stewardship."

Graham added quietly. "We thought we were doing something for God. We thought we were doing something for humanity. We thought we were doing something for the Christian church. And I think we have."

The reporter's next gambit involved secrecy—Billy Graham's secrecy. Already, Hodierne had hinted that a need to escape public scrutiny might have been the reason behind so many corporate name changes. It also could have been behind Graham's self-imposed restriction of WECEF publicity. Now he wanted to know why secrecy had obscured for so long the purchase of WECEF's mountain land.

In truth, the WECEF purchases were as private as possible. According to official records, a Dallas lawyer named Jerry John Crawford was the buyer, and the acreage was transferred to WECEF only after some time had passed. Hodierne knew—or should have known—that the appearance of any famous person in a real-estate deal elevates the cost. A recent case was the purchase of the Florida acres on which Walt Disney World is now situated. Eventually, the price per acre rose from hundreds to many thousands of dollars—but that was only after all the early steps had been carefully hidden by the Disney people.

When Hodierne asked why Graham had not followed the Disney pattern of having different companies buy up various parcels, Emery replied: "This wasn't that big a deal."

And so it went on that lovely mountaintop, with the birds singing madly while the two sides thrust and parried, until finally, Billy said: "I think there are just two different points of view, and I don't see any ethical problem. I don't see any moral problem. I don't see any legal problem. . . .

"I'm just sorry that it happened and sorry that you feel that you were somehow misled, because I don't believe, if you had asked us directly, that we would have misled you in the slightest."

Hodierne countered by wondering how Billy could have failed to note that the *Observer* account of the "breadth and scale of your ministry" would be leaving out "$15 million worth of endowment funds and 2,600 acres of prime land."

"Well, you know," a tired Graham replied, "I actually thought you already had all of that. I was never asked about it, even. You or Mary never asked, but you didn't ask about a lot of things."

A useful session or a wasted session? Would the explanations offered by Graham prevail, or would the newsman's suspicions dominate the *Observer* story?

## The June 26 Article

On Sunday, June 26, 1977 an *Observer* headline read: GRAHAM'S $23 MILLION FUND. A more accusatory second-deck headline declared: HOLDINGS NOT REVEALED TO DONORS.

Those words rode across a six-by-nine-inch block of type on page one of the *Observer*'s Sunday edition. By-lines indicated that Mary Bishop and Robert Hodierne, the same pair who penned the earlier praise fest, were its authors. Its lead paragraph said: "The Billy Graham ministry in the last seven years has amassed $22 million in land, stocks, bonds, and cash it has carefully shielded from public view."

An even wordier article on an inside page told of land being
"secretly bought" by a Graham organization from a company
whose president "was reputed to have been in the business of
helping mobsters disguise money they acquired illegally." Its
black-faced, italicized, queen-sized headline read: OWNER HAD
MOBSTER TIES: HE LATER SOLD LAND TO GRAHAM GROUP.

What was that supposed to mean? What kind of brazen thinking could join Billy Graham with a mobster figure who had ties
with a mob figure? It had the essence of a "hot tip," but it had
absolutely no value as hard news. The reporters had been unable
to confirm any kind of connection between Graham and a
"money-laundering" operation. Apparently, wiser heads among
the *Observer*'s editors prevailed, because the puffed-up "mobster ties" headline vanished from later editions. The original
headline was relatively noncommittal. In fairness, I must add that
the management of the *Observer* has insisted all along that it had
no intention of blasting Graham. Unfortunately, night-side
deskmen and editors across the country had only the stark words
of the story, as transmitted by the Associated Press, on which to
base their judgments. Looking for a juicy tale to hype their
Monday-morning front pages, they penciled in heads and sub-
heads even blacker than those published in North Carolina. By
combining the hint of fraud with the hallowed name of Billy
Graham, they connected real eye-grabbers.

As the story moved further and further from its source, the
headlines became more and more sensational. Hurried readers
across the country were informed, for instance, that:

BILLY GRAHAM'S HOLDINGS ARE NEARLY $23 MILLIONS
GRAHAM ADMITS AVOIDING TALK ABOUT LARGE FUND
BILLY GRAHAM MINISTRY AMASSES $23 MILLION
BILLY GRAHAM TRIES TO KEEP FUND SECRET
GRAHAM PORTFOLIO NEARS $23 MILLION
GRAHAM ADMITS HUGE SECRET FUND.

In North Carolina, the name of Billy Graham is rarely tossed about lightly. Imagine, then, the shock that hit Charlotte with the publication of the GRAHAM'S $23 MILLION FUND story. In two brief paragraphs, the *Observer* had described WECEF, without mentioning its name, as "an accumulation of wealth" which had been "amassed" by the Billy Graham ministry "over the last seven years."

Within three sentences of the opening words, the authors had informed (acutally misinformed) readers that "the two million contributors a year whose gifts to Graham's ministry average $10 each have never been told of the fund, which makes the ministry far wealthier than ever reported." This wealth had been *concealed*, they intimated.

Another surprising claim, made in the third paragraph, was that Graham had spoken publicly about the fund for the first time "after the *Charlotte Observer* discovered its existence and asked about it."

I have studied those statements thoroughly, and they are simply not true. Nor were the paper's intimations of Graham's hoarded wealth true. But how were the paper's thousands of readers—and eventually the readers of the many other papers that carried the story—to know that?

To be sure, the *Observer*'s reporters made some cosmetic admissions. As a corporation, WECEF "appears to be perfectly legal and, in fact, is normal, good money management," they said.

Nor were the uses of WECEF money criticized; its objectives, including the two Christian evangelism and education institutes, apparently passed muster.

But by the time the reader had reached these favorable phrases, the words went virtually unnoticed in the excitement aroused by the loaded opening and its provocative headlines. So no matter how thin you slice it, the article intimated that Billy

Graham had skimmed a fortune off of contributions to his ministry.

When Ruth and Billy read the story, I think they must have been torn between pity and regret. T. W. Wilson, Graham's associate, who had sat through the front-porch conference, shook his head in wonder and weariness. "They didn't use a thing we told them," he said. "I don't understand it."

I have presented these glimpses as taken from a taped two-hour interview in an attempt to illuminate the tension that exists to some extent every time Billy Graham meets the press. I have tried to show that good investigative reporters are inquisitors and must be inquisitors. I have also tried to show that Graham, having the legal right to say nothing, chose to reveal his financial affairs to an unprecedented degree.

To what end?

## The Facts

Perhaps this is the place to discuss the factuality of certain elements of the *Observer* story. The *Charlotte Observer* implied that its discovery of WECEF was both exclusive and new. The Charlotte stories broke on Sunday, June 26. But the Asheville stories had been published on June 23. The Asheville stories were news, emphasizing Graham's plans for building a local institute for the study of the Bible. They outlined the history, organization, and management of WECEF, through which the purchase had been made.

In contrast, the Charlotte story, which ran three days later, emphasized only the "big money" aspect of the fund and implied the fund had had an undercover existence for seven years since its inception. The fact that a proposed Bible institute would be built in the *Observer*'s circulation area was not mentioned until the twenty-first paragraph. The Wheaton Center, to which the bulk of WECEF funds had been pledged, was not mentioned at all.

Little national attention had been paid to the Thursday stories in the Asheville papers, a. I their facts and figures were ignored by the news services.

When the *Observer* came out with fewer facts but more innuendo, the story went out on the Associated Press wire, spreading from city to city and from country to country, until its echoes reverberated around the globe.

I now call your attention to the *Observer*'s statement that "Billy Graham spoke publicly about the fund for the first time this past week after the *Charlotte Observer* discovered its existence and asked about it."

Actually, Graham *had* spoken about WECEF and its plans much earlier and in some detail. I submit these indisputable facts, which the *Observer* chose to ignore: On December 14, 1971—*six years* earlier—the Religious News Service, a bona fide news-gathering service, distributed a release to its thousands of clients under the heading: BILLY GRAHAM CITES NEW PLANS FOR ASSOCIATION IN INTERVIEW.

The interview release said: "A trust separate from the Billy Graham Evangelistic Association was set up to enlist estates and money to be used for evangelical work around the world, Mr. Graham revealed. Its income would be used to aid Christian education, small seminaries, Bible schools, and hospitals."

The same report also mentioned "the proposed evangelism center and library which the Graham Association plans to build," saying that it would not be a place "glorifying Billy Graham, but would include a student center where seminarians and others could come to study evangelism."

That was in 1971. The story was carried by the *Minneapolis Star* and by other newspapers around the country. So much for the allegation that Billy had kept secret the fact of the new trust that was separate from the BGEA, and that he hid the fact he intended to build an evangelism center and library, for which a site was being sought.

Another newspaperman, Pete Geiger, a reporter and religion writer for the Akron, Ohio *Beacon-Journal*, has challenged the *Observer*'s claim to have "discovered" a hidden Graham fund.

Back in 1972, Geiger met Billy Graham in the airport at Charlotte, North Carolina, for an extended interview. They were driving into the city when Geiger realized he had forgotten his tape recorder. "It's not much out of the way," he told Graham. "Would you mind going by my motel so I can pick it up?"

Graham said, "That'll be just fine."

Geiger told me: "Given my nature, that request was a most unlikely thing for me to do—to impose on somebody in that fashion. And to impose on Billy Graham like that is just unthinkable. As I look back, I can't tell you why I did that. But I did, for whatever reason."

So they picked up the tape recorder.

In the course of the recorded interview that followed, Geiger asked Graham: "Tell me about your finances."

May I say here that two things have long astonished me: the intrusion of reporters into the private finances of other private citizens and the profound courtesy of Billy Graham in discussing subjects which are not necessarily anyone's business but his own.

So Billy told Pete Geiger about his finances, including those of the Billy Graham Trust (to be renamed WECEF), headquartered in Dallas, Texas, and made up of businessmen and clergy chaired by Christian layman Maxie Jarman, one of the nation's outstanding executives. Its purpose, Graham said, was to support missionary and evangelistic projects around the world. "I think it's going to be growing, but it's only a year-and-a-half old," Graham concluded.

Geiger published his interview with Graham in June of 1972, six months after the earlier WECEF announcement was distributed by the Religious News Service.

One night in 1977, Geiger and his wife flicked on their car radio and happened to pick up the "Hour of Decision" broadcast. By chance, it was the program in which Graham was responding to the *Observer*'s story by explaining the origin and purposes of WECEF.

"When he started talking about this fund," Geiger told me, "I said to my wife, 'That strikes me very strange. I've heard that before. The words he's using to talk about that fund, I've heard them before . . . .'

"My wife said, 'How could that be? This is something that was supposed to be a secret.'

"I said, 'I guess maybe it wasn't a secret, or I wouldn't know about it.' "

Geiger told his wife that he would bet those words would be on the tape he had made of his interview with Graham, 'way back in April of 1972.

If he could find the tape . . . .

He did. It was all there.

Geiger has told me that he felt the *Observer*, which was owned by the same newspaper chain as his own publication, should have an opportunity to correct their error about "discovering" the WECEF millions. Obviously, it had been reported long ago. So he sent them documentation and copies of his notes.

The *Observer* chose to ignore them.

A time of prayer during the 1977 ground-breaking ceremonies at Wheaton College for the new Billy Graham Communications Center. *Below:* Upon alighting from a helicopter after a tidal-wave disaster in Andhra Pradesh, India, Graham is stopped by a distraught survivor begging for help.

Graham presenting a check for relief to Governor Patwari, of Madras State. BGEA gave a total of $250,000 for Indian relief following the tidal wave in 1977.

In Hungary, on his first mission to a Soviet-bloc country, Graham donned a native sheepskin coat and hat and enjoyed goulash with a local resident.

Billy Graham and his party visit a state farm near Budapest in 1977. *Below:* Responding to a request for an autograph at the Sun Street Baptist Church in Budapest.

Billy meeting well-wishers on his recent visit to Poland. *Below:* Meeting with local reporters while on tour.

Billy addressing a meeting of the National Religious Broadcasters. *Below:* George Beverly Shea (left) and Cliff Barrows at an American crusade.

Billy's father, William Franklin Graham, Sr., and his mother, Morrow Coffey Graham. *Below:* Billy and Ruth enjoying a minute together.

The Graham family group at Montreat a few years ago. *Below:*
A recent Graham family picture, including three daughters,
two sons, and twelve grandchildren.

From left to right: Gigi, Ruth, Anne, and Bunny. *Below:* Billy and Ruth in front of their Montreat home.

Billy and Ruth on the front porch of their home—a favorite spot for fair-weather entertaining.

# 9

# WECEF: A Clean Bill
# of Health

*I can assure you that your contributions were handled legally and with the highest sense of Christian ethics and spiritual concern.*

Billy Graham

The toll exacted from Graham during this spiritual and temporal crisis must have been considerable. I don't believe that Billy ever complained directly about its burden, but one afternoon at Montreat, Ruth said: "I could see what it was taking out of him. Particularly, I could see the wasted hours that he had to devote to discussions with people who needed an explanation. Sometimes, those long-distance phone calls went on for hours—hours that should have been devoted to his writing and studying."

Allan Emery, Jr., who was with Billy during that front-porch conference at his home, put it even more strongly, when I approached him.

"I just don't see why he keeps answering the questions," Emery said angrily. "I think it's so ridiculous. The story was totally wrong. There isn't a bit of reason for it." Emery sighed, adding the trace of another feeling to which he had become resigned. "He trusts people so," he concluded.

Surely, Graham was entitled to a full measure of sleeplessness. If the charges were believed, the public reaction could ruin the grand educational program he envisioned as a necessary extension of his ministry. But even more important, in the view of many, would be the loss of the moral influence that Billy Graham represented in America.

Anticipating the future, the most immediate consequence could be the loss of revenue from the hundreds of small, voluntary contributors on whom the work of the Graham ministry totally depended. Not once, since his "boy preacher" days, had he ever banked a crusade surplus to create a reserve fund of stocks and bonds. Incredible as it may seem, this multimillion-dollar enterprise went broke purposely at the end of every year by spending all of its income for extra radio and TV time, and then depended entirely on God's grace for the replenishing of its coffers.

In midyear of 1977, loss of operating funds for his far-flung enterprises was an immediate worry. Daily contributions are the lifeblood of any evangelistic association. With the pressures of inflation straining the resources available for God's work, a further loss of revenue could be disastrous.

A second worry was for the evangelist's dream and for WECEF itself. Far from being a repository for surplus money, which many papers seemed to suggest, WECEF was in fact desperately underfunded, considering its commitments to the Wheaton Center, to the Asheville school, and to world evangelism.

If donors came to believe—as some did—that the Graham treasury contained hoards of surplus capital, WECEF might never be able to fulfill its pledges.

Graham's real concern was much broader than who was right and who was wrong. His association had now grown to the point where it employed more than four hundred people, of whom more than one hundred were in far-ranging widely spaced mission fields, out of daily contact with the Minneapolis headquarters.

Billy knew how deeply the *Observer* story had cut into his own peace of mind, and he sensed how disturbing its potential collision with their labors must be. Would it hurt their ministry? Would they slack off? How many projects planned for God's glory and the advancement of His kingdom might be curtailed? Everywhere, members of the association wondered what would happen next.

News from England, a sensitive barometer of the feeling of Graham supporters, was bad. In the weeks after the tale implying hoarded wealth jumped the Atlantic, contributions in the British Isles fell off precipitously.

Graham decided to respond.

Critics have accused him of having a slick public-relations department. He has none. Only one part-time associate helps media representatives with their stories. So no phalanx of idea men and image builders could be mobilized. Rather, team members went to their knees and to their Bibles.

Graham has a genuine reluctance to spar with faultfinders. On this occasion, for good reason, his response was energetic.

On July 1, he issued a statement denying the implication of secrecy. Declaring that the fund's holdings, as well as a list of its gifts, were known to every regulatory body entitled to them, he effectively rebutted his detractors. It was the beginning of a policy-reversal that would presently shake church and parachurch charities to their roots. Soon, the BGEA would disclose its own contributions and expenses, setting an example of candor and integrity rarely paralleled in American church history.

In his statement, he called the *Observer* story "grossly misleading." Later, he would dismiss the allegation of "mobster ties" as "merely ridiculous."

He named WECEF's executive committee, honored businessmen who serve without compensation and who control all of the WECEF assets. They were and are: William Mead, Dallas, chairman of the board of Campbell-Taggart, one of the largest bakery combines in the world; Dewey Presley, Dallas, president of the First International Bancshares, Inc., the tenth largest banking firm on earth; and George Bennett, Boston, recently retired treasurer of Harvard University and president of the State Street Investment Corporation.

The *Observer*'s story had dismissed those men as nameless and faceless, saying only that Graham's "inner circle of business advisors controls the money."

"I am very proud of the integrity with which this fund has been handled, and the purposes for which it has been used," Billy declared. "It has been a labor of love on the part of dedicated Christians."

Like all second-day stories, his statement never overtook the scandal of those first adverse headlines.

I suspect that a residue of hatred, envy, or whatever else you call it, had survived the Watergate bloodbath and that it abetted and even encouraged much of the criticism. Most of the censure of Graham came from people who had no real knowledge of the facts. The public—a portion of it, at any rate—had enjoyed watching the humiliation of its most famous citizen, the president. They wanted an encore. How fitting if a friend of the president, especially one so generally admired and trusted, could be pulled from his pulpit and dragged in the mud.

By the middle of August 1977, other critics were in full cry. Graham chose to meet them head on. His early denial had obviously not sufficed, so he chose the forum of his own radio broadcast, the "Hour of Decision." His shield was the truth. His sword was his sincerity.

On August 18, he delivered a moving address on the theme of "Our Financial Commitment to You." This was the broadcast that *Akron Beacon-Journal* reporter Pete Geiger had heard. After the broadcast, Graham's words were printed in a thin, sixteen-page booklet, smaller than a postal card, which was mailed to his supporters.

I have space for only a few of its phrases. His first words were: "Since the beginning of our evangelistic ministry, we have been deeply concerned about the financial integrity of our work. We believe we are accountable to God for all money entrusted to the Billy Graham Evangelistic Association. We consider ourselves stewards before the Lord. . . ."

Explaining this stewardship, he told his audience about:

. . . discontinuing the embarrassing custom of taking love offerings.

. . . praying for enough support to enable BGEA to help other mission efforts.

. . . tithing every dollar contributed to BGEA, so they might help less fortunate organizations.

. . . the guidance afforded BGEA by its board of directors of twenty-five men and one woman, which included "distinguished lawyers, bankers, businessmen, a seminary president, and distinguished clergy, including two outstanding black clergymen, one of whom was vice-president of the NAACP."

. . . the recent two-year study of BGEA and its affiliates by one of America's great law firms, to insure the observance of every possible safeguard and practice for prudent financial management.

"I can assure you," Graham said, "that your contributions are handled legally and with the highest sense of Christian ethics and spiritual concern."

For the remainder of that half-hour broadcast, Graham named some of the far-flung causes BGEA had assisted—a halfway house for convicts in Mexico, a TB clinic for nomads in the Middle East, a clinic in Bangladesh—and he described more fully than ever before the saga of WECEF, from its birth to its present maturity, and the great dream that sustains it.

"We are limited in the many visions and dreams that God has given us," he said. "We are limited because of physical strength, time, and finances."

But he was not pessimistic. "Doors are opening right now, as perhaps never before. This is an age of unprecedented harvest. I am told that as many as 50,000 people a day are becoming Christians."

In conclusion, he mentioned the diminishing availability of TV and radio stations, the astronomical rise of costs, and the mounting constraints that are being placed on religious programming.

"It is a question as to how much longer we can have the freedom to hold evangelistic crusades in many parts of the world," he said.

"We are ready to spend our strength and our energy," he concluded, "if you will stand behind us with your prayers and your financial support. God bless you."

No audience anywhere had ever heard such an address. No evangelist, no preacher, no public figure had ever revealed so much of his financial history and his visions for tomorrow as Graham did in that candid address.

Its effect was instantaneous.

Letters of support poured into Minneapolis. Temporarily, at least, Satan was stopped in his tracks.

In the fall of 1977, BGEA's international ministries reported that their autumn appeal letter had brought a low response. "It was the press reports about finances," Maurice Rowlandson, who was director of the London office, told the team when they gathered in January in Jamaica.

"But then," he said, "everything changed. At Christmastime we enclosed, with the prayer letter, Mr. Graham's statement of 'Our Financial Commitment to You.'

"And I am able to tell you tonight the most exciting and thrilling thing," he said. "We received the most magnificent response from that letter that we have ever had in London! It exceeds the nearest figure by almost ten thousand dollars—and that was eleven years ago!"

Rowlandson continued, "So many have written in and said, 'Thank you for that letter. . . . it has changed the whole view I had of the way the association was conducted.'

"And so we praise God that Billy Graham was able to write that letter," the British director told the other men and women of the team—those who had also endured the weeks of anguished worry over whether funds would continue to come in to support their ministries.

Elsewhere the story was the same.

The low period of the summer was followed in the fall by a succession of great moments for the Billy Graham ministry.

### The July 1978 Article

Apparently, the *Observer*'s campaign would continue, for board members of both BGEA and WECEF soon reported that they were receiving telephone calls from reporter Robert Hodierne. His questions usually concerned the purchase of Porter's Cove, in Buncombe County. His queries assumed an unnamed irregularity in corporate procedures and prudent business practices.

His second shoe was about to drop.

It dropped on Sunday, July 23, 1978; one year and one month after publication of the initial story. Again, it was a page-one story in the *Charlotte Observer*.

Written by Robert Hodierne, now billed as a member of the *Observer* Washington bureau, it made these points, implications, allegations, innuendoes, or call them what you will. In his forty column inches of closely set type, he asserted:

- Five years ago, a Billy Graham tax-exempt foundation (WECEF) had paid $2.75 million for a piece of mountain land.
- The property was bought through business associates of Billy Graham's family, who had turned a $25,000 investment into a $650,000 profit in three months.
- The price paid for the land was more than the amount local appraisers thought it was worth.
- The deal raised federal tax law questions.
- Those who profited from the sale were also involved in other real estate investments with Graham's mother, brother, sister, and brother-in-law.

In sum, the financial monkeyshines implied in the 1977 story were now focused by implication on Billy Graham's own kith and kin.

Even a careless reader could not escape this latest intimation of financial skulduggery in the *Observer*'s detailed account of buying and selling God's acres, of past and present business relationships between Graham's closest relatives and friendly commission men, and of profits which were allegedly split and paid privately to unnamed persons, probably of the Graham family.

Billy Graham chose to lay his integrity on the line by responding immediately. On the day of the story's publication, he declared that "it was filled with unsupported and untrue innuendoes and insinuations." And, he added: "To my knowledge, no member of my family or organization has made a cent on the purchase. The Internal Revenue Service has audited WECEF [the buyer of the land] for the period when the purchase occurred, was aware of the transaction, and took no exception."

Again, a funny thing happened.

This time, almost nobody paid attention to the *Observer* revelation. It was as if the general press, having been burned once, declined to be hoodwinked again by unsupported, circumstantial trumpery. A national newsmagazine scheduled the story, then took a second look and rejected it.

Instead of detonating around the world in the manner of the earlier *Observer* write-up, it fizzled like a wet firecracker. No wave of hurt, angry, or curious letters inundated Graham's Minneapolis headquarters. As the days passed, even the *Observer* seemed to lose interest.

Billy Graham wrote a coda to the *Observer*'s slurs by initiating a thorough investigation of the WECEF realty transaction. Employing outside law firms, he invited them to conduct an independent inquiry.

When they submitted their reports, and Billy Graham read their solemn conclusions, he must have breathed deeply with relief. The message he sent to his BGEA board of directors read:

"The Charlotte *Observer* 'flap' (which you may or may not have heard much about), I hope is over. We did a thorough internal inquiry, bringing in outside, prestigious law firms in addition to our lawyers, to be sure that none of their innuendoes were true. We are now totally satisfied that no members of my family or organization received a cent in WECEF's purchase of the property for the Bible Training Center in North Carolina. We are also totally satisfied that there were no violations of IRS regulations in the transaction, as was implied in the *Observer* story. The story seems not to have received much attention, except in a few areas."

### On With the Lord's Work

At last—at long last—the Lord's work could go forward.

Gears began to mesh as the implements of Graham's ministry throbbed with new life. The slowdown was over, the devil beaten back.

Finally, there was time to lay the capstone of Graham's career. As he neared the fourth decade of his public ministry, the Wheaton Center in Illinois and the Asheville Bible school became the principal focuses of his concern.

The concept for both institutions follows the precedent-breaking tradition of all earlier Graham ministries. Other evangelists have founded conventional universities. At one point, this course was strongly backed by some of Graham's friends. A multimillionaire had offered him 1,000 acres of land and millions in cash if he would establish a Billy Graham University in Palm Beach, Florida. After much prayer, the offer was rejected, because Billy concluded that accepting it would dilute his evangelistic ministry.

On the contrary, the Wheaton Center and the Carolina Bible school would intensify it. At Wheaton, the walls were going up. A scholars' library of books about evangelism, probably the most complete on earth, had been purchased. Technical apparatus was on order to instruct prospective students in the technology of communications and graduate students from around the world were already enrolled. Among them were two hundred Third World students now living on scholarships provided by the Graham ministry. Some were refugees smuggled out of Uganda when General Idi Amin's tyranny threatened to wipe out that nation's Christian youth. When Uganda is free again, many Wheaton-trained Christians will be ready to return to their homeland to provide leadership.

In passing, it should be remembered that WECEF's commitment to this enterprise is now at least $15.5 million. Obviously, financing a dream is no small undertaking.

Graham's first public revelation of the character of the Carolina Bible school appeared in a story written by Bob Tyrrell and published in the *Asheville Citizen*. Its construction would await the completion of the Wheaton Center, he revealed, and although plans were well along, the first building that would be erected on the 1300-acre mountainside would be a caretaker's house.

The Bible school is expected to be unique in several respects. "It probably won't have a faculty except one or two people," Graham told Tyrrell. "But teachers will be brought in from all over the world. And a person who wishes to study, say, the Book of Acts, will be able to come for two weeks or six months or a year and study it.

"The school will also offer courses in speech, for that is most important in the spreading of the Gospel. No credits will be given. It will not be an academic institution," Graham continued. "If a busy businessman takes his two-week vacation and comes here to study, we will have a course for him."

Both novice and veteran Christians will be welcomed. A new Christian, no matter what his status may be in the secular world, is a babe in the spiritual realm. In this new school, courses will enable him to perfect his faith and deepen his understanding. In one sense, the school will be a place for meditation, contemplation, and retreat; in another sense, it will become the source of intense intellectual and spiritual illumination.

"We have had a tremendous lot of evangelism in this country the last few years," Graham says. "Now we need to go deeper into the Bible and discipleship. This is the last goal I have before the Lord takes me to heaven."

Escalating construction costs are now Graham's most nagging problem. Although the WECEF flap left many supporters with the notion that the foundation was generously financed, the truth is that its treasury is desperately strained. Graham's annual financial report showed a WECEF balance of $15.5 million for 1977, but half of that is promised to the Wheaton Center.

"A fund of $50 million might be adequate for all the projects we have in mind," Graham has said. "We are trusting the Lord to provide."

Let me explain my personal understanding of why WECEF was born.

First, Billy Graham had a dream that his ministry should culminate in the establishment of two extraordinary educational institutions.

In the 1960s, he had begun to see signs which indicated that the technological and electronic evangelization of the world was reaching its limits. Already, his sermons, motion pictures, and publications were in many languages and available on every continent. Moreover, other evangelistic organizations, following along the trail he had cleared or spreading out on their own, had assumed a portion of the burden.

One element alone remained in short supply. This was manpower, a cadre of believers possessed by the faith that could move mountains and trained in every communication skill. He believed that his schools could recruit and educate such a cadre.

He and his team and his board of directors studied the flow of funds that was regularly available to BGEA. They came mostly from listeners to his radio and TV broadcasts. But over the years, many contributions had originated in foundations, or in bequests from more than 1,000 estates. Some contributors asked Graham to use their gifts for specific causes. Others sent their tithes trusting that he would know better than they how to spend God's money.

Simultaneously, poorer evangelistic missions by the score turned to BGEA, asking for help, which was forthcoming as long as their qualifications satisfied and the money was available.

But even as they dispensed their surplus, Billy and the BGEA board were aware that giving away money is a serious business.

Their stewardship over these funds and their "good husbanding" of the gifts they received, they felt, required a type of management different from that of their evangelistic-oriented undertakings.

So a foundation arm of the Graham ministry was conceived. In 1970, it was set up as a legally separate organization with an altogether different function. Though it would be closely related to BGEA, it would be "its own person" in its decisions, without a single salaried employee (at least to start with), and it would be devoted to accepting special kinds of gifts and other funds and investing or deploying them on the basis of decisions made by its own executive committee and board of directors.

The foundation was set up in Dallas, Texas, for sentimental and business reasons. Billy has been a member of the First Baptist Church of Dallas for over two decades and still calls Texas his second home. More importantly, Dallas was the business base of some of the astute money managers whose financial acumen would be needed. I am thinking in particular of Bill Mead, the chairman of the board of Campbell-Taggart, Inc., which operates many massive business enterprises.

So the foundation was based in Dallas for the convenience of its executive committee. The BGEA scraped the bottom of its treasury and found funds from foundations and estates that had been given for the exact purposes for which WECEF had been established. There was also money that had not been earmarked for crusade or radio or TV evangelism. All of it was turned over to the new WECEF board of directors. None of the contributions to BGEA's preaching ministries were touched.

WECEF's first name was the Billy Graham Benevolent Fund—a name which wrongly implied that cash resources were available for any and all needy causes.

To reduce these unfulfillable expectations, the fund was renamed the Graham Foundation, but this notion was wrong, too, because it suggested something far grander than what had been visualized.

Another name change made it the Billy Graham Evangelistic Trust, a title that came closer to describing its exact nature, which was managing the holdings entrusted to it. But one problem remained, and it brought about a final renaming. Billy has always disliked having his own name singled out. This was true when BGEA was first established, although his young advisors outvoted him at the time. They carried the day again when the same problem arose in connection with naming the Wheaton structure. Graham fought against having his name placed on the building, but the college's board of directors overwhelmed him with their sincere and sensible arguments. Thus, evangelism's greatest facility will be called, as of now, the Billy Graham Center.

So, finally, the trust achieved its ultimate identity with a name that announced its intent: the World Evangelism and Christian Education Fund. The name change did not alter in any way its purpose of enlisting funds from trusts, foundations, and estates, or its organization and management.

To be sure, some goals have been rethought, modified, or expanded. For instance, Graham's original thinking about his Asheville center included a halfway house for young drug addicts. Convinced by evidence that the soundest way to kick the hard-drug habit is to experience a new birth, he and Ruth hoped to provide a refuge staffed with Christian counselors. For the moment, this project is in abeyance.

For the record, WECEF is registered with the Internal Revenue Service. It is administered by a small executive committee which meets several times a year, often by means of conference telephone calls. A fourteen-member board of directors, of which

Billy Graham is the nominal chairman, meets annually. Its members are all elected by the BGEA board. The majority of its board members are also members of the BGEA board, from which WECEF obtains much of its funds.

WECEF is audited annually, and its holdings (as well as those of BGEA and all affiliated organizations) were published in complete detail in 1978 as audited by Ernst and Ernst, one of the nation's largest and most respected firms of certified public accountants.

As this survey is being written, WECEF is on its way to fulfilling its mission. In 1977, it contributed $7,719,556 to the Graham Center at Wheaton College. Its year-end balance was $15,579,418, all of which will be used to complete the Graham Center and to start the layman's training institute in North Carolina.

When these projects are completed, additional funds must be raised to support the Third World students attending the school of communications at the Billy Graham Center at Wheaton College. Funds will also be needed to continue BGEA's support of organizations that have proven their worth in the field of missions, evangelism, and Christian education.

How ironic that a program so benevolent, humane, charitable, and forward-looking should be turned against Graham and his ministries. How galling that the press, which was the agency that lifted him from obscurity in 1949, should become the devil's agent in 1977.

# PART TWO

## *The Family Graham*

# 10

# Billy and Ruth

By late 1978, I had satisfied myself that the Mickey Cohen caper and the WECEF flap were spurious attacks. Along the way, I had checked into every other big and little controversy I could find that might reflect on Billy Graham's integrity. You will read my conclusions in chapter sixteen.

But I wanted more. I wanted an affirmation of my gut feeling about the essential goodness of Billy and Ruth Graham, which had propelled me into my yearlong review of crusades and crotchets, of longings and life-styles.

So I returned to my scrapbooks, clippings, and transcriptions of past interviews, and I discovered a leitmotif I had missed: I discovered a love story.

I should have picked it up earlier from Graham's remarks, from private communications, from public asides during crusade sermons, and from the observations of other reporters. What I had missed is the story of two people who are in love with the Lord and with each other. Their names are Billy and Ruth.

But there was more. There was the story of how their twin loves had created an amazing family under incredibly difficult circumstances. As soon as I became aware of it, I sought the details. I wanted to know the particulars of their support for each other through the thirty-five years of a marriage that had ripened, without headlines, into the fruit of an unprecedented world ministry and the blossoming of girl children into women and boy children into men.

Once I perceived the truth, I saw the story everywhere, its theme running like a golden cord through the tapestry of three generations. Throughout his stardom, Graham has provided a moveable feast for reporters and commentators. No "superstar" has ever engaged the public so frequently and candidly at press conferences, in private interviews, in TV appearances, and in countless addresses.

One year ago, I heard him speak to 1,000 ministers. He had chosen a serious topic but, as has happened scores of times, his thoughts strayed. In the midst of a serious comment, his thoughts turned inward, and he blurted out the pain he felt over having to leave Ruth so often. Obviously, his distress was real. Then he tried to get back to his subject, and he failed. For ten seconds, you could have heard a pin drop. Suddenly, he grinned boyishly and admitted, "You know, I've completely forgotten what I was talking about." That moment was a revelation.

Trailing this new theme, I read through my reference materials, which ran back across the years. I found a tattered copy of a thin book published early in his career. It was by Billy Graham and contained sermons Billy had delivered to Youth for Christ rallies. Its dedication read: "This book is dedicated to MY LIFE'S COMPANION, whose sacrifice in standing by the 'stuff' makes my ministry possible."

What that inscription lacked in elegance, it made up in sincerity. Billy and Ruth were undoubtedly already experiencing the frustrations of a trying way of life. He was traveling almost constantly. She was living with her parents and mothering her first daughter. The "stuff" to which he alluded must have included many vexing problems.

I found other signs of inner struggle. More than two decades ago, he told biographer Stanley High, "The Lord certainly knew what He was doing when He chose Ruth for my wife and number-one advisor."

A faded book, published in England early in his career, told of an appearance by the Grahams at a banquet in Glasgow. When Ruth was introduced as one of the guests, the speaker described her as an evangelist's wife who had made many sacrifices in behalf of her husband's work. Rising quietly, she responded, "I want you all to know that I would rather be an evangelist's wife than anything else in the world. And I want you to know—maybe you have guessed it—that as far as being this particular evangelist's wife, I'd rather have Billy Graham part time than anybody else in all the world full time."

Later, Billy wrote a memorandum to me about his home: "Through the years, Ruth has made my home a place of love, joy, and tranquillity," he said. "Her deep faith in God, her constant study of the Scriptures, current events, and social problems have always been a source of inspiration. We have long talks on many subjects. Some of my best thoughts have actually come from her."

After the birth of his daughters, he wrote, "Other evangelists have been unfortunate with their children. Ruth has insisted on staying home most of the time while I travel. She has been both father and mother. She handles our finances. She pays our bills."

My search uncovered a blurred carbon copy of a diary Billy kept during the 1950s. Prior to his 1956 crusade in New York City, he wrote: "Today, Ruth and I took our last stroll to see our four sheep and to lie on the grass, talking, quoting Scripture, and praying together. What a wonderful companion she is—so full of Scripture for every occasion. Certainly our marriage was formed and planned in heaven. I shall miss the children during the next few weeks. I shall miss this mountaintop and would like nothing better than for the Lord to say that I should stay here for the rest of my life. But duty calls."

The diary also said this:

"As I went to the train yesterday, my little family saw me off, and there was a lump in my throat. During the past few months, I have been home more than at any other time and have gotten to know my children. To think of leaving them, even for a brief period, pulled at my heart."

Other later entries were even more revealing, as will be seen presently. At this point, I should explain that one of the qualities that first drew me to the young evangelist was his passionate advocacy of the institution of the family. In crusade after crusade, I heard him address himself to the Christian duties of fathers and mothers, stressing their responsibilities to each other and to their progeny.

Searching for the patterns that might have shaped the man, years ago I visited the parental farm and interviewed his father and mother. William Franklin Graham and Morrow Coffey were married in 1916. Both of them were of rugged Scottish stock, and profoundly religious. On the first night of their honeymoon, I was told, they knelt together in their hotel room and dedicated their lives to God.

Their ancestry was all-American. Their forebears had settled in America before our revolution. A signatory of the Declaration of Independence, Ezra Alexander, and a president of our nation, James K. Polk, were in William Franklin Graham's family tree. During the Civil War, Morrow's father, Ben Coffey (blue eyed and fair-haired, like his grandson), had stopped a Union bullet at Gettysburg and was seriously wounded.

Morrow Coffey had been gently reared, but she quickly mastered the difficult chores required of a farmer's wife. She kept books for the Graham dairy business. She saw that good literature was always available in the home for her children. She supervised their devotions. And she always had a hot breakfast ready for her men when they completed their morning's milking, often as early as 2:30 A.M.

She was, and still is, a remarkable woman. At a birthday party given Billy by some of his Charlotte admirers, Billy cut his cake and dedicated the first piece to his mother. "Sixty years ago," he explained, "she picked beans all afternoon. I was born late in the day. Then she got up the next morning and finished picking beans."

Billy's father, William Franklin Graham, is described by biographer John Pollock as being "dark-haired, with a fine bass voice, and a farmer through and through. In early manhood, he had experienced a religious conversion as vivid as that of St. Paul on the Damascus road . . . He was as straight as his back in business dealings . . . he scorned relaxation and hated travel . . . Yankees were suspect . . . and any stranger not Presbyterian, Baptist or Methodist, he rated peculiar. His world was the South, placid, sunny, but smarting from the Civil War."

Visiting the brick-pillared home, which had been built in 1928, when Billy was ten years old, I stood in the kitchen where the future evangelist had recited Bible verses to his mother, and I sat beside the old table that nearly always held a basket of tomatoes and a salt cellar to satisfy their eldest's appetite. Then I had walked out to what remained of the rustic grove where Frank Graham and his neighbors had gathered to pray that God would send a revival to Charlotte; the same revival, when it did come, at which Billy Frank, as his parents called him, was converted.

It was during that visit that the father told me of his stalwart pride in all of his children, of his rugged enforcement of obedience with a leather belt (Morrow Coffey used a switch), and of his undeviating expectation that his children would be totally honest, moral, and faithful to the Lord Jesus.

It would be a mistake to assume that the lives of those four little Grahams were shaped exclusively by ironhanded coercion. Graham *père* used a carrot as well as a stick. Lots of carrots. When the boys were young, they received such gifts as cats, dogs, goats, and a horse. They were carefully taught how to aim and fire a Daisy air rifle, then a .22, and finally a shotgun. And when Billy left home to drive to Chicago and Wheaton College, he rode in the most coveted bonus any parent could bestow, a car of his own. It mattered little that his chariot was Pa Graham's own somewhat creaky and cranky 1937 Plymouth, refitted and refinished and deeded to his beloved son.

Later, I visited the home of Ruth's parents in Montreat, a cozy and comfortable structure to which they had retreated after being forced out of China by events leading up to World War II. In that and subsequent visits, I learned the circumstances that shaped events on the opposite side of the earth, where another human pair was about to give to the world a girl named Ruth. This family contained L. Nelson Bell, Presbyterian missionary and physician par excellence, and his wife, Virginia. They would be stationed for several years at Tsinkaing, North Kiangsu, China. Bell was a Virginian of Scotch-Irish descent. His ancestors included ministers, doctors, and teachers. One great-great grandfather was of such advanced learning that when he fell from his horse and bruised his head, he arose unable to speak in English but spoke fluently in Latin and Greek. Other forebears served in George Washington's army, and more recently, a cousin named Woodrow Wilson had moved to Washington, D.C. to live in the White House.

Bell's religious training was the gift of earlier generations. His father had been elected a ruling elder at the age of nineteen. His mother held a profound belief in the efficacy of personal prayer. In their home, family prayer was the first order of weekday business, and the last at night. The Bible was their court of appeals for all rules of discipline and deportment.

As a youth, Nelson Bell had loved two things, baseball and books. His excellence at the former provided a career briefly as a professional baseball player with a Baltimore team. His perusal of missionary sagas excited his imagination and first fired his ambition to serve God among the heathen Chinese.

Virginia Myers Leftwich, Ruth Graham's mother, was raised in a house just five blocks from the Bell home. She and Nelson met in a class at the Waynesboro, Virginia, high school. She was twenty-one months his senior, but he was large and mentally advanced for his age, and a natural leader. When she was eighteen and he was sixteen, they became engaged. Her interest in religion matched his own. Her blonde hair and gray eyes were enhanced by a vivacious nature that made her a winsome personality. She and Nelson played tennis together, acted in local plays, and sang in the church choir, much like other gifted young people. Friends predicted that she would be an ideal wife when young Bell became a Virginia lawyer.

But Nelson had felt a strange stirring. One day, a friend suggested that he consider going to China to work in the mission field. At that instant, he reported later, he knew what his life work would be. He changed from prelaw to premed. He decided to become a surgeon and serve the unsaved.

Winning a medical degree with high honors, he married Virginia, and practiced medicine in a mining town to gain experience. They arrived in Shanghai in 1916. Thus, China gained a great hospital administrator and surgeon. And, many years later, Billy Graham would gain a wife.

Reading my yellowing notes, I perceived for the first time the extraordinary underpinnings of the Graham-Bell union. Family worship, family strength, and family integrity were in their very genes.

The story of their meeting at Wheaton College has been told many times. Ruth had come there from China via a Presbyterian high school in Korea. Bill had transferred to Wheaton after graduating from a Florida Bible school. History says they met, they fell in love, they became engaged.

Billy related his story of their courtship to a British audience many years ago.

"It was a cold spring afternoon when Johnnie Streater introduced me to a beautiful young campus queen," he said. "Our eyes met for the first time. I was impressed, timid, and bashful. But something went straight to my heart that I never could describe. The love bug had bitten me.

"A faraway expression came into my eyes. Her every wish was a command from that moment on. Classes and studies were forgotten when I thought or talked about her. Her letters to me were read scores of times. The slightest indication that she might return my love thrilled me from head to toe. And though we have been married now for many months yet we are sweethearts still."

Ruth's recollections are somewhat different. "Well, if he fell in love with me right away, he sure didn't show it," Ruth told me during an interview. "You see, he'd been engaged to another girl, and she had called it off. That was a rough time for him. So he said—he told me later—'Lord, if You want me to have this girl, You'll have to win her for me. I'm just not going to try to court her.' And he was very matter-of-fact about it. But when I realized why he was like that, I understood."

"What was your first reaction?" I asked her.

"I thought, 'Well, this is the strangest courtship ever.' He just seemed so indifferent. But I learned why the night he told me he loved me. Then he told me all about the girl who had jilted him. He was just gun-shy."

I asked Ruth, "When did you begin to realize you were made for each other?"

"When we had our first date. We went to hear the *Messiah*. I can remember going back to my room and telling the Lord that there was something about Bill that was different from any man I'd ever met. I said, though I'm not sure I vocalized it, 'Lord, if

You would let me spend my life helping this man, I would consider it the greatest honor possible.'

"I didn't really know him well enough to love him, but I was just so convinced about him. The Lord had first place in my life, no doubt about that. In fact I was eager to get back to China as a missionary and tried to convince Bill that he should go to China, too. But God had something more important in view. Our love came as we got to know one another. When I learned that he really cared, it didn't take long for the love to follow."

"So you met him and he took you to a concert and told you he loved you. How long did that take?"

"About two weeks, I think, but I'm not sure that he actually used the word *love* that first night. He was driving, and right in the middle of a sentence, he jammed on the brakes. A truck in front of us had stopped for a red light, and we slammed into the back of it. That is the only time I've ever known Bill to do something that dumb."

Then there was the matter of Billy's first pastorate after graduation and marriage. It was in Western Springs, Illinois, and it wasn't a church in the conventional sense, but merely a concrete foundation dug into the yellow clay and then roofed over when the congregation ran out of money. But Graham had agreed to serve as its pastor and to try to build it up. Ruth was not pleased.

"I was shocked," she told me recently.

"But didn't he consult you about it?"

"He didn't consult me a bit. But the reason was that he'd suddenly taken a wife and all at once there was that financial responsibility, and the church would pay him forty-five dollars a week. I felt he was being sidetracked, and he may have been. But God can overrule being sidetracked."

Their parsonage was a small apartment on the second floor of a house in adjacent Hinsdale. It was already furnished. Billy had rented it before they were married.

"So he took you there, and there you were?"

"There I was. Right!"

Ruth explained her feelings. She told Bill that marriage was a partnership. "I don't recall any heated discussion," she says. "I guess I just understood instinctively why he had done it."

In due course, God did overrule Billy's pastorate at Western Springs, for he was offered an opportunity to become a traveling evangelist for the newborn Youth for Christ organization. "It was a step in the right direction," Ruth recalls. "I felt he would be reaching many new people."

I remembered that his outreach had begun on a Chicago radio station, with a program called "Songs in the Night." Ruth said, "We accepted it as a challenge, and there was a lot of work involved, but its success let Bill reach multitudes outside the church. I knew that God had called him to minister to them, and I felt that God had given him the gift of communicating the Gospel to the unconverted."

"How could you be so certain?"

"I'd heard him preach in halls and little churches during our college years. But it wasn't just his preaching; it was talking to him and feeling there was something different about him. He had a purposefulness. I knew he was a man under orders, as it were. When I first heard him preach, he spoke much louder and much faster than he does now. In fact, I found him very hard to listen to. He was sort of like the person who made up in thunder for what he lacked in lightning."

His Youth for Christ job required new domestic arrangements. And the act of sacrificial loving suddenly became a real fact in both their lives. He would have to travel almost constantly. Her mission field would be her home. Their separation would probably last for weeks at a time, perhaps months. The prospect did not delight them, but it did not daunt them, either. So Ruth closed the apartment and moved in with her parents in Montreat. Billy went on the road.

Ruth declares that even before she and Billy were married, she knew that a normal family life would be impossible. "Instinct told me," she says. "I knew that God had laid His hands on Bill for a special ministry."

Publicly and privately, he has frequently credited Ruth with the vision of his larger ministry. It meant that she would tend the home fires while he traveled. Mrs. Billy Sunday, the wife of an earlier world-famous evangelist, had once lamented, "I spent all of my time with Mr. Sunday on the road. As a result, I lost my children." Ruth foresaw that the same thing might happen to the Grahams, if they failed to exercise precautions.

Billy says her decision made her "both father and mother." At a New York banquet in 1966, Billy was named the Father of the Year and given a citation. His response named Ruth as the one who really deserved it. "She was the father," he said, "as well as the mother."

Ruth maintains that sacrifice works two ways. She has given up Bill for months at a time, but he has given up his children. "If I had it to do over," he says, "I would spend much more time with my family."

They agree that what has happened, had to be. "I've always wanted to tell others about the peace, joy, happiness, and security I found in Christ," he says. "I remember that when God called me, I rebelled. Today, I am an evangelist because I cannot be otherwise. Humanly, there are other things I would prefer to do, but inside there is a small voice saying, 'This is the way. Walk ye in it.' And so I must walk."

Graham knows that God is guiding him and Ruth; indeed, that everyone who walks with God is guided hour by hour and day by day. I once questioned him closely on this point, for it explained so much of his and Ruth's way of life. He replied:

"I mean that God guides those who are living and who are moment by moment following Jesus as their Lord and Saviour. If you are in God's will, everything that happens will be of God. I was flying once through a thunderstorm and one of the plane's motors went out. I remember that I felt out of God's will at that moment. It was a terrifying feeling, to be out of God's will and in that terrible storm. I prayed and confessed my sin and mistakes, and I remember the great sense of forgiveness that came over me. I had a feeling of wonderful security that suddenly flooded my soul."

I have now reached the point where I must try to explain a matter of much theological importance. I refer to what an evangelical Christian calls God's will, or God's leading, and to the conviction of Billy and Ruth that they are following it.

I once asked Billy: "How can you tell the difference between the way your ego or your emotions direct you to go and a course that might be directed wholly by God's will?"

He referred me to 1 Corinthians 2:12, 13. "To me, those verses mean that such things are spiritually discerned," he explained. "In other words, only a spiritual man can know God's mind. It is impossible for me to explain how this can be. Yet, there *are* things we know because the Holy Spirit is inside of us and giving witness to those things. For instance, it's difficult for me to explain the new birth to unbelievers. That is what Nicodemus wanted to know. He asked Jesus, 'How can a person enter his mother's womb and be born again?' He yearned to understand it. He begged Jesus to explain it. But Jesus said 'No, you can't understand it!' You see, Nicodemus was an unbeliever. The unbeliever cannot understand such things. He must first walk through that door of faith into the kingdom of God. *Then* he knows."

Billy and Ruth were believers long before they met. The primacy of Christ in their lives was as natural as hunger or thirst.

Jesus Christ ranked ahead of all others. His will became Billy and Ruth's will. His leading told Billy to preach. His leading told Ruth to raise their family.

The result was a fierce personal commitment. Billy honed his message to a sharp cutting edge and preached it around the world with astonishing success. Writing recently in the *Texas Monthly,* Bill Martin said: "His message has not changed through the years. Unlike Peale and Robert Schuller who urge us to be as great as we can be through positive and possibility thinking, or Oral Roberts, who promises us that something good is going to happen, or Reverend Ike who assures us that one never loses with the stuff he uses, Billy Graham starts on a downer. In sermon after article after book, he gloomily ticks off the fruits of man's rebellion."

Edward V. Hill, pastor of the Mount Zion Missionary Baptist Church in Los Angeles, condenses Graham's message into a baseball simile. "Billy Graham has a four-base ministry," he explains. "At first base, he reconciles men to God. But once he gets you there, you don't head for the dugout. You try for second because that's where men who are reconciled under God are reconciled to each other. But you don't stay at second base very long because you hear the cries of the hungry and the poor from over at third. So you run to third base to try to alleviate their distress. But you don't stop there, either. Billy Graham wants you at home plate because that's where you learn that the Lord is really coming and you're heaven bound. When you know all that, brothers, you're safe at home. You really are."

Ruth's commitment was to raising her family. That obligation has never changed. Phil Donahue once asked her if she was a liberated woman. She replied, "I certainly am." To her, a liberated woman is one who is freed of the burden of working *outside* the home. Raising a family is strenuous, nerve-popping, patience-straining work. It is also as important as breathing.

Ruth believes it should be a full-time job. She heartily agrees with Pope Pius XI, who said, "The family is more sacred than the state, and men are begotten not for the earth and for time, but for heaven and eternity."

With good humor but quiet determination, she rejects the Biblical interpretation which has God saying in Genesis 2:18, "It isn't good for man to be alone. I'll make for him a helpmeet." The word *helpmeet* should be replaced by the word *helper*, she feels, or perhaps by the paraphrase used in the Living Bible, which says: ". . . I will make a companion for him, a helper suited to his needs." The wife is created, she insists, to be a help, meet for her husband.

In her search for God's will and leading, Ruth has worn out six Bibles and is near the end of her seventh. In Julie Eisenhower's astute chapter in her book of essays *Special People*, she says of Ruth, "Her Bible is so worn and soft that she can roll it like a magazine. She turns each page gently so it will not tear. She has read and re-read it. The hundreds of underlined verses and the margins filled with tightly written notations . . . attest to the extraordinary way in which she communicates with God."

The Book of Proverbs is her Dr. Spock. "It tells all anyone needs to know about raising a family," Ruth says, and Billy agrees. His own sermons and magazine articles attest to his own concern for fatherhood as well as for the nuclear family.

"The family is the prime source of human progress," he has written. "In it, the child's education begins. In it, the old and sick and weak find refuge. In it, we have the implementation of God's Word which ordered His children to 'be fruitful, and multiply, and replenish the earth.' "

At first, the injunction to multiply was deemed not relevant, at least by the physician who had treated Billy's painful case of metastatic mumps. Fruitfulness, he explained, was probably a casualty of the mumps virus. I have before me a frayed document written by Billy, which describes his reaction when that prognosis was reversed. He was on a preaching mission in Peoria, Illinois when word came from Ruth that she was pregnant.

"The news sent me up on cloud nine," he says. "Ruth told me we could expect our first child in September. As soon as I got to the hotel, I called her and wired flowers. It was one of the most thrilling and exciting days I can remember. I got on my knees and asked God to give Ruth and me wisdom to rear children who would come to know Him and be a credit to the Christian faith."

Their first three children were girls. When the fourth was due, Billy was in Texas. Again, Ruth's message brought him home. "I rushed home from Texas and took Ruth to the hospital," he recalls. "We talked right up to the birth, when she was hurried into the delivery room. After a few minutes, a nurse came out and said, 'You are the father of a baby boy!' I gave a yell of delight so loud that I was heard all over the hospital. We had longed for a son, and now I had a son. Ruth insisted that we call him William Franklin Graham, Junior. I agreed only if he would always be known as Franklin. So he's always been Franklin to everyone."

Billy's delight in his progeny has never abated. Christmas is a time for special joy, for then the children come home with their broods, and the log house on the mountain echoes with the gaiety of a united family.

Each holiday season, the Grahams take a group photograph that is used as their next year's Christmas card. Last year's card pictured twenty-one persons. Occasionally, Billy shows the original photograph to a visitor, taking care to point out each daughter and son, each son-in-law and daughter-in-law, and each of his thirteen grandchildren. And he names them all correctly. Not many grandfathers can do as well.

When a stranger examines the photograph taken at any recent

Christmastime, he sees a group of uncommonly handsome men, women, teenagers, and children assembled in a comfortable home. No show of strain is visible. Every face is happy. Here is togetherness on a holy holiday.

Watching the Graham clan in the living color of a TV Christmas special, it is difficult to realize that Ruth and Billy, so surrounded by loved ones and so much admired on every continent, have arrived at this safe shore only after a somewhat stormy passage. Indeed, there were times when God's leading seemed to offer more pain than pleasure.

What could go wrong with a marriage tailored so conscientiously to God's plan? The answer is, plenty!

Loneliness can happen, for instance. In her book *Transformed*, Helen Kooiman wrote about Graham's Anaheim, California crusade and of a woman who had finally realized her dream of meeting the evangelist. After the introduction, she told Ruth, "I've always wished I could shake your husband's hand before I died." To which Ruth replied, plaintively. "Sometimes, I feel the same way."

If the day ever comes that the Grahams decide to release their diaries, personal correspondence, or Ruth's poems, a host of admirers will be delighted and surprised. One snippet from Billy, written after having Ruth with him for a few days in a crusade city, says, "I kissed Ruth good-by today and she left for Montreat. I won't see her for the next three weeks. It was only a few minutes until I was already homesick for her. Everywhere I turned in the room, I could see her."

Some of their bad times were accidents and some were illnesses. Not many grandmothers fall out of a tree while putting up a swing for a grandchild. Ruth managed to do it. The resulting concussion was serious enough to deprive her of memory for many anxious days, more specifically to wash her mind free of the imprint of the hundreds of Bible verses she had memorized and from which she drew her daily breath. So she prayed, "I can stand anything else, Lord, but don't take away my Bible verses." Slowly, He slipped them back into her mind.

The greatest pain accompanied the deaths of Ruth's parents, Virginia and Nelson Bell, in the mid-1970s. Each was a force in the growth of Billy, Ruth, and the children. A room in their home had been Ruth's refuge when she began her education as an evangelist's wife. A loan from Dr. Bell had helped buy a cottage across the street, into which Billy and Ruth moved with their children. Always, a visit to the Bell kitchen brought relief from loneliness, sound advice on child rearing or theology, or fellowship and prayer that sought God's will. The presence of grandparents and their availability as baby-sitters facilitated many of Ruth's visits to crusades. In short, the Bells were irreplaceable. Their loss was traumatic.

Julie Eisenhower was the first writer, I think, to tell the world about Ruth's hacking cough. It began to bother her about fifteen years ago and has persisted. It became a medical puzzle for every physician who studied it. A nuisance and sometimes an agony, it can turn a quiet conversation into an ordeal. Ruth's speaking formally in public—she gets hundreds of invitations—becomes almost impossible.

Of late, competent specialists say tentatively that it may be caused by an unprecedented condition in which live nerve ends are exposed within her throat. The search for a remedy continues. As well as she can, she grants interviews and addresses seminars and Bible classes with stimulating common sense and cheerfulness, hoping that God's mercy and a medical miracle may someday relieve her of this persistent thorn in her flesh.

"Whatever the cause," Julie Eisenhower wrote, "the persistent hacking often kept Ruth—and Billy—awake until dawn. Finally, she was forced to move into a bedroom adjoining his."

Nor has Billy been spared. His health is not now, and never

has been, robust. Ruth says, "He gets the *craziest* things." His medical record describes bouts with kidney stones, infections of the intestines, eye, nose, bladder, and prostate. And there are more. You name it and he has had it or will have it soon. He cannot remember when he didn't live with high blood pressure.

Add the rigors of almost constant travel, jet lag, bad water, foreign food, too little sleep, the pressure of evangelizing night after night, of raising money, of decision making. If Ruth suffers from loneliness, Billy suffers from fatigue. His diaries and correspondence are sprinkled with the noises of exhaustion. So are many of his platform announcements and press conferences.

"What a meeting," he wrote in an old Indian diary. "I was so tired I could hardly stand on my feet. I had to shake my head several times during the sermon to keep from blacking out."

Another entry: "I feel that I am waging a constant battle when I am preaching. When I finish a sermon, I seem to be drained of strength. The forces of hell always line up to confront me."

After one recent crusade, he went to a friend's apartment and slept for two days.

As the years march by, his dependence on Ruth is reflected in the tone of his comments. His first big evangelistic success in London, England was called the Haringey crusade, and Ruth was with him for three happy months. "Her encouragement, her counsel and her prayers supported me more than anything except the Lord Himself," he wrote later. "Certainly God has chosen her to be my life's companion. Many times, at the arena, she would be the last to leave. She was counseling people sometimes past midnight. One night, there was no one left in the building when she finished, and she had to hitch a ride back to our hotel."

Years later, he used words that fairly glowed in describing a steamship journey they took to another crusade. "It was like a second honeymoon," he told a reporter for the *London Times*. "I am a million times more in love with Ruth than we were when we first married."

Still more recently, he joined David Frost before the mike in a famous give-and-take interview that subsequently became a book. Frost is one of the world's most skilled interviewers, as his televised sessions with Richard Nixon demonstrated. Some of his questions to Billy tended to lead him toward admitting a taste for the good life. One of those questions blew up in Frost's face.

"I know that material possessions don't matter much to you," he told Graham, "but if a burglar were to get into your house somehow, and he told you he would leave just one material possession or gift, if you asked him nicely, what would you say you wanted to keep?"

Billy's answer was waiting on the tip of his tongue. "My wife," he said evenly. And the audience cheered.

Lately, a more poignant note is creeping into Billy's interviews. His appreciation of Ruth seems to have deepened and broadened.

Looking through recent magazine pages, I find these items: "My wife has been rearing children all her life, but that is over. Now I shall give more of my time to her. She is going to travel more with me. I shall love her more and be more tender to her because, for the first time in her life, she really needs me. And you know something? I love it. We love each other at a deeper level than we ever dreamed possible in our younger years."

Again: "When my wife left me yesterday, I broke down and cried. I just couldn't bear to think of being three or four weeks without her."

I talked to Ruth Graham recently. We had been reviewing the happy marriages of her four oldest children and the newly announced engagement of her son Ned. Would she gamble again, I

wondered aloud, on a marriage whose principals were separated
so often and so long?

"I must say that it was never indifference to each other or lack
of love that caused us to live such separate lives," she said. "We
made a commitment to the Lord and followed the Lord's leading. In response to that, He gave us extra love for one another
and extra understanding. It wasn't always easy, but Christ never
promised that it would be.

"We love one another today so much more than we ever
dreamed was possible," she added. "When you are first married, a lot of sentimentality and romanticism get mixed up with
your caring. After thirty-five years together, you really begin to
understand the richness of love."

Need more be said? I pushed my search through court records, newspaper files, transcripts, and finally into human
hearts. I found love and heroism.

"I don't want to get to heaven without any scars," Billy
Graham once told me. He won't.

Already, his body bears unsuspected wounds, but they have
not prevented him from conquering his weaknesses in order to
follow God's leading. He did this not for honor or gold, but
because he was *called*.

Ruth wears secret scars, too, confessed only in her prayers.
But she also has conquered because she, too, was called. And
she is honored—I know I am not mistaken—by the multiple
miracle of five believing children.

Some are called to be preachers, some teachers, some
evangelists, and some are called to be holy mothers. In some
undiscovered Dead Sea scroll, there must be a notation defining
holy motherhood like Ruth Graham's and stipulating rewards.

In the middle of an interview, I asked her how she did it.

"You'd best ask my children," she said.

I promised I would.

# 11

# Gigi (Virginia)

*Born: 1945*
*Married: 1963*

Modern child training has become a growth industry and a major educational project among community colleges and social agencies, but in the average home, child rearing is a lost art, along with chipping arrowheads and weaving pine needles.

The vacuum left by this deficiency in family life is demonstrated by an explosion of parenting experts, the most enduring being the celebrated Dr. Benjamin Spock.

Ruth and Billy Graham, once they embarked on the sea of matrimony in 1943, encountered the same reefs and riptides that agitate every marriage. Like millions of couples who came before them, they were almost wholly innocent of the rules and regulations of bringing up baby. But they owned a precious Guidebook. And they were committed to total dependence on its Author.

With the birth of Gigi in 1945, they began to search out and study those tidbits specially directed to young parents. From the first, the Bible was their counselor, admonisher, and guide. The consequences were astounding.

I invite you to meet the Graham children.

I suggest there is a precious reward herein for anyone who confronts his or her actual or remembered problems of parenting

with the assurance that the promise of Proverbs 22:6 will be
fulfilled: "Train up a child in the way he should go: and when he
is old, he will not depart from it."

When I talked to Ruth Graham about her children, I asked her
to bring me up to date on questions that have been asked in the
past by puzzled friends. For instance, why had her daughters
married so young? Why had they not finished college? I reminded her that some psychologists now theorize that young
people who leave home early are really trying to escape from an
environment they hate.

She answered by telling me about Gigi, her first child and the
first to marry. Long ago, she had refused to reveal these details.
Now, six grandchildren later, she relented.

"Bill had preaching engagements in Germany," Ruth said.
"That summer our family lived in a house in Switzerland that
was loaned to us by a friend named Tchividjian. He was a de-
lightful host, and on Saturdays he would phone and say, 'Would
you do me the honor and great pleasure of having lunch with us?'

"He had six children of his own and they had wonderful man-
ners. We had five little Grahams, and I was reluctant to take
them to his home, but we did. We went over for lunch and the
children were so well behaved, you wouldn't believe it."

So the Grahams ate with the Tchividjians every weekend. The
adults ate at one end of a long dining room. The children sat at
the other end, presided over by their senior member, Stephan
Tchividjian, age twenty-one. Gigi Graham was fourteen.

Stephan made an incomparable supervisor. He had a sense of
humor, he was firm, and he filled his car with laughing kids each
Saturday afternoon and showed them the sights. Ruth remem-
bers that Billy surprised her one night by saying, "Wouldn't it be
great if Stephan and Gigi married someday?"

She replied, "You've got to be kidding." She knew that Gigi

was madly in love with a boy back home.

"But out of the blue," Ruth recalled, "two years later, we got a long letter from Stephan, asking permission to marry Gigi. Stephan enclosed a personal letter to Gigi and asked us to send it on to her at college. It was his formal proposal."

The situation was without precedent. Billy was a thousand miles away, but Ruth found him via telephone and told him of the unanticipated proposal. After thinking it over, she liked the idea. "I just knew they were hand picked for each other," she recalled. Billy had reservations. So instead of sending Stephan's letter on to Gigi at college, they agreed to hold it until she came home for the approaching Christmas vacation.

"When we showed her the letter and she read it, her eyes got as big as saucers," Ruth remembered. "She said, 'Mother, this must be of God.' And she repeated those words every morning for several days, but every night she'd be crying."

Finally, she announced, "I've got to see Stephan."

Billy, newly arrived for the holidays, telephoned Stephan in Switzerland and invited him to Montreat. He was there three days later.

While they waited, the family was uncomfortably at odds. "We'd talk about the marriage," Ruth said, "And Bill would say, 'No way!' I'd argue, 'But you don't know Stephan,' and he'd reply, 'But I do know Gigi.' "

Ruth realized that their final decision needed the blessing of a united family. Gigi was so inexperienced; Stephan was a young man of business. Gigi was 100 percent American; Stephan was Indo-European. The age difference and the cultural disparity could become ingredients in a disaster. Ruth got out her personal Bible and sought instruction. Then she found a Prayerbook Bible verse which said, "God maketh men to be of one mind in an hous." Praying hard, she asked God to make her house of one mind.

The climax came when Stephan arrived from Switzerland. Billy met him at the airport. Later, he told Ruth, "I see what you mean. He is the perfect one."

Seventeen-year-old Gigi saw Stephan and knew immediately, without a shadow of a doubt, Ruth recalled: "Suddenly, we were of one mind."

Today, Stephan and Gigi Tchividjian live in a suburb of Fort Lauderdale, Florida. They have six children. He has changed careers, trading banking and business for the vocation of being a Christian psychologist. "He's getting his PhD at Marquette," Ruth told me. "He's a terrific father and she's a terrific little mother. They balance each other. They moved to Florida because they wanted their children to be thoroughly grounded in the Bible while they were young. And they go to a super school down there that's run by a Presbyterian church."

I know of no other romance so unique or so ordered by biblical principles. As for the influences that shaped the character of Gigi and subsequently played their role in producing the remarkable fruit of this marriage, I have asked Gigi to speak for herself.

When I think back on my childhood, Mother was always there. We did everything together, as friends and companions. I can remember her out in the yard doing yard work and planting flowers. We built a rock wall together, and we fixed a dam in a stream, and we went antiquing. Then we'd all pile in the Jeep and go for a slumber party at the little cabin up on the mountain.

In those early days, she didn't attend Sunday school, much less teach it. She didn't attend the Bible-study classes or teach Bible study—she stayed home and cared for us when we were little.

When we grew up, then she started teaching the college-age Sunday school. In one place my husband and I lived, we were made to feel guilty if we didn't attend two or three Bible-study groups each week. I don't think you can be that busy and still be an adequate mother, especially if the father is not at home.

The first thing I can recall about Daddy is a time that I was being bad and he came home from a trip when I didn't know he was going to arrive. Boy, did I feel guilty! Mother always built up our excitement and anticipation for Daddy's return, and there I was being naughty. I was very embarrassed. I think my embarrassment was caused by my feeling of respect for Daddy. He was away so much, but somehow he and Mother instilled in us the feeling that children ought to respect their Daddy. I had a healthy respect for him as a child. I still do.

Daddy was very warm and loving to us all—with Mother and with us children—and I never saw him embarrassed by it. I can remember that when I was married and nine months pregnant, he'd still pull me down on his lap and hug me. I think of him as warmly and openly physically affectionate with Mother, too—hugging her, kissing her, snuggling up to her. I feel that's important in a family. I know that I learned something from the modeling I saw in my family. It's what I wanted in my life, too.

In many ways, Daddy is an optimistic pessimist. We had a little joke at home about that, and Mother made him a pillow that had this motto on it: "If anything can possibly go wrong, it will." That was Daddy! We have quite a bit of rain in Montreat, and some days he'd look out at the rain and get lower and lower, until Mother would finally say, "For pity's sake, Bill, turn your chair around and look at the fireplace instead!" It's a family joke that if Daddy comes home, the rain will start. It always does. Last spring, he flew down to visit us in Florida. The weather had been beautiful all week, but this big thunderstorm rolled in and his plane had to land in a tornado! I couldn't believe it.

I used to pray that the Lord would give me the man of His choice, but being the daughter of a man who traveled so much, I also prayed that my husband would stay at home. And Stephan does that, but sometimes he has to be gone for two or three weeks at a time, and then I see how difficult it was for Mother when we were growing up. I don't know how she did it.

She must have been longing for Dad to be home during the holidays. One Christmas he was in Korea, and she went out of her way to invite friends to visit us, so we wouldn't miss Daddy so much.

Daddy constantly covered us in prayer, and we felt that. And there were the prayers of a lot of God's people. Of course our grandparents prayed for Daddy every day, and we always heard that. Just knowing that people like that were praying for us gave us a beautiful sense of security.

To me, the most important thing in raising a family is each person's personal relationship with Christ. All the other things follow from that. And then, I would want each member of my family to know and feel the things that I felt in my home—such as total acceptance of the way I was. What I did wasn't always accepted, but I was. You need to feel secure, and even with Daddy away, I think we felt that way.

Having my grandfather there was very important during my growing-up years, because he was a definite male influence that gave us security. Grandfather never disappointed me spiritually. In fact, I can't remember him ever disappointing me in anything.

The only thing Mother and Daddy didn't do enough of when we were young was argue in front of us. We never heard a cross word. One result was that when I married and we had our first argument, it shook me up, because I thought that wasn't supposed to happen. But then as Stephan and I got older, we realized that Mother and Daddy had their arguments, but they kept them away from us.

Mother told me recently that when she was expecting Ned, there was a period of several months when she was depressed, but it went away when Ned was born. I asked her, "How did you get through those nine months without any of us knowing that you were depressed and down?"

She just smiled and said, "Oh, you learn to hide a lot of things."

I remember seeing Mother with tears in her eyes only two or three times, even when Daddy would leave to be gone for a long time. She had little tricks to get her mind off it. When he would leave, she would have piles of work to do—big jobs to keep her busy for a couple of days.

Stephan and I have six children now—four boys and two girls. I do as little as possible outside of the home, like Mom did when we were young. There are exceptions, when someone in our community will ask me to do something. Mother and I did a seminar together a year or so ago on "Why Have a Home?" In fact, I'm working on a little book that is going to have that same title. But I believe my place is at home for now.

There are times when I look longingly at other grandfathers going to Disney World with their grandchildren, and I wish so much that we had the kind of normal family life that would have allowed Daddy to be just a normal Daddy every now and then. That's why I try to take the children back home to Montreat as often as I can. We go home for Christmas, and we were there last August. These are the times when we feel the most like a normal, everyday family, and they are special to us.

To me, Daddy is honest and straightforward. He has one purpose, and he's truly humble. I've been amazed by his humility at times. "No, no," he'll say about a book he's written, "it won't be a success. Nobody will buy my little book." Some time ago, after he became well known, he met some people when he was out of town. The next time he was in their town, he called them on the phone and said, "Hello, this is Billy Graham. Do you remember me?" They just couldn't believe he would say that. But that's how my Daddy is!

# 12

# Anne

*Born: May 21, 1948*
*Married: to Dan Lotz, a dentist in Raleigh, North Carolina*

Anne, the Graham's second daughter, is named for Anne Morrow Graham, in tribute to Billy's mother, Morrow Coffey Graham. When I talked to Ruth about Anne, I was already aware of the stir her daughter was making in her adopted hometown of Raleigh, North Carolina.

As always, Ruth's remarks became a reflection of the ideals advanced and supported throughout the upbringing of all her children.

So I shall step aside quickly to permit my interviewee's own words to set the stage for Anne's refreshing memories. She began Anne's story with her courtship and marriage.

"She married Danny Lotz, who is a dentist. Earlier, he was captain of the North Carolina University basketball team the time they were first in the nation. She met him when the Fellowship of Christian Athletes was meeting here in Black Mountain. When she came back from her first date, she said, 'Mother, I met the coolest guy tonight. I don't know anything about him. I don't even know his name. But he is six feet and six inches tall.' She's a tall girl, and I think it was almost love at first sight. He's eleven years older than Anne, and when he proposed, we didn't insist on her finishing college. He was already older, and why should we make her wait?

"This may be heresy, but I'm not all that impressed by a college education. Some of the most interesting people I know never went to college but they tried to make up for it by reading. They are fascinating people. Some of the dullest I know went through college, then quit reading, and that was it.

"I told the girls, read widely and read constantly, and you'll be educated. And they are.

"Anne teaches a Bible class in Raleigh that has about five hundred members and a waiting list of two hundred fifty. She started it when she was a member of the Junior League and every member had a special project. She asked them if she could make her project a Bible class. They had never considered such a project, so they called for a secret vote, and the result was unanimous. She got to start her class.

"I think she got burdened for the women of Raleigh. So many of them had family and emotional problems, and some were going through charismatic experiences.

"I know that speaking in tongues can be a gift of the Spirit, but there are also pseudo-experiences that are psychosomatic or Satanic. I've seen all three. You know, sometimes the law of diminishing returns requires you to expect bigger and better experiences, and so you get experience-oriented rather than depending on sound Bible doctrine. You become spiritually depleted. That leads to trouble.

"At any rate, Anne was burdened to help people. I begged her not to do it. I said: 'You've got a husband and three children and help in the house only one day a week. You can't do it. You haven't got the strength.'

"She said: 'Mother, if ever I've felt called of God to do something, this is it.' So I said: 'Well, I'll pray for you, but if ever you feel that it's distracting you from your home or that Danny and the children are missing something because of it, you know which comes first.'

"So she started her class, and it has grown, grown, grown. Those women get *taught*. She's had to resign from the Junior League because there's no time for any other activity. And the leadership of the city is coming. She could never get out of bed in the morning, but now she gets up at five o'clock so she can get her studying done before Danny and the children are awake. And she studies late at night and while they are in school. When she's with them, they get her full attention.

"The last time I was in her home, it was the neatest I'd ever seen it. The children were the best behaved and the happiest. And Anne was so well organized. She always was a frail person, and she's even better off, physically. It's just amazing."

As I later listened to Anne, her whole personality seemed to coalesce into a finely tuned communications instrument, with body, mind, and spirit blending to express her truth. Her words were a torrent, laced together with force and authority, yet buttered with engaging charm.

I remembered a young Billy Graham who spoke rapidly in a hypnotic gush of sound that bound the ears to slavish attention and which convinced, even as they were succeeded by other images, while fresh concepts flooded the brain.

Anne is her father's daughter.


I rarely talk about Daddy, because our family life is the one private thing he has left. He's sharing everything else with the world, and this part of his life is something that's ours alone. People may think we're not a close family, since we're awfully spread out, mileagewise, but we're close in spirit, and we absolutely adore our Daddy.

Our whole family has a warm, close relationship. My relationship with Daddy and Mother has taught me so much about my relationship with the Lord, too. I think of them and I think of the Apostle Paul. In one of his letters, he says that "to follow me is to follow Christ.'' He must have been some man to say that! With my parents, I can honestly say that growing up in obedience to them was to follow Christ. I pray that I can be that sort of example to my own children.

No parents are perfect, but ours love the Lord, and they shared that love with me. They may have made some mistakes, as everybody does, but I haven't seen too many of them.

Having a famous father isn't always easy for a child. Once we were all on a train, and the train was derailed in Kentucky. We had to get off and take a little plane to some other place, and I remember that people came up to Daddy even then. I didn't like that at all.

Then one time when we were driving to Charlotte to see Mother Graham, we stopped at a restaurant for lunch. A couple came over and introduced themselves to Daddy, and I remember my heart saying *no, no, no!* Then this couple told us how they'd come to the Lord under Daddy's ministry and joined a church. They had never had lunch out before, but somehow the Lord seemed to direct them to stop for lunch that day. When they saw Daddy in there, they were certain that the Lord had made them stop. Something like that warms your heart. It's the people who pull on him and drag on him and ask for his autograph that irritate me. But I can't remember ever seeing Daddy irritated about it.

We missed Daddy when he was away, but we knew he was always interested in us. I think the Lord gave him a discernment and wisdom and insight into each one of us, so that the time he did have with us was very special, in that we felt extremely loved and important in his sight. He made each of us feel that he was proud of us, and that each of us was his favorite. I still feel that way. I think my heavenly Father is so important to my life now because I see Him in Daddy. My earthly father taught me a lot about my heavenly Father.

I can never remember a time when Daddy has forgotten a birthday or an anniversary of mine. Wherever he is in the world, he always calls me on my birthday. I can count on that just as I can count on the sunrise. He's so faithful and so considerate in things like that.

I guess the most special times in my childhood were when we traveled with Daddy. I remember going to Fort Lauderdale for several weeks one winter when I was six or seven. I can remember driving down in somebody's convertible and then driving up and down the beach. Those were special family times.

Perhaps the trip that meant a lot to me personally was a trip alone out west with Daddy. It was before the Fresno crusade, when he and I went by train from Asheville to Billings, Montana. It was such a special time, having meals together and enjoying each other's company.

In Billings, we met Cliff Barrows and his daughter Bonnie and continued out along the Snake River, down past Mount Rainier, and on to Fresno. Daddy had the crusade there, and I came back with Uncle Cliff and Bonnie.

That particular trip was quality time. We were together about ten days. There was no particular incident during that time that I remember—it was just being with him, being loved by him, having his attention for a while. I was twelve or thirteen at the time, and it was important to me.

Daddy's homecoming was always special, but it was especially so for Mother. Their relationship—I don't know how to explain it—but I know that Mother's not really alive until Daddy walks into the room. Her close friends will tell you that, too. They say they can tell when he's home, because then she just radiates. Their relationship is precious, and that has blessed me, because I see it becoming warmer and closer and more loving, now that we children have left. A lot of people don't know what to do with themselves when their children leave, but Mother and Daddy are falling in love all over again.

Just before last Thanksgiving, Daddy and Mother both had to leave for different places. They were supposed to return home at about the same time, but Daddy got home before she did, and she didn't show up. When he went to meet the plane, she wasn't on it, and he was in a twit.

All this time, Mother has been the one at home, never knowing where Daddy was, and now he was at home and didn't know where she was! He was so upset that he called me late at night, saying how worried he was. I reminded him that planes sometimes get rerouted, and tried to calm him down.

It turned out that she got home safely the next day. She had been at the airport in Atlanta, reading a good book that Daddy had given her, and she had simply missed the call for her plane. She had to wait until the next plane, which was the following morning. Daddy was really worried, and I don't know if he'd ever been in a position like that before. I thought it was good for him to have the shoe on the other foot for a little while, myself!

I only remember Daddy getting really mad about one thing I ever did. He was away so much that he always tried not to get down on us when he was home. This was when Goldwater campaigned for the presidency. I was feeling my intellectual wings at this point, and became an absolutely avid Goldwater fan. A friend invited a group of us to hear Goldwater speak in person, and I was delighted.

When I got there, somebody latched onto me, and I ended up on the front row of the platform. Before I knew it, someone said, "Billy Graham's daughter will say a word." There I was, fourteen years old, in a hall filled with people waving signs and blowing horns. They pushed me up to the microphone, and I looked out at all those people. I can even remember exactly what I did next: I read one of the placards in front of me. It didn't take more than thirty seconds, but the point is that Billy Graham's daughter had publicly said something that meant she was endorsing Goldwater, which implied, of course, that Daddy was, too.

Daddy was staying out of the whole campaign, and was really upset at me. He even went for a couple of days without speaking to me. But then it became a joke between Mr. Johnson and Daddy when Mr. Johnson's daughter joined the Catholic church. They decided Mr. Johnson couldn't control his daughter on religion and Daddy couldn't control his on politics.

When Daddy heard how the whole thing happened, he understood. That was the only time I can remember him so mad that he wasn't reasonable.

Daddy's so extremely affectionate, and that blessed me when I was growing up. He would hold our hands and kiss us. Even today, he pulls us down on his lap. He's just a loving person, and he's that way with all us children and with his grandchildren. He'll pull them onto his lap and hold their hands and ask them what they've been doing—and a child can feel and appreciate that type of love.

The night that Danny told me he loved me, I went into Daddy's room to say goodnight and told him what Danny had said. Daddy pulled both of my hands to him and looked me in the eye. "Anne," he said, "I'm sure that this is the man you're going to marry. I know that Danny's the one for you."

Well, when your father tells you something like that, you think twice. Danny set up his dental practice in Raleigh and drove every weekend to see me, and we were married the next September.

Daddy knew me so well and could see Danny had qualities that would complement me. He did a great job picking my husband! I've never had one regret. It's been up and down, as all marriages are at times, but deep in my heart, I know that this is where God would have me and that Danny was the one He had selected. He must have used Daddy to bring it into focus for me.

Our children are John, age nine, Morrow, six, and Rachel Ruth, four. They're at the age when you can teach them easily. Each night before they go to bed, they have their Bible story, and they are also involved in Sunday school. They know their Bible stories, and I've taught them Scripture verses.

Mother used to make us memorize reams of Scripture verses when we did something bad. I remember my brother had to memorize so many verses before he could have a friend up. I haven't done that yet, but I teach the two youngest ones very simple verses.

I think it's important to teach them Scripture, and I get up early to do it, because first I have to get right with the Lord myself. I pray that the Lord Jesus is becoming a living person in their eyes in our home, so it's very natural to talk about Him during the day.

In Montreat, reading and training were every day. Mother made sure of that before we went to school. Yet, I never really appreciated it unless Daddy was there to lead us. Not that Mother didn't do it right, but he would expound it as he read.

But you can't improve on the way Mother and Daddy taught us in our home and brought us into a relationship with the Lord. Each of us has come to know the Lord in a really personal way. I know I can't imitate that with my children, but I mean to follow it as closely as possible.

I also have a class here in Raleigh. It's the Bible Study Fellowship, which is an international organization. And it's a super Bible study that is extremely disciplined and deep—much like the college or seminary level, but for lay people. I teach a women's class, and we have five hundred in it, with a waiting list of two hundred fifty.

To have the Lord Jesus within you, you have to ask. When I was very young, at the age of three, actually, at Mother's knee I asked the Lord Jesus to come into my heart. That wasn't a real intellectual experience, because at three you're not very intellectual. But as far as I knew, I was responding to what I knew the best way I could.

Mother had an experience like that when she was small. And you just grow in the Lord from that time on. Some people have an experience like the Apostle Paul's, and some people have an experience like Daddy's, when he was eighteen years old. Others are born again or reborn in different ways that are more drastic or sensational, which might be bad, because you depend on your feelings when the Bible actually says if you ask the Lord to come in, He will. You take that on faith in God's Word.

So that experience was mine when I was small. I never had an experience afterwards. I feel as if I just grew and responded the best I could each time the Lord revealed Himself in a different way. Actually, I've just been following the Truth and following the Light.

# 13

# Bunny (Ruth Bell)

Born: December, 1950
Married: to Ted Dienert, Philadelphia advertising executive
Home: Paoli, Pennsylvania (but moving soon to Texas)

Bunny is the youngest of the Graham daughters. Named Ruth
Bell Graham, for her mother, she lives near Philadelphia.
Perhaps because of her proximity to eastern journalists, she has
had to bear more than her share of media attention.

Invariably, reporters have been startled by her charm and
beauty. An article in *Good Housekeeping* magazine once described her as "not at all the dowdy, oppressively pious type of
stereotype one might expect of a preacher's daughter. Instead,
she is strikingly pretty . . . slender . . . long, blond hair . . .
porcelain skin . . . blue eyes like her father's. She wears bright
lipstick and blue eye shadow and swinging clothes."

Bunny's mother agrees with the description, except for the
"swinging clothes" reference. "They are not swinging," she
asserts firmly. "They are simply stylish."

Regardless, Bunny has a mind of her own as well as a clear
understanding of its impact. A recent note from her discusses
her mental set (about matters of importance to her) as being what
she calls "pugnaciously opinionated." And again, her mother
uses a softer phrase. "I'd say she is strong-minded," she says.
But this small fissure in the family is no generation gap.

My first question to Ruth was one she had already answered

233

a thousand times: "Where in the world did she get that name?"

"When she was born, she looked just like a little rabbit."

Listen to Bunny describe her life.

We had such a happy home. I don't think Daddy was a sentimentalist, in the conventional sense. I'm sure there were many forgotten anniversaries, and certainly many forgotten birthdays, because Daddy's mind was on so many other things that it was easy for him to forget those special days.

Mother was very much concerned about not adding any burdens. Whenever he calls—even today—she'll say, "Hi, honey," and she'll never tell him there's a problem at home or that one of the kids has just slit his throat. Certainly, with all five of us at each other constantly, there were problems. We had some accidents, like when the Jeep turned over and all five of us rolled down the mountainside. Yes, it happened. Gigi can tell you about that. She was driving. She slipped off the side of the road and all of us went down the hill. She was only thirteen at the time, and Mother had just told her not to drive.

But when it came to Daddy, Mother was very particular about easing his burdens. Especially when he came home. We couldn't have friends out to play with us, and his rooms were private, so he could study undisturbed. To try to convey this to someone else makes it sound as if he were sort of a nuisance and Mother made him a nuisance, but he was just special. To us, Daddy was really important. I don't mean that in a worldly sense, either. We thought he was terrific, and because he was busy and because his work was so important, we had to take special care of him.

I never heard Mother and Daddy argue. I never heard them fight. But now that I'm married and can sort of read between the lines, I know what Daddy meant when he said, "Ruth" in a special kind of way.

I can remember distinctly that he spanked me three times. I

think he did it only those three times, but all were for very good reasons: once for lying, once for kicking Franklin in the head, and once for telling Mother that I hated her.

We were in Switzerland for the summer and Franklin and I had been fighting all morning, so Mother sat between us while we were either having lunch or having prayers. Franklin reached behind her back and hit me. I reached in front of her and hit him back. She thought I had started it and was punishing me by having me go to my room. As I left, I turned around and told her I hated her. Much later, we talked it over. She still doesn't think I was right in saying that I hated her, but she does agree that there was injustice.

I kicked Franklin when I was sitting on the hood of our Jeep as Mother was getting ready to drive up the mountain. Franklin wanted to sit there, too, and I didn't want him. I told him no, but he tried to climb up on the top, and I kicked him in the head. That's why Daddy spanked me. Daddy always punished first and explained later. But after it was all over, we'd pray together and ask for guidance, and he would always gather me in his arms and tell me that he loved me.

Mother made it a point to make Daddy's homecoming special. She talked about it for days ahead. It was something to look forward to. It was an exciting time. We all went to the train station, if he was coming in on the train. Or we all went to the airport, or we were at the door to meet him. No one was allowed to visit—our playmates, I mean—while Daddy was home. We weren't being deprived, this was just a special time because Daddy was home.

They were always so affectionate with each other. She would walk by his chair and he would grab her and pull her down on his lap and they would hug. Yes, we were very much aware that they were in love with each other. Always, they were affectionate, very affectionate.

I do wish Daddy could have a little more freedom to come

home when he's needed. One thing sticks in my mind, and Daddy and I have discussed it. It's over now, but when Mother fell out of a tree, I flew home to take care of her. The doctors were afraid that she had a concussion and there might be hemorrhaging. Then when she was recovering and still on crutches, her own mother died. Daddy was in the middle of a crusade. We called him to tell him what had happened, and at first he felt that he could not leave the crusade, but then he did come. He was there for the funeral, and then he flew back to the crusade. Mother didn't project to us that she minded, but I did. I felt that he should have stayed with her. But I don't want to make Daddy seem like a hard-hearted ogre, either, for he isn't. Only I think Mother needed him, especially at that time.

We definitely are a close family. When we are all together, like at Christmas, we all pick up right where we left off and everybody is everybody else's best friend. My closest girl friends are my mother and my two sisters. It's very special.

We were close and we were happy, too. I've never heard a cross word between my parents. My husband and I have cross words occasionally, and that worried me at first, because I thought it was abnormal. It isn't, of course.

My mother's mother and father, the Bells, really helped raise us. Their living across the street when we were little was a blessing. I'm a great deal like my grandmother. They were just great, and I think they were a great influence on all of us four older children. [Ned was still a very small child when both Nelson and Virginia Bell died.] Even now, sometimes, it is difficult for me to talk about them. We just miss them so much. They were unbelievable. They don't make people like them any more.

I greatly admire Daddy's own discipline and dedication to the point of sacrifice of his own wants and wishes. This applies to so many things, like wanting to do things with the family. Recently, he said if he had to do it over again, he'd spend more time with his family. But he gave that up for his ministry.

After we all got married and had children, we once asked Mama, "How is it that you raised five children and never screamed at us?"

She said, "When I was going through it, I prayed that God would make you all forget the times that I yelled or got angry." And I think this applies to Daddy, too, because he had to sacrifice the family times. *But God has been so gracious and has protected us from any bitterness or any feeling that we were neglected or deprived.*

I think it's unfair, the way some people say Daddy's "feathering his nest." Mother and Daddy made sacrifices to send us away to school. Nobody in our family has ever lived high. When Daddy travels, he stays in good hotels and sometimes he travels first class on overseas trips so he can sleep, but what people don't know is that most of those hotel rooms are given to him free or half-price.

If he'd had his hand in the till, he would have retired a long time ago. And what could he have done with the money? We don't have a mansion or a yacht or a fleet of Cadillacs. So I think that kind of criticism is unfair. All Daddy wants to do is follow his calling.

# 14

# FRANKLIN

*Born: July, 1952*
*Married: 1974*
*Home: Boone, North Carolina*

Preachers' sons are a special breed, plagued by unique problems and harassed by stringent expectations. The sons of "superstars" must also endure a host of pressures unknown and unsuspected by run-of-the-mill youth.

The two sons of Billy and Ruth Graham have had to withstand the stresses of both categories. Their survival represents an extraordinary tribute to both parents.

William Franklin Graham (called Franklin), their fourth child and first son, was promptly named for Billy. As might be expected, his arrival caused great rejoicing and lofty expectations. The load imposed grew heavy during adolescence. One day it became more than young Franklin could bear.

"Franklin was our beloved prodigal," his mother told me.

"Did he rebel against your strictness?" I asked.

"None of the kids has ever rebelled against Bill or me," she replied, "but Franklin did rebel for a while, and I think maybe he was rebelling against being a preacher's son. Anyhow, he was pretty wild."

"In what way?"

She drew a long breath that sketched the memory of too many years of parental pain and uncertainty. She explained carefully that Franklin was always a believer, but he loved his version of fun. This is the story she told:

"I'm not going to confess Franklin's sins for him, but one time I got a call from a policeman here in Montreat. He said, 'Mrs. Graham, I was chasing Franklin and he slammed the door in my face.' The door he was talking about was our front gate, with its electric lock. He was chasing Franklin up the mountain and Franklin had gotten inside and slammed the gate. You can imagine how that policeman felt. I said, 'Well, come on back up. I'll have the gate open and we can talk it over.' So he came and we talked.

"You know, Franklin did make me study real hard as to what to do about him. And I thought, how did God treat *His* children? We don't always please Him. Sometimes we are really spiritual con artists, when we give to the Lord because of what we want Him to give back to us—or we try to convince Him that what He wants is what we think we need.

"So what does God do to His children? Well, He loves us. He knows that we know what's right and what's wrong. All of our children have been taught that from the time they were so high. They know exactly where we stand. So the only effective thing a mother can do is to love them and listen to them and pray.

"I really feel that the time for talking to a child is during his preteens, when he is growing up. The Bible says, 'Thou shalt teach thy children when they walkest by the way, here a little, there a little.' Someone has said that if you try to pour liquid into a narrow-necked bottle too rapidly, much of it is spilled and wasted. The same thing happens when teaching a child. It must be a little at a time.

"By the way, I've discovered that *they're* the ones who want to do the talking. They've got things they want and need to talk out, so shut up and listen. There are exceptions, but basically, you'd best just shut up and listen.

"The hardest part is that they always want to talk about midnight. That's when I'm cross-eyed. I remember our girls would come in and crawl up on the bed and talk and talk. Or I'd sit up and wait for Franklin to come in. Usually, he'd feel like talking, too, and he'd sit down and he'd talk. One night he said, 'I know why you wait up for me. It's because you want to smell my breath.' I said, 'If that's what you think, I'm sleepy. I'm heading for the sack.' So I quit waiting up for him.

"But I really feel that relationships are much more important than rules. I'm not talking about the Ten Commandments. I'm talking about house rules. A relationship comes first. I know mothers who have destroyed relationships with their daughters by picking on them to be neater in their rooms and things like that. The relationship is more important than any neat room.

"I think the boys and I have a good relationship. I know it. Franklin's really found himself and married the most wonderful girl, and he's working for the Lord. He's working on a mission project that is just thrilling, and I know he'll want to tell you about it."

Mother's always bright and sparkly—even when she worries herself sick over some problem or when she only gets an hour or two of sleep at night. She might be worrying about some student at college or some member of her Sunday-school class, or me, when I was growing up and wouldn't get home until four o'clock in the morning. Mother never went to bed until all of us children were in. Sometimes I would come in at three or four, just to see if I could catch her asleep, but the light would always be on in her bedroom. I'm sure she'd been awake for hours, worrying about where I'd been.

I resented that some, but I knew that's just a mother's instinct. And the next morning, no matter how much she'd worried, she'd always have that bright, sparkly face, as if she'd had twelve hours of sleep. You know, she's had a horrible cough for years and she suffers from headaches, but she always has that bright, cheerful personality, and I believe it comes from her daily walk with the Lord. The whole family knows it.

One of my earliest memories is of Father returning from a trip. Two of my sisters were out in the front yard, and I remember how excited we were that Daddy was coming home. I believe he had been to Africa, because he brought us a little stuffed lion and some other presents.

He'd go hunting sometimes when he was home. He's inclined very much toward the outdoors, but his position and his work schedule are such that he's never had that much time. But one of my best memories is when he took me camping. He bought me my first sleeping bag and we went up on the side of the mountain and camped out. I was so proud of my new sleeping bag! I guess maybe I was six or seven years old. I was just as tickled as I could be.

We lived on the side of the mountain, and when I was nine years old, Daddy gave me my first rifle. I hunted constantly. I hiked every day. I camped every weekend. I had my rifle and my backpack, and I'd always head for the mountains. I'd shoot rabbits and squirrels, anything that hopped, flew, or crawled. You know, when you're a boy and have three or four hours of sunlight left after school, and there are no neighbors to play with, you go to the woods. So I headed for them every afternoon.

I went to a public school in Black Mountain until the ninth grade. Then I went to a school on Long Island called Stony Brook for three and one-half years. They were more advanced than we were, and they put me back a year. The middle of my junior year up there, I came home, and they put me ahead into my senior year. Then I went to a college in Longview, Texas, for about one and one-half years, but I didn't do too well and wasn't very happy. That's when I dropped out and went into the Middle East to work.

Later, I went home and attended Montreat-Anderson College for two years and got a two-year degree. Then I married and enrolled at Appalachia State University at Boone, North Carolina. I graduated this past summer [1978] with a degree in business administration.

When you are the son of a famous man—or even if you're not—sometimes other children will give you a hard time. One reason I chose to get my education here in North Carolina is that here I've never had that kind of trouble. North Carolina people look on my father as just a home boy who has done well, and they are proud of him. But they never think of him as great or big. They just think of him as Billy, so they've never treated me as anything special—just as Franklin Graham, a local citizen. I've always appreciated that.

At a very early age, Mother and Daddy treated me like an adult. When I was old enough to go to college, they felt I was old enough to make my own decisions. Of course there were some things in which they always had the last say—as in any home situation where the parents are paying the bills. And there were some times where they demanded to have the final say. But they always treated me as an adult.

They sent a tremendous amount of prayer into my life, and I think they let me make decisions because they knew that Almighty God was looking after me and had His angels overseeing me. Some people think they were too liberal because they gave me a lot of leeway, but it let me gain the experience of making decisions on my own.

When I was eighteen, I wanted to buy a little sports car, but Daddy wasn't willing to finance it. He let me go to the bank and borrow the money, and he cosigned the note. So I had the experience of paying it back each month, and after about six months, when I couldn't make the payments, I had to sell it. He could have easily bought the car, but it was a better education letting me borrow the money and then fail.

I never really rebelled against my parents. Sure, there were petty things, but not to the point where we didn't speak to each other or went around pouting. That never happened. I was trained to respect my parents and to honor my father and mother. If they laid the law down, that's the way it had to be. If I didn't understand it, they'd explain. You could be hardheaded and not want to accept their decision, but that was just too bad.

I hold a private pilot's license that I got when I was in college. But when you're married and have two children and you're trying to go to school at the same time, you don't have a lot of money to do those things.

I did go to Alaska to help build the pipeline on the North Slope. The month I got there, they closed it. So I stuck around for a few weeks with nothing to do, and then got a job with a construction crew. We built about fifty houses for Eskimos. That was an adventure.

Now I'm head of a small organization called the World Medical Mission. We started it last year and I took over this summer. Our purpose is to supply mission hospitals with surgeons for a short time of service, maybe four to six weeks.

Most denominations have their own hospitals in various parts of the world which are staffed by missionary doctors who come to them for two to four years. They need more doctors. The doctors I've talked to say they'd love to go into the mission field, but they've got wives who feel differently, and children that are in school, or they have sick parents that they can't leave. As Christians, they feel they ought to tithe their money and their time and would like to give one-tenth of their time to the Lord. So they'll go anywhere on the mission field for four to six weeks. So we're doing it. No other organization is doing it. As yet, nobody has tried to motivate the Christian medical community to support missions on a national scale. There's no organization to promote it, oversee it, organize it, and help get everything together. That's why we're trying to do it.

Right now there are needs in twenty-three mission hospitals for surgeons. Not doctors in general, but surgeons. There's a tremendous need just for surgeons. Once we get set up and learn how to handle surgeons, we'll take on another specialty and recruit other kinds of doctors. We've chosen surgeons first because they can pay their own expenses with no problem, and most of them take a month or two off each year anyway, so they've got the time to give.

But we're looking only for committed men, men who go to the field for one purpose—to be a servant both to the people that they administer to and their own colleagues. We aren't there only to treat their wounds and heal the sick, but to introduce them to Christ. If a doctor's main purpose is to practice medicine and not preach, we don't want him. Our mission is strictly spiritual.

I'm expecting to have about 50 surgeons saying they will go by early 1979. With information already in hand, I can use about 24 surgeons in our first year, and we know of needs that exist right now in about 100 countries around the world.

We are supported by private donations. Our office is donated. Our space is donated. Our overhead is almost nothing. I'm not taking a salary. We're starting off one step at a time. It's up to the Lord. We're doing His work, and if He wants to let it move, then it's up to Him. If He wants to hold it back for some reason, then that's fine with me.

My intention is to set it up, to get it financed, and then to find someone else to run it. I don't feel that I have the experience or the expertise. So right now, I'm just setting it up. The Lord may have other plans for me or He may want me to stay with them. But there are other things I would like to do.

For instance, there's a small outfit called the Samaritans,

founded by Dr. Bob Pierce. It's very small, but they are involved in a new concept of ministry that is exactly what the Good Samaritan story was all about. They want to help the people that everybody seems to have bypassed. Dr. Bob Pierce used to travel around the world and find these missionaries that couldn't express themselves well, or didn't have support from the big churches because they couldn't get up front and talk. They'd stutter, or maybe they were ugly to look at, but they were doing a great work in the field. And he would back them to the hilt. He took me on some trips with him, and that's the type of work I hope to get into.

I'd like to do a little work with my father. As I grew up, he wasn't at home that much. If I'm ever in a position where I can travel with him, I'd like to go with him, even if I could only carry his suitcase. He's getting older, and with the kind of schedule he's keeping, the Lord could take him home at any minute. I would just like to spend some time with him, and I'd just like to carry his bags or maybe shine his shoes or whatever. If that would help him, I'd like to do it.

I plan always to be in full-time Christian work. As for the type of evangelism my father is in, no. I've never felt that God called me to that. God appoints His men to do His work. What my father does is not inherited. God appointed him to that. If you are the son of a great man, you are always compared. Nothing I have done is equal or even close to what my father has done, and I'll never strive for that. I want to serve the Lord in anything that He has for me.

# 15

# Ned

*Born: January, 1958*
*Engagement announced: 1978*
*Home: Montreat, North Carolina*


Nelson Edman Graham (Ned) is the youngest son in the Graham family. He is named for his mother's father, Nelson Bell, and for V. Raymond Edman, the president of Wheaton College and Billy's mentor and counselor during and after his undergraduate days.

Born in 1958, Ned came late to Montreat. There was a span of a half-dozen years between him and his brother Franklin, and over a dozen years between him and his oldest sister, Gigi. One result was that he spent much of his time (the others were married or away at school) almost as an only son.

When I interviewed him, he was living temporarily at the Graham home and limping badly from torn knee tendons, the result of an incautious step off an Asheville curb. He was also very tired of explaining to sceptics how such a mundane accident could happen to a robust athlete and teacher of the arcane skill called rock climbing.

Ruth had told me earlier of his passion for the outdoors in a charmingly indirect manner. "Right now," she said, "he's a salesman at a mountaineering equipment store in Asheville, and he's absolutely thrilled with it. Actually, he sells sporting equipment and teaches rock climbing. I don't know how long I can afford his being a salesman, because he called me recently and said, 'Will you please buy some stuff? Our store didn't quite meet its quota and we need some help.' "

"But that's Ned," she added.

What else is Ned? Many things. Just listen to Ruth:

"He's taking a year off from school, until he knows what he wants to do in life. We told him we'd put him through school, but he'd have to support himself if he quit. When he first quit, I thought it would be good for him to go to some other city and work. He was in Kansas City that first summer, and he worked hard. But I'm glad he came home. You know, a lot of kids don't want to come home.

"He's been a boy who gets tremendously involved in different hobbies and then abandons them. For a while, that bothered me, but he's learned so much through each experience. He went to school in England for a year, and he got wrapped up in photography. Then he went to Stony Brook on Long Island and he got interested in all the martial arts. And he mastered them. He was little and they picked on him, but a young man—I think he was from Cuba—tucked him under his wing and taught him how to kick with his heels, karate, and all that, so he could protect himself. He really had to floor a couple of fellows before they respected him. They understood that kind of language.

"Next, he got interested in swimming and he won several events. His coach wanted him to train; he thought he was Olympic material. But Ned said, 'There's no way I'm going to stay in the water for eight hours a day.'

"Right now, he's into rock climbing. He's absolutely wild about it. He wants to go to Yosemite next summer and climb El Capitan. I was telling Bill how expensive some of that climbing equipment can be. But what can a mother say, when she knows that if he falls, he'll kill himself? He got his nylon climbing rope for about one hundred dollars, but it's a lot cheaper than a funeral. Anyhow, I can't think of a healthier hobby.

"Ned is all right," Ruth concluded. "We've had long talks, and I think he needed this time out of school just to surface for air and to think things through. His relationship with the Lord is solid. It's growing. He just doesn't know yet what he wants in life or what the Lord wants him to do."

My questions to young Ned, who is strictly a product of here and now, were less about his family and more about his personal ideals and hopes. But, of course, dreams are always a reflection of the family matrix in which one is reared.

I cannot say that I found Ned to be a typical young American. I did come to believe that he was an extraordinary young man whose responses did much to reassure this veteran journalist about the future state of our nation.

Here are some of the things he told me.

I do miss Dad at times, which is natural when his physical presence isn't here, but it's not upsetting. I suppose it's because, for one thing, Mother has done such a wonderful job. She's offered so much love. Then, when Dad is with us, his presence is so strong and so deeply felt that I appreciate it. His being so busy is no struggle. Not at all. They've both done a wonderful job.

My mother carries a lot of other people's problems. You know, she worries for other people—not worrying about her children so much any more, but rather the people she comes in contact with. I think I'd like to give her peace of mind, *total peace* of mind. And that would include a chance to be with Dad without his having to rush off here and there. I think that would please her greatly, but she would never admit it.

I get most of the support for my interests from my mother, because she's at home and I can talk to her. My dad gives me total support, but normally his mind is focused on larger and more important things. He can't really understand as fully as my mother, and Mother is here and can take time with me. She's always enjoyed learning about something new, such as my interest in saltwater fish. This is not fishing, but a study of the fish themselves, of their habits and relationships. I did this study for college credits with the fish in aquariums of my own when I was at school. I enjoyed it very much, because it gave me a chance to escape—no, that's not the word—but you enter into another little world. I did a paper on it. Lately, I haven't had a chance to do any more work in that area. Besides, it's expensive. I think I had about twenty fish I was studying.

Through friends, I had a chance during one summer vacation to go to Alaska to work for a professional fisherman. This same man owned a construction company, and we cleared about thirty acres of brush with two axes and a broken chain saw. And we laid the foundation for a church. It was a very satisfying experience. It's sort of a different world up there. On the way home, the engine of my truck blew up, and we had to hitchhike from the Yukon to Montana, which is about 2,000 miles or so. I brought my Husky puppy with me. He's still with me—a beautiful dog.

I left school until I could be sure I was motivated in the right direction, until I knew where I wanted to go, and had my sights set. I'm not sure, but I believe that the Lord still has work that He wants me to do outside of school. When I go back, it will be with a specific purpose and a destination. In everything that I do, I like to use my full potential. I try to achieve some excellence, whether it be rock climbing, the martial arts, or studying saltwater fish. I'm always attempting to reach some degree of excellence for my own satisfaction.

I want to go back to school at some point, maybe next year. I'm thinking of studying forestry at North Carolina State University. They have a very good department, and Kim, my fiancee, will be able to get into a nursing school near there. She's in her third year now.

I don't believe that young people are giving up on the world, as some people say. My generation isn't giving up at all. I believe we have self-motivation and self-confidence. Not that we'll solve the world's problems, but that we can cope and deal with the problems of the world. You need a Christian viewpoint, of course. You don't conform to the world, but you learn how to live in it. I don't believe that you can look at the world today and have hope, unless you do have a Christian outlook.

I'm living at home right now because I've already had travel and adventure, to a degree. My home has always been a warm place. It has always meant security, I suppose. Also, I enjoy the times I have with my mother. I guess I just thought it would be important for me to come home to be with her before I get married and go off to some other place. Besides, I like my home. We all do.

# PART THREE

*Rumors and Reality*

# 16

# Rumors and Reality

*The flying rumors gathered as they rolled,*
*Scarce any tale was sooner heard than told;*
*And who told it added something new,*
*And all who heard it made enlargements, too.*

Alexander Pope
*Temple of Fame*

*The words of a talebearer are as wounds, and they go down*
*into the innermost parts of the belly.*

Proverbs 26:22

People have always been curious about Billy Graham, even before he became a celebrity.

He was a mere schoolboy when they first began to gossip about him back in the countryside west of Charlotte, North Carolina. A juvenile flair for Halloween pranks and miscellaneous deviltry might have been the cause. His matchstick frame and his height, especially then, always attracted attention.

He was barely into his thirties when he became a nationally known personality. But unlike the standard, American production-model celebrity, he was a man of God, which added to the tantalizing mystery of "what's he really like?" So from 1949 until this very day, his affairs have been on the tips of millions of tongues. Americans wanted an instant "Mr. Clean" (as do people everywhere), and he filled the bill.

Inevitably, his growing influence forced him to run a gauntlet of pitfalls and mantraps that have unhinged earlier evangelists.

The phenomenon is interesting. Apparently, our culture forbids us to tolerate manifest virtue. We prefer heroes who are slightly gamey. Emerson understood this when he wrote, "The world cannot move without rogues."

In literature about American evangelism, the evangelist's world has most assuredly been moved by rogues, the prototype of which is Sinclair Lewis's itinerant preacher named Elmer Gantry. Since his birth in 1927, Gantry's personification of the religious racketeer has entered our consciousness so profoundly that any new Christian Galahad is now immediately suspect.

Billy Graham has not escaped.

He fought the Gantry image successfully for years, but eventually, as his eminence increased, so did the number of his detractors. These last two years have witnessed the birth of a bumper crop of brickbats.

In my travels about the United States and in my conversations with all kinds of people—folk who had no notion of my interest in the evangelist—I heard them repeat, over and over, outlandish cock-and-bull prevarications. A fact of life seems to be that a scandal comes trippingly to the tongue, in Shakespeare's expression, but rarely does a recital of personal piety.

Almost never did I hear a falsehood corrected, or even suspected. So I added that chore to my search for the truth. The results follow in a sort of compendium of chitchat, tittle-tattle, and scandalmongery. Listed alphabetically, it is my hope that their accessibility will nail some of our journalistic *Paul Prys*.

# ATTENDANCE, CRUSADE

**The Rumor:**

> *Attendance at crusades is falling off, and it would seem that Graham's appeal as a crowd-getter is diminishing.*

**The Reality:**

Comparisons never tell the story. For the record, Graham's first 1978 crusade was held in Las Vegas, a relatively small city, where only 10 percent of the people are churchgoers. Average attendance was 12,000. In Toronto, Canada, the average nightly attendance was 26,000. In Memphis, it was about 37,000.

In Kansas City, the crusade was held the week before Labor Day, a traditionally tough time to fill seats. Competition came from the nightly games of the Kansas City Royals baseball team, who were playing down the street in a tight, down-to-the-wire race for the American League's number-one spot. Kansas City attendance in 1978 was less than the 37,000 who came nightly for the evangelist's last visit in 1967. On the other hand, the crusade's School of Evangelism, a week-long seminar for ministers and lay persons, was the second largest in BGEA history, attracting 1,600 students.

Other crusade meetings of 1978, held in Manila and India, attracted crowds of close to 100,000 each.

A few years earlier, attendance at the crusade surpassed all known records when, in 1974, more than 250,000 people packed themselves into the world's largest stadium during Graham's Greater Rio crusade. An even larger crowd was reported in attendance at a racetrack in Korea, where estimates by police and other authorities varied from one million people up.

## BGEA: ANNUAL REPORT

**The Rumor:**
> *The BGEA resisted issuing an annual report until it was forced to change its policy by governmental pressures.*

**The Reality:**

Constitutional guarantees of the separation of church and state have always excused religious organizations from revealing their income and outgo. This is still true. Billy Graham was one of the first to understand that the mood of the country had changed, that the public wanted to know what parachurch organizations do with the contributions they receive, and, specifically, what percentage of their total income is spent for fund raising.

The expense of obtaining a complete audit by an outside firm of accountants is considerable. Most parachurch organizations have chosen to spend their money on people, rather than on bookkeepers. However, Graham believes that complete disclosure is desired by the public. The model he followed is the one used by most publicly owned enterprises. First, it provides discussion of business dealings, then presents a consolidated financial declaration.

Here are the principal items as reported in the annual report of 1977 of the Billy Graham Evangelistic Association. It is the first one issued by BGEA and, I believe, the first of its kind issued by any similar parachurch organization.

Surprisingly, its release to the media attracted little attention. *Time* magazine gave it a brief story under the title of "Billy's Bucks."

Hereunder is a roster of some of the association's soul-winning activities.

*BGEA* The Billy Graham Evangelistic Association has these affiliates: World Wide Pictures, World Wide Publications, Blue Ridge Broadcasting Corporation, Christian Broadcasting Association, and BGEA of Canada. The corporation known as the World Evangelism and Christian Education Fund (WECEF) is not an affiliate and does not have a separate ongoing ministry, as do the affiliates, but its financial statement is reported separately.

*Cost of administering* The report states that the association and its affiliates expended 89 percent of their funds for evangelism ministries, 5 percent for fund raising, direct mail, postage, and 6 percent for administrative costs and overhead. The costs of local crusades are not included, because each is a separate, local project, locally managed, with its total operation revealed to the public by an auditor's report. Neither Graham nor any of the nine associate evangelists receives a love offering or honorarium from a crusade or any other engagement.

*Counseling* Following up those who make a decision for Christ is a vital part of every crusade. During 1977, over 14,000 counselors were trained by the BGEA staff for this work. Such training includes two four-hour classes plus a written or oral session before the trainee qualifies.

Inquirers are provided a series of books (studies of the Book of John) and then participate in a correspondence course, in which their papers are graded and returned by the home office in Minneapolis. Special lessons are available for children under the age of twelve.

*Nurture* After any crusade, nurture groups are organized in every part of a city and provided with study materials for thirty-nine weeks. This is a "Roots" program, with six booklets for personal witnessing, follow-up, enrichment seminars, and leadership training. Often, team members return to a crusade city for rallies in support of a crusade's continuing ministry.

*Schools of Evangelism*   Since 1967, almost 50,000 men and
women have been trained in crusade Schools of Evangelism.
Ministers, preministerial students, and key church leaders are
invited to participate in five days of lectures and workshops. To
date, the largest enrollment was in Manila, where 5,000 church
leaders attended.

*Television*   A major part of the BGEA budget goes for prime
television time. Its cost rises constantly, even faster than hous-
ing. In 1977, over 4,200 hours of prime time were purchased.
Also, a Christmas special was produced, which added additional
expense. During telecasts from crusade cities, religious books
are offered free to viewers, of whom 1,967,572 responded with
requests.

*Radio*   This activity started in 1950, with Billy Graham, Cliff
Barrows, George Beverly Shea, Tedd Smith, and Grady Wilson.
Through 1977, 1,418 programs have been on the air, for a total of
nearly a half-million hours. AM, FM, and shortwave stations
have carried messages throughout the United States, Canada,
Australia, Europe, Asia, and the islands of the sea. Listeners
have formed thousands of prayer groups to pray for various
crusades and special ministries. During Graham's 1977 crusade
in Manila, his sermons were broadcast on 27 stations in 11 languages.

*Films*   World Wide Pictures is a nonprofit corporation, set up
to produce and distribute evangelistic films that are available in
English and 18 other languages. In 1977, Billy Graham films were
shown 36,000 times in churches on a free-will offering basis, and
for free in another 700 showings in prisons, hospitals, nursing
homes, and so forth.

*Decision* Magazine   Beginning publication in 1960, *Decision*
has become the world's largest religious publication. It grew
from an initial press run of 225,000 copies to more than 5 million.
It has editions for the United States, England, Canada, Australia, New Zealand, France, Germany, Spain, Japan, and China,

and a special edition in Braille.

*World Emergency Fund*  This fund was started in 1973. Since then, over $1,458,000 has been distributed to needy people in many countries. All of this fund goes to sufferers from famine, flood, or other natural disasters. No administrative cost or overhead is ever charged. Every cent of every designated dollar relieves suffering.

*International Offices*  International offices are in Buenos Aires, Sydney, Winnipeg, London, Paris, Frankfurt, Hong Kong, Tokyo, Mexico City, and Madrid. They are locally incorporated and directed. They manage their ministries, raise their own funds, direct the publishing of local *Decision* magazines, show films, and cooperate in crusades held in their lands. The association only partially subsidizes these offices. The goal is their ultimate financial independence. The BGEA gets no revenue in return.

*Fund Raising*  BGEA has never employed a professional fund raiser, nor has it rented its mailing list to any outside organization. The organization's list is for the sole purpose of the ministries of the association.

*Deferred Giving*  Some years ago, a deferred-giving program was established, to permit donors who make gifts to the association to receive a tax benefit and an income for life. This program is fully funded. To date, every dollar received from the issuance of gift certificates has been deposited in the trust department of a bank, not to be touched as long as payments are owed to the givers. This practice of 100-percent funding for each gift is exceptional among charity organizations and it guarantees every payment due to the donors.

*Finances*  Figures given here have been rounded off to the nearest hundred thousand dollars. No detailed breakdown of receipts or expenditures has been attempted. My intention has rather been to show the relationship between revenue and expenditures of BGEA and its affiliates.

**Revenue**

| | |
|---|---|
| Contributions received by BGEA and affiliates. | $28,226,000 |
| Revenue from estates, film showings, distribution of religious books, radio-station operation, investments, and so forth. | 10,203,000 |
| Total Revenues | $38,429,000 |

**Expenditures**

| | |
|---|---|
| Expenditures for operating and administrative costs for support of ministries in radio, TV, films, distribution of Christian literature, *Decision* magazine, world emergencies, direct mail, postage, and so forth. | $41,630,000 |
| Balance | ($ 3,201,000) |

Obviously, this financial report shows that the BGEA and its affiliates spent more money on its ministries in 1977 than they received in contributions and revenues. Most of this, Graham has explained, was caused by unexpected inflation of prices for television time, which in some instances, rose by several hundred percent.

Late in 1978, he declared that he intended to maintain his well-known, pay-as-you-go financial policy. "We'll not go into debt," he declared. "Instead, we'll cut back on some of our ministries." Earlier, he had publicly regretted that his organization had grown so large. "If I had it to do over," he said, "I'd try to keep our ministries smaller."

In all probability, other parachurch organizations will soon follow BGEA's example and make similar financial reports. Meetings have already been held by top officials, including

BGEA's executive vice-president, George Wilson, who is a leading spirit. Their goal is to provide a clear, authoritative accounting to the public, but one which will not impose an unreasonable financial burden on the reporting organization. Such disclosure is needed today, Graham feels, because the religious boom around the world could produce a crop of *Elmer Gantrys*, about whom the public should be warned.

## BGEA: ASSOCIATE EVANGELISTS

**The Rumor:**
> *Outsiders have complained that it is impossible to
> break into the elitist circle of the BGEA, espe-
> cially the group of associate evangelists, which
> allegedly is made up of Graham's cronies.*

**The Reality:**
Cronies, no. Friends, yes. Any leader's team consists of
people he can trust and whose ability is known. Those of us who
worked in the Pentagon during World War II were sometimes
disturbed by the large number of field commanders who came
from General Eisenhower's West Point graduating class. Frequently, they were promoted over the heads of scores of older
generals. But the commander-in-chief *knew* the men he chose
and needed their skills.

Graham's nine associates come from growing up with him in
high school (brothers Grady Wilson and T. W. Wilson); from
working together in the Youth for Christ Organization during and
after World War II (Cliff Barrows and Leighton Ford); from
attending Bible school with him (Roy Gustafson); from his first
crusade on the continent of India (Abdul Akbar-Haqq); from the
difficult pioneer days of desegregation in the South (Howard
Jones and Ralph Bell); and from an early extension of his ministry into Canada and England (Canadian and Oxfordian John
Wesley White).

Today, each associate evangelist makes a unique contribution
to every big-city crusade, but each one also has his own ministry, which is shaped by his special talents. Their individual proj-

ects range from minicrusades to writing books, from Bible-teaching tours to prison revivals, and from personally counseling people in need to preaching on jungle atolls.

Like Graham, each associate is an evangelist, but each is able to use his talents to the fullest through the opportunities made possible by the supporters of the BGEA

## BGEA: BOARD OF DIRECTORS

**The Rumor:**

> *The BGEA board of directors is composed of old Graham associates plus a few cronies and other trained seals, who would jump through a hoop at Graham's command and are figureheads in the operation.*

**The Reality:**

Nothing could be a greater error than to call this board a group of trained seals or cronies.

Yes, they do include a few longtime Graham associates, but they also include a college president, a former postmaster general of the United States, a former ambassador to the United Nations, an ex-treasurer of Harvard University, various financial experts and business consultants, pastors of great churches, executives of large business corporations, physicians, and lawyers.

Here are the names and affiliations of BGEA board members. Read them. Judge for yourself if they are the kind of men who would "jump through a hoop" for Billy Graham.

### Billy Graham Evangelistic Association Board of Directors:

Mr. A. Harold Anderson. President and owner, J. Emil Anderson & Son, Inc., Chicago, Illinois. Elected 1967.

The Reverend Clifford B. Barrows. Vice-chairman and music director, Billy Graham Association, Greenville, South Carolina. Elected 1950.

Mr. George F. Bennett. Treasurer, Billy Graham Association, president, State Street Investment Corp., Boston, Massachusetts. Elected 1973.

Mr. Wallace E. Berg. Secretary, Billy Graham Association, vice-president, Midwest Federal Savings & Loan Association, Minneapolis, Minnesota. Elected 1973.

Mr. Francis A. Coy. President, Coy & Associates, Cleveland, Ohio. Elected 1973.

Mrs. Mary C. Crowley. President, Home Interiors & Gifts, Inc., Dallas, Texas. Elected 1974.

Mr. Allan C. Emery, Jr. President, Billy Graham Association, Servicemaster Industries, Inc., Boston, Massachusetts. Elected 1967.

Dr. Leighton F. S. Ford. Vice-president and associate evangelist, Billy Graham Association, Charlotte, North Carolina. Elected 1957.

P. Kenneth Gieser, M.D. Senior physician, Wheaton Eye Clinic, Wheaton, Illinois. Elected 1960.

The Reverend Billy Graham. Chairman of Billy Graham Association Board, Montreat, North Carolina. Elected 1950.

Dr. Edward V. Hill. Pastor, Mount Zion Missionary Baptist Church, Los Angeles, California. Elected 1973.

Governor Harold LeVander. Attorney, LeVander, Gillen, Miller & Magnuson, South Saint Paul, Minnesota. Elected 1973.

Mr. Guy Martin. Guy Martin Oldsmobile, Woodland Hills, California. Elected 1967.

Mr. Bill Mead. Chairman of the board, Campbell Taggart, Inc., Dallas, Texas. Elected 1960.

Mr. Carloss Morris. Attorney, senior partner, Morris, Termini, Harris & McCanne, Houston, Texas. Elected 1957.

Dr. Harold J. Ockenga. President, Gordon-Conwell Theological Seminary, Hamilton, Massachusetts. Elected 1958.

Mr. W. Dewey Presley. President, First International Bancshares, Inc., Dallas, Texas. Elected 1971.

Roland G. Scherer, M.D. Physician-surgeon, Green Valley, Arizona. Elected 1957.

Mr. Robert C. Van Kampen. Banking and business consultant, Santa Barbara, California. Elected 1958.

Mr. William B. Walton. Vice-chairman of the board, Holiday Inns, Inc., Memphis, Tennessee. Elected 1978.

Mr. W. Marvin Watson. Business consultant, Daingerfield, Texas. Elected 1971.

Dr. John W. Williams. Vice-president, NAACP, pastor, Saint Stephen Baptist Church, Kansas City, Missouri. Elected 1973.

Mr. George M. Wilson. Executive vice-president and assistant treasurer, Billy Graham Association, Minneapolis, Minnesota. Elected 1950.

Dr. Grady B. Wilson. Vice-president and associate evangelist, Billy Graham Association, Charlotte, North Carolina. Elected 1950.

*Board Members Emeritus:* John Bolten, Sr.; David M. McConnell; C. R. Wall, M.D.

### Officers

| | |
|---|---|
| Chairman | Billy Graham |
| Vice-chairman | Clifford B. Barrows |
| President | Allan C. Emery, Jr. |
| Executive vice-president, assistant treasurer | George M. Wilson |
| Vice-presidents | Leighton F. S. Ford |
| | Walter H. Smyth |
| | Grady B. Wilson |
| Vice-president of finance, controller, assistant secretary | Joel B. Aarsvold |
| Secretary | Wallace E. Berg |
| Treasurer | George F. Bennett |

### Executive Committee

Allan C. Emery, Jr., chairman
George F. Bennett
Francis A. Coy
Guy Martin
Bill Mead
Carloss Morris
Robert C. Van Kampen

The executive committee meets six times a year. The board of directors meets three times a year. The board of directors and officers of the Billy Graham Evangelistic Association were elected at the annual meeting in January, 1978.

## BGEA: SIZE AND SCOPE

**The Rumor:**

> *The Billy Graham organization is one of the biggest and richest corporations in the United States.*

**The Reality:**

Absolutely nowhere near it. The combined annual budget of all the Graham operations worldwide totaled only about $40 million in 1977. Reporters for the *Charlotte Observer* calculated that, in the Carolinas alone, there were at least 60 publicly owned companies taking in more dollars than that each year.

But the Graham organization seems to have a way of getting a lot of mileage out of comparatively little money. By 1977, the BGEA had conducted over 230 crusades, in nearly every state of the union and some foreign countries, attended by a total of 100 million people! They had produced more than 100 films and had a weekly radio broadcast, carried over 900 stations. In the course of the year they sent out nearly 100 million pieces of mail, including *Decision* magazine, which goes currently to more than 3.5 million readers in the United States and Canada, plus six foreign-language editions. In support of these activities, some 90 percent of the BGEA budget of $27.7 million in 1977 came from individual contributions. The BGEA had a staff of 478 in 1977.

## BGEA: THE TEAM

**The Rumor:**

> *The team concept of running a growing organiza-*
> *tion has resulted in crossed-up lines of authority,*
> *low morale, and high turnover.*

**The Reality:**

Graham's initial responsibility as an evangelist is to conduct successful crusades. His first team was assembled under the Billy Graham Evangelistic Association in 1950. Its first members were Billy Graham, George Wilson, Grady Wilson, Tedd Smith, George Beverly Shea, and Cliff Barrows.

Barrows was the crusade song leader.

Shea was soloist.

Smith was a pianist.

Grady Wilson was a jack-of-all-trades and executive assistant, serving as advance man or substitute preacher.

George Wilson was the business manager.

Each had his own job to do. No lines of authority were needed, for each knew the scope of his assignment and executed it efficiently. To be sure, growth has complicated the problem of management. However, these kinks have been straightened out.

As for morale and turnover problems, it may be unique in American annals that the same five young men who started their enterprise twenty-eight years ago are still happily engaged in executing their ministries with unprecedented harmony.

## BIBLE SCHOOL

**The Rumor:**

> *Cynics are suggesting that the Bible school, announced for a site in the mountains between Montreat and Asheville, may never be built.*

**The Reality:**

During the *Charlotte Observer*'s investigation of Graham's finances, their reporter asked him: "How would you evaluate the chance right now of getting the Bible-study school off the ground?"

Graham replied: "I would hope within the next five years." Allan Emery, BGEA board chairman, said: "I would estimate three years."

In my judgment, the answer depends wholly on finances. If contributions are available, if we do not run into a depression in the United States, and if inflation does not eat more deeply into the value of the dollar, Emery's answer is probably accurate for the beginning of building.

Plans have already been completed by architect Charles A. Franzman, of the Atlanta firm of Harland Bartholomew and Associates, who are the landscape and planning architects. Franzman has stated that Porter's Cove (where the institution will be situated) "is the finest piece of property for Dr. Graham's purposes that I've seen anywhere. It has the best of both worlds. City and country in one. You turn the corner from the Interstate and you are on totally private property. Any developer would give his right arm for a piece of property like that. It has public utilities and remoteness, and to have an interchange at the entrance makes it a tract that people go around searching for and never expect to find. It is most exceptional."

# CARTER, JIMMY

**The Rumor:**

> *Jimmy Carter won't invite Billy Graham to the*
> *White House.*

**The Reality:**

That rumor is not true, but contacts have been relatively infrequent. Billy saw President Carter once during his first year as president and has been invited back. He has talked to him on the phone on other occasions. There are reasons for the limited contacts. Billy and Jimmy come from the same religious tradition, and it is probable that Carter would want to avoid giving the impression that he was packing the White House with Southern Baptists, just as John F. Kennedy was cautious about inviting Cardinal Cushing to visit him. Similarly, at this stage of his career, Billy is attempting to keep a greater distance from political involvements, and has not sought to see Carter, although the two men have enjoyed a long association.

## CATHOLICS

**The Rumor:**
> *Billy Graham's "gone Catholic."*

**The Reality:**

I would say that the Catholics have "gone Billy Graham." The transformation has occurred between the 1957 crusade at Madison Square Garden, when Catholics were prohibited by their church leaders from attending the meetings, and 1977, when Billy Graham was honored by being invited to conduct a crusade on the Notre Dame campus, the nation's most prestigious Catholic university.

Catholics have learned over the years that Billy Graham can anchor the faith of Catholics as well as Protestants. The charge against Billy Graham comes from some of the more extreme fundamentalist groups, who object to the fact that Billy has permitted priests to be included among crusade counseling staffs and has permitted those who come forward to designate a Catholic church if that is their choice.

Graham says that as he has learned over the years about Christian faiths other than the Southern Baptist tradition in which he was raised, he has become more tolerant. He says: "I have found that my beliefs are essentially the same as those of orthodox Roman Catholics, for instance. They believe in the Virgin Birth, and so do I. They believe in the blood atonement of the cross, and so do I. They believe in the Resurrection of Jesus and the coming judgment of God, and so do I. We only differ on some matters of later church tradition." During his 1978 visit to Poland, a Catholic country despite its Communist government, he preached in several Catholic cathedrals.

## CHURCHES BACKING CRUSADES

**The Rumor:**
> *The established churches of the community would never get involved with anything like a Billy Graham crusade.*

**The Reality:**

How much more establishment can you get than the Archbishop of London, the Archbishop of York, and eventually the Archbishop of Canterbury, who shared the platform with Billy Graham during the Greater London Crusade of 1966? In fact, the major churches in a community are often the mainstays of a local crusade effort.

Billy told me recently that at the time he started preaching in the 1940s, probably not more than 25 percent of the churches in a city would support a revival. But when the Graham team went to Cincinnati in 1977, 80 percent of the churches of that city were involved in supporting the crusade. "And that's about average across the country," he said. Add that up, and it comes to a lot of churches.

## CLOTHING, PERSONAL

**The Rumor:**

> The closets in the Graham home are "bursting with expensive clothing and seventy-five-dollar shoes."

**The Reality:**

Not according to Ruth Graham. Ruth is amused by the description of closets bursting with clothes. "As for shoes," she told me, "his shoe rack is two boards that I had the carpenter build on a slant under the window of his closet. He has maybe three or four pair of Hush Puppies and a couple of pairs of tennis shoes for running. His sons-in-law send him those because they know he ought to run, but he runs in Hush Puppies. I think he has one pair of patent leather for dress. That's about it. And one pair of loafers, which I like.

As for the suits, Ruth told me that he does have suits that are picked out for him especially for television, but said he doesn't wear those for normal dress. His normal-dress suits, Ruth buys at Sears, where she says she can get polyester, which doesn't wrinkle as expensive suits will, and where she can still get "a jacket and two pair of pants for eighty dollars." These, she says, Billy will wear for "three or four years, until they are flapping around his ankles."

The "bursting" closet she describes as being six feet by eight feet, with built-in drawers at one end. "Above that we hang his sweaters, jackets, separate trousers, and some shirts. The other end is full-length, so we hang his suits, topcoat, raincoat, and maybe a gown for graduation. Above that is a rack for his luggage, so when he goes to pack, he doesn't have to go to the attic."

# COMMUNISM

**The Rumor:**
> *Billy Graham has "gone Communist."*

**The Reality:**

Billy Graham certainly has not "gone Communist," but he has gone to preach in Hungary and Poland, and there is a strong possibility that he will go elsewhere behind the iron curtain. He says that the existence of a church separate from the state has become more pronounced in recent years in the eastern European countries and that the door to preaching the Gospel there is slowly opening.

Graham is quite aware that he has critics who believe that he is compromising with communism if he preaches to people in a country with a Communist government. But long ago, even in America, he had moved away from his early position of equating Christianity with Americanism and of denouncing Communists from the pulpit. His mission, he says, is to preach the Gospel to people who have never had a chance to hear it, wherever he can reach them.

## COMPUTERIZED RELIGION

**The Rumor:**
> *The Minneapolis offices specialize in a mail-order*
> *ministry, sending out computerized letters in re-*
> *sponse to the thousands of spiritual inquiries they*
> *receive.*

**The Reality:**

It is certainly true that the BGEA worldwide ministry makes great use of the mails, and it is also true that the organization has kept up with the times in the use of computers. But "counseling by computers?" No.

The 40,000 to 50,000 personal letters that come into the Minneapolis offices in a week are all read by individual pastor counselors. These are real people. They have found that about half of the letter writers ask questions similar to those asked by many other letter writers, and in these cases parts of the counselor's answer can be transcribed using programmed automatic typewriters.

Each letter is then read and signed personally by the pastor counselor who prepared it. No letter goes out over Graham's signature unless he has personally prepared it. Some letters from the daily mail are flagged for special attention, such as perhaps a personal phone call to the writer or to someone else who might be able to help him. Others are placed in the headquarters' chapel, where staff members may read them for special prayers.

## COUNSELING AND NURTURING

**The Rumor:**

> *A magazine article has alleged that most of the inquirers who come forward are really Graham-trained shills, whose function is to lure reluctant converts from their seats and to fill the aisles and the space before Graham's platform so it will look good on television. Other critics have claimed that most of the people who come forward are brushed off by the Christian community when they attend a church, and so fall away.*

**The Reality:**

Both charges demonstrate ignorance. The people who join those coming forward are badge-wearing Christian counselors, who have been trained for weeks to answer any question an inquirer can ask. As a rule, a counselor director (at each aisle) assigns one of them (by an inconspicuous gesture) to each inquirer, matching them for sex, age, and nationality.

As for introducing an inquirer into church life, this has always been a major concern. Many methods of welcoming a new Christian have been tried. Every city presents some unique problem. BGEA's current procedure is beautifully illustrated by one of the most difficult situations in recent history, when 5,000 counselors were trained for the November 1978 crusade in Manila's Rizal Park, and a total of 22,000 inquirers came forward.

"Careful counseling lies at the heart of effective evangelism," reports Roy Robertson, who was Graham's director of training in the Philippines. "Here in Asia, we dare not rush. Everything takes more time. The skillful Asian counselor may first ask about one's family background. . . . then the Gospel must be clarified, followed by a prayer of personal commitment.''

At Rizal Park, the average counselor spent close to a half-hour—although many spent an hour or more—going over the above ground. On the final Sunday, the response was so great that each counselor had to serve several persons, and inquirers queued up to await their turn. "The Gospel is preached to multitudes, but the people come to Christ one by one," Robertson says.

The follow-up of inquirers has become a major crusade enterprise. Essentially, it is an effort to help babes in Christ become mature Christians. Its principles are simple. Its performance is very hard work. Follow-up and nurturing in Manila involved mailing to each inquirer an encouraging letter from Billy Graham, and mailing to each pastor a list of inquirers who had stated a preference for attending his church. This was done by hundreds of volunteers. Typewriters were borrowed. Thousands of decision cards and other forms were printed and distributed. Hundreds of people in this co-labor corps worked around the clock for fifteen days. The night crew often worked until dawn when, Robertson says, "It was too late to go home by public transportation and too expensive to go by taxi. Many slept on the floor, couch, or table, and went directly from the follow-up office to their own jobs later that morning."

Nurture classes were formed in scores of churches, each class consisting of a group of a dozen or so people living in the same neighborhood and led by a trained Bible teacher of their own age and background. Toward the end of the follow-up campaign, Manila had 461 nurture groups. As a typical result, of the 65 inquirers whose names went to the Philippine United Church of Christ, 60 became active in church life. Another group grew to 50 people and formed its own church. Twenty girls in a college dorm organized their own nurture class.

Inquirers came from a wide background. One early report showed that commitments to Christ were made by ten Muslims, forty or so Buddhists, forty-six Vietnamese refugees, a half-dozen American servicemen, travelers from Pakistan, Indonesia, and India, a movie star, and many prominent businessmen.

Counseling and follow-up activities are never seen by American viewers in the crusade specials they watch on TV. Only rarely do reporters know or understand what goes on before or after. As has been said, a crusade can be likened to an iceberg; the preaching service is the tip, visible and in Technicolor. The great bulk of the crusade remains unseen and unsung. In this observer's opinion, this is the area in which lives are really changed.

## CRUSADES ARE DISRUPTIVE

**The Rumor:**

> *Instead of being a cohesive force for strengthening and linking the Christians within a community, the activities of the Billy Graham team and the evangelist himself leave behind an atmosphere of outrage, jealousy, and quarrelsomeness.*

**The Reality:**

The opposite is true. While some pastors do withhold their endorsement, a large majority provides enthusiastic support and participates in the nurture phase of a crusade, during which an earnest effort is made to enlist those who come forward into active church membership.

The last Billy Graham crusade to be held in the United States, as this is written, was at Kansas City, Missouri, in August of 1978. Four leading Kansas City churchmen recently commented on the Kansas City crusade.

Dr. B. Edgar Johnson, general secretary of the Church of the Nazarene, said, "I see the exciting participation of the Kansas City religious community. There has been a wholesome united cooperation across denominational lines. If there has been opposition, I haven't known it. I've been very pleased with the response from night to night. It exceeds my expectation for this time of the year."

Dr. Milton Ferguson, president, Midwestern Baptist Theological Seminary, commented, "I see the hunger of people for stability and confidence in these difficult times being satisfied. People are putting their lives and energies into the things that count."

Dr. Jesse Roberts, pastor, Broadway United Methodist Church, said, "This is a spiritual shot in the arm. People of various denominations are getting together, and that's good. Billy Graham doesn't always preach the kind of theology that goes with all the denominations, but there is a fellowship here around the Gospel."

The Reverend Ted Nissen, pastor, Colonial Presbyterian Church, added, "We feel a sense of Christian kinship that we didn't have before—an interdenominational closeness. People are coming to Christ, and that's important, but Christians are also getting enthused and rededicated, and I expect that to last."

## CRUSADES, HOW CITIES ARE CHOSEN

**The Rumor:**
> *The big-time Billy Graham crusade show comes barreling into town—wanted or not—and runs roughshod over the wishes of local churches.*

**The Reality:**
Completely wrong. There could not be a Graham crusade without massive support from local churches. This is an understanding that Billy Graham reached very early in his ministry. He will not go to any city, except by invitation of local churches. Before accepting any invitation, no matter how persuasive it may be, he will pray over the matter until he knows that the churches really mean it.

The concept works in two directions. The success of the crusade is deeply dependent on the involvement of the multitude of local church members, who become the foot soldiers of both the outreach and follow-up phases of the crusade effort. But every crusade is also intended to bring membership and revival back into the local churches. Billy Graham has never identified himself as an independent operator, but always as a churchman. From the beginning, his greatest concern has been not merely to persuade Christians to come forward, but to incorporate them into the Christian community and its fellowship.

# DEPRESSION

**The Rumor:**

> *The "Aging Lion of Evangelism," as he has been called, is becoming more and more depressed about the world's state. From time to time, discouragement overwhelms him, causing him to shun people, to sulk on his mountaintop, and to withdraw even from his family and friends.*

**The Reality:**

Some time ago, a reporter for *Christianity Today* asked Graham if he suffered from "down times," and how he handled them.

His answer: "Of course I have 'downs.' Most of my Christian life I have read the Psalms daily. The writers of the Psalms constantly had their downs as well as their ups. This was true of some of God's greatest servants. But in the midst of downs, God is always present, and there is an underlying joy that words cannot express. Sometimes, downs are caused by a physiological condition. For example, I have high blood pressure. One of the side effects of my medication is a tendency toward depression. But I can face that and recognize where it is coming from. It causes me to pray and to ask for God's grace."

## DOCTRINES, HAVE THEY CHANGED?

**The Rumor:**

> *Graham's changed his mind about Christ being*
> *the only means of salvation, and now believes*
> *that pagans can be saved by worshiping their own*
> *gods.*

**The Reality:**

Billy Graham is firm and inflexible in his belief that Jesus Christ is the only way of salvation. This belief, expressed in John 3:16, is, and always has been, the bedrock of his entire ministry as an evangelist.

The impression that he had somehow wavered in this fundamental belief came out of the magazine story headlined "I Can't Play God Any More," in which the writer understood Billy to say that he no longer believed that pagans in far-off countries were lost if they did not have the Gospel of Jesus Christ preached to them.

Graham explained to me: "Contrary to what the article suggests, I do believe that non-Christians are lost—whether they live in far-off countries or in America." He said, "My statement that Jesus Christ is the only way of salvation pertains to the whole human race . . . . My prayer is that Christians everywhere will rededicate themselves to the task of spreading the Gospel of Christ to every corner of the earth in this generation."

# DOUBLE LIFE

**The Rumor:**

> *Graham leads a double life: the public Billy Graham, who preaches goodness and love, and the private man, who is a secretive, paranoic recluse.*

**The Reality:**

Billy Graham at home is exactly the same Billy Graham that you would meet on the road, as any of the innumerable writers and reporters who have visited him at Montreat would testify, including two reporters who did the five-part *Charlotte Observer* series on Graham in 1977 and the subsequent story on WECEF.

Writer James Robison, who did an extensive interview with Billy for the *Chicago Tribune Magazine* in 1977, said this: "Graham seems to hide nothing in his detailing of his daily routine. Is nothing private? It's hard differentiating between the public and the private lives of Billy Graham—or maybe they're one and the same. Is he always on stage with an act of humility? Or is he always this humble and unpretentious?"

Billy himself speaks of his shyness and his wish to be out of the spotlight, and his tendency to be a homebody. He has said: "I don't like being recognized all the time and pushed and pulled at. I'm a private person. Most people think of me, I suppose not knowing me, as an extrovert. Inside, I'm an introvert."

## FEAR, USE OF, IN PREACHING

**The Rumor:**

*Billy Graham uses fear of final judgment as a motive for conversion.*

**The Reality:**

Billy says: "I do not believe we use the motive of fear any more than the love of God." He notes that Jesus' own teachings are full of warnings. "He loved men, but He loved them enough to warn them of wrath to come."

In 1954 Billy Graham stated his view of God in this way, and I have since heard him preach this view time and again:

I am going to present a God who matters. And who makes claims on the human race. He is a God of love, grace, and mercy, but also a God of judgment. When we break His moral laws, we suffer; when we keep them, we have inward peace and joy. I am calling for a revival that will cause men and women to return to their offices and shops to live out the teaching of Christ in their daily relationships. I am going to preach a Gospel not of despair, but of hope—hope for the individual, for society, and for the world.

# FINANCING, CRUSADE

**The Rumor:**

> *The Graham crusade team moves into a town, collects thousands of dollars that might otherwise have gone into the collection plates of local churches, and then leaves with the cash.*

**The Reality:**

Untrue. One of the revolutionary innovations in evangelism was made by the Graham team following the 1950 Atlanta crusade. All crusade collections are handled by a local committee of churchmen in the city where the crusade is held. After the expenses of the crusade have been met, no more crusade collections are taken, and a public accounting is made of all funds received. Further, the evangelist and his staff are placed on fixed salaries paid by the Billy Graham Evangelistic Association. These procedures, and others set up nearly thirty years ago, are still followed.

Most of the early money scandals arose from the practice of calling for "love offerings," which were in payment for an evangelist's specialized talents and time. A few people remember to this day the plea for "paper money only—I don't want to hear no coins." Billy cleared the air when he abolished the practice of love offerings in his ministry, placing himself and his team members on salaries paid by the evangelistic association.

The BGEA never makes money from a crusade; often, the crusade costs the BGEA money, particularly those held in other countries. As soon as local expenses have been met, the taking of offerings is either discontinued or their purpose is specified, so that each contributor knows exactly the cause to which he is invited to donate. This cause might be to help a struggling crusade committee in a distant city, to help finance a motion picture or film special, or it might—as in Cincinnati in late 1977—be replaced by a plea for the audience to contribute to their own churches or to a list of charities approved by the local committee.

# FINANCES, PERSONAL

**The Rumor:**
> *Billy Graham is a multimillionaire.*

**The Reality:**

Billy Graham is not even a millionaire, although he undoubtedly could be, if he wanted to be. The Grahams's major personal asset is a mountaintop farm in North Carolina that they bought in 1950 for a little less than $13 per acre. Four years later, with the financial help of friends, they built a home on that land, at a cost of about $43,000. The property has escalated in value many times over since the early 1950s, when Graham settled his family there.

Graham also has a private source of income from the reinvestment of approximately $250,000 received when land inherited from his father was sold to make way for a suburban Charlotte shopping center. In addition to these personal assets, he draws what must now be one of the world's most publicized salaries, $39,500 a year, from the BGEA board. He also draws $200 a month in unreimbursed expense money from the BGEA, and receives an unspecified amount from his syndicated newspaper column. During a crusade, his expenses are paid, usually through arrangements made with a local crusade committee.

He consistently refuses opportunities to increase his income through such means as commercial endorsements, large honorarium offers, and consulting positions. He gives away all of what would be his largest source of revenue—the royalties of his best-selling books.

## FINANCIAL RESPONSIBILITY OF BGEA

**The Rumor:**
> *The Billy Graham organization has accumulated a $23 million nest egg, and still they go out asking people for their $5 and $10 bills to help carry on their evangelical work.*

**The Reality:**

There is no nest egg. The WECEF funds are entirely committed to purposes other than the daily evangelistic work of BGEA. In terms of the general contributions that come into the BGEA, no check marked for a particular use is ever diverted to any other use. In cases where a particular use is not specified, it is understood that the donor is trusting the BGEA board of trustees and executive committee to place the funds where they are needed, whether this be in meeting radio and television costs or helping with mailings or disaster relief or overseas missions.

# HEALTH

**The Rumor:**

*Graham's health continues to fail, and he is on the brink of retirement.*

**The Reality:**

When I saw him in Las Vegas in 1978, he announced, "I never felt better in my life." (But two months later, when I saw him in Montreat, he was recovering from a staph infection that had invaded his nose and caused him to dash to the Mayo clinic for treatment.)

Actually, while Graham's health is not failing, it is true that throughout his adult life he has been plagued by health problems. He suffers from high blood pressure, but aside from that, as Ruth put it, he has a tendency "to get the dumbest, wildest things wrong with him." Since 1960 he has had pneumonia four times. He has only partial sight in his left eye, as a result of a swelling behind the retina in 1959. His salivary glands on the right side were removed in 1971. He's had two prostate operations and surgery for kidney stones. In 1976 he developed thrombophlebitis, and in 1978 he had that painful infection of the sinsuses that required treatment at the Mayo clinic.

Billy tries to keep up a program of exercise and good diet as a hedge against illness, but this hasn't always been the case. I rode around town one night with Billy and two aides, looking for Kentucky Fried Chicken. When we found it, we sat back in the car and ate it all, complete with French fries. Hardly the best dinner for a man who preaches himself soaking wet every night!

That was the case for years and years, but Billy now watches his diet closely. He eats very little red meat, for instance. When he is home in Montreat, Billy usually has a big breakfast. For lunch he will have a bowl of soup or a salad and some cottage cheese and fruit. He says that Ruth usually fixes a vegetarian dinner. Every year he goes to the Mayo clinic for a complete physical workup, and he keeps his weight steady at 172.

Billy often says that his persistent health problems are "God's way of knocking me down." He has said, "I think that God has allowed sickness to come on me, to many preachers, to keep us humble and to keep us dependent on Him." In an interview with television's talk-show host Phil Donahue, he put it this way: "Every time I've thought of myself as a little something. . . . I get sick or something happens . . . . God has a way of keeping me down."

# HOME, A FORTRESS

**The Rumor:**

> *Billy and Ruth live in an "opulent mountaintop fortress."*

**The Reality:**

The writer who made that statement has never met Billy Graham personally, and he obviously has never seen the Graham's home. It is a beautiful home, clearly created with a great deal of loving care. But it is neither "opulent," nor a "fortress." In style, it is a rambling log house. As Billy puts it, "a big, old, country house, more like a mountain lodge than a house."

Billy and Ruth began building the house in 1954, after four of their five children were born, and the house grew as the family grew. It now has ten rooms, including Billy's study and the rustic porch that is a favorite Graham family gathering place. With the children now grown, Ruth feels the house is too large for herself and Bill, but they want to keep it as a center for the family and the grandchildren, who now number fourteen. Ruth is redesigning the old heating system so that rooms that aren't being used can be closed off in the winter to conserve fuel.

As for the "mountaintop"—yes, it is. The property where the Graham home is located stands at an altitude of 3,600 feet above sea level—about 800 feet above the village of Montreat—and is reached by a steeply inclined narrow road.

Billy and Ruth Graham bought the property, approximately two hundred acres of wild, mountain land, in 1950 for the astonishingly low price of $4,500. At one time the property had been farmed. On the land were "two little cabins, eighteen springs, and one hundred twenty apple trees," Billy recalls.

In the years between the time that Billy and Ruth bought their land and the time they were able to build their home there, Billy used it as a place for study, meditation, and prayer. He recalls that in order to keep fit in those days, he would trot the full mile from the Graham's small house at the base of the mountain to the top, where their land was located.

As for the fence which someone likened to the "Berlin Wall": The fence around the Graham property is an ordinary six-foot tall chain link fence, the kind seen in suburban residential areas all over the country. Its installation was recommended by the Federal Bureau of Investigation.

# HOME, DOGS

**The Rumor:**

> *The Graham fortress is patrolled by vicious dogs,*
> *"trained to kill."*

**The Reality:**

The Graham family dog at the time they bought the Montreat property was a Great Pyrenees named Belshazzar. They have also had other dogs—German shepherds, Saint Bernards, collies. Billy once told me that, on coming home from long and wearying travels, one of his greatest delights has been "to take hikes around our mountain on the many trails with our big dogs." I saw only one dog the last time I was there in 1978—a German shepherd that Billy said has a loud bark but "is so friendly I think he would lick you to death." Is that what you call being "trained to kill"?

Since Billy and Ruth moved to their mountain home, dogs have come and gone. One pair was specially trained to guard, but certainly not to kill. They were German shepherds from Alsace-Lorraine, and were a present from the father of the young man the oldest Graham daughter had married. It was a generous gesture of helpfulness, elicited by various mail and telephone threats. Several years ago, these dogs were presented to the Buncombe County sheriff, as trackers and sentry dogs. Newspaper stories indicated that they were worth thousands of dollars each. Apparently, they were worth much less than that, for subsequent reports indicated that the animals were more of a nuisance than a help to the lawmen. Other dogs, gifts from relatives and friends, continue to come and go, but not one has been trained to kill.

## HOME, GUARDS

**The Rumor:**
> *Billy Graham employs security patrols and care-*
> *fully screened bodyguards.*

**The Reality:**

There are no bodyguards! The perpetrator of this story may be thinking of the Graham's caretaker, George, a former navy man who also serves as a volunteer deputy sheriff. George's brother Homer, a former security guard at a nearby college, works at the Graham office in Montreat. The caretaker's wife also works at the house two days a week. The Graham's son, Franklin, found all three employees, whom Ruth describes as "pure gold."

## HOME, HOW FINANCED AND BUILT

**The Rumor:**
> *The Grahams obtained their "very big and very expensive" house in some way that is "a financial mystery."*

**The Reality:**
It's no mystery at all. Most of the materials for the Grahams' home were donated by friends who were concerned about the Grahams' loss of privacy in the small stone house on Assembly Drive in Montreat. As Billy grew more famous, tourists swarmed into town to catch a glimpse of him or his family.

At that time Dr. Rupert McGregor, who was president of the Presbyterian Assembly at Montreat, began to contact friends, and they contacted other friends, gathering money to build a permanent home for the family. It isn't unusual at all for a congregation to pool resources to build a home for a minister.

Billy describes the house "as one of the greatest things we had ever done." He said "It gave us the privacy we needed as the momentum of our work has gathered, and the pressures became greater."

He recalls how it was constructed. His study was built by a friend in Greensboro and shipped to Montreat. The kitchen equipment was given by a friend in Nashville. Lumber for framing came from friends in Charleston. Ruth scoured the mountainsides, searching out old cabins (for the most part abandoned) and purchasing the massive hand-hewn logs from which they had been built, for use as siding for the house. Brick used in the house came from an old school in Asheville that was being torn down. "When we moved in, the house looked as if it had been there a hundred years," Billy said.

## HOTEL SUITES AROUND THE WORLD

**The Rumor:**

*Billy Graham maintains lavish hotel suites around the world.*

**The Reality:**

Nonsense! Various hotels offer him suites of rooms. It's good business for them, and it's a savings to the BGEA or local crusade committees when this type of arrangement can be made. An arrangement with Holiday Inn was originally established by the chain's owners, who were born-again Christians that Billy first met long ago in Memphis. Conrad Hilton later met Billy and made the same offer. The Marriott chain also offers accommodations to Graham.

In fact, when Billy and Ruth are in a crusade city, they try to arrange to stay at a smaller, out-of-the-way hotel, where they will have more privacy and where Billy can get in an afternoon swim as exercise without attracting attention.

One of the authors who charges that Graham maintains a "suite of rooms at the Hilton" claims he "has been in them." He probably doesn't realize that Billy occasionally accepts a Hilton suite in order to provide a room for a press conference. Another author writes that during the 1966 London crusade, Graham stayed in five-star hotels. I was there then, and I can say from firsthand knowledge that he actually stayed in a very modest hotel, which happened to be opposite the Kensington Garden end of Hyde Park.

# INTEGRATION

**The Rumor:**

> *Billy Graham has avoided taking a stand on integrating his crusades because he feared it would lose him his broad base of support in "rural, white America."*

**The Reality:**

The opposite is the case. Graham called for whites and blacks to come forward together very early in his ministry, long before the word *integration* was heard in America. "The ground is level at the foot of the cross," he would say.

On March 15, 1953, he undertook the first deliberately integrated crusade, at Chattanooga, Tennessee, ignoring forecasts of trouble. In those early years of the integration movement, he frequently and publicly stated his conviction that the Bible did not support segregation. From 1954 on, he insisted that every crusade be integrated.

Moreover, Graham has used his crusades to create an example of integration. In 1966, the year of decision in the integration movement, his organization undertook a crusade in Greenville, South Carolina. Billy told an interviewer that he chose to go to Greenville "partially on the basis of the race question." He said, "I wanted to hold an integrated crusade there, to show the nation, by television, as we were able to do, that it could be done in the heart of the deep South." These words certainly are not those of a man who was "avoiding a stand on integration."

## LIBERALISM

**The Rumor:**

   *Billy Graham's "gone liberal."*

**The Reality:**

   If the term *liberal* means any departure from New Testament Christianity and the substitution of a speculative philosophy of religion, the answer is emphatically not so! Since 1949, Billy Graham has consistently preached the infallibility of Scripture and has emphasized that the New Testament is the enduring Christian criterion.

   This position was unchanged in late 1977, when he said "My view is that the Bible is without error in its totality. I can't prove it, but I base it on faith." He added this comment: "I know some people will object to that. I would like to say also that this does not affect my Christian fellowship with people who hold different views, provided they hold to the diety of Christ, the Virgin Birth, the Atonement, and the Resurrection—the cardinal doctrines of Christianity."

   Graham himself rejects the terms *fundamentalism* and *liberalism*, commenting that neither is found in sacred Scripture. Thus, Billy says, "I much prefer to be called simply a Christian, rather than to be identified by what are latter-day labels."

## LIFE-STYLE

**The Rumor:**

> *Billy Graham associates only with the rich and the famous, the high and the mighty.*

**The Reality:**

Billy spends very little time golfing with presidents or with movie stars, but if he does, it makes news. He says, "If my picture is taken just once a year with the president, then they say, 'he's always hobnobbing with the president.' I spend eighty percent of my time with just ordinary people."

Ruth Graham confirmed this recently, when speaking on another subject. She said, "Bill really longs to have more friends up [to the house]." She said, "When he comes home, he has such a short time—five days this time—and he has all his messages to prepare." But, she added, "He's been saying to me, 'Ruth, let's start having the faculty up here—three couples for dinner or lunch.' He loves to meet people—but there is so little time."

## LIMOUSINES

**The Rumor:**

> Billy Graham *"runs around everywhere in chauffeured limousines."*

**The Reality:**

"That is absolutely false," George Wilson says emphatically. Billy Graham's transportation used to be arranged by local committees in crusade cities, and their choice of vehicles may have included a limousine. He has also ridden in the limousines of politicians or other dignitaries who often welcome him to a city. After traveling as a passenger in singer Johnny Cash's limousine one evening during the Las Vegas crusade, Billy admitted on a national television broadcast the next day that he had "felt a little uncomfortable." The Grahams themselves own two cars: a Jeep and a Volvo. In recent years, transportation during crusades has been arranged by local automobile dealers.

## MAIL-ORDER DEGREE

**The Rumor:**

> *According to press reports, the son of a United States president suggested that Billy Graham's title of Doctor was obtained from a mail-order university.*

**The Reality:**

In his 1966 book *Billy Graham* author John Pollock writes: "In 1948 Billy Graham received his first honorary Doctorate, a D.D. from King's College, New York. About twenty honorary degrees have been bestowed on him since, and others he has declined. Because none has been earned he prefers to be addressed as *Mr.* Graham, or simply Billy."

All of Billy Graham's degrees have been honorary, conferred on him by grateful people who have been touched by his radio and television programs, his books, newspaper columns, and his worldwide crusades. For instance, Stetson University, a Baptist institution in De Land, Florida (and the first institution of higher learning in that state), demonstrated its high regard for Billy Graham's place in the annals of evangelism and the Christian ministry by giving him such a degree in 1958. The citation which accompanied the presentation said:

DOCTOR OF DIVINITY, WILLIAM FRANKLIN GRAHAM: Preacher, Evangelist, Minister to untold millions, we honor you for your lifelong devotion to the way of Jesus Christ. We join you in the prayer that His blessing may be on you and your work and on us in the years that are yet ahead. As we place this University's highest approval on the work that has been begun, we trust that it may be continued and that many others may yet be helped in their hours of decision. And now under the authority of the Board of Trustees, I confer upon you the degree Doctor of Divinity with all the rights, privileges, and obligations thereto appertaining wherever in the world you may go.

# NIXON, RICHARD

**The Rumor:**

*Billy Graham refuses to recognize Richard Nixon's perfidy and still pals around with him.*

**The Reality:**

Billy has visited at the Nixon home in San Clemente, but very seldom. He says of Nixon, "I've known him for a long time. I knew him for twenty years. He was a close friend. I feel that I didn't misjudge *him* but that I misjudged what he would do under certain pressures."

Billy Graham's loyalty to friends, and his tendency always to believe the best of people, is well known. The closeness of the Graham family's ties to the Nixon family are revealed in Julie Nixon Eisenhower's tribute to Ruth Graham in her book *Special People*. It is unlikely that the Graham family would ever abandon friends in a time of trouble. Of Watergate, Billy says, "I've never been privy to what happened, and he [Nixon] has never seen fit to tell me."

According to Bill Dalton, of the Ypsilanti, Michigan, *Press*, "Graham makes no apologies for becoming closely involved in American politics, saying, 'We need more Christians in Washington. Richard Nixon is still my friend and I've seen him twice since his resignation but have not counseled him. A religious leader does not desert a person because he is in trouble."

But if Nixon used Graham, Graham also used Nixon's influence on at least one occasion. It was when he thought the administration was not giving enough attention to black problems. He told the president, "I'd like to bring some black leaders to see you."

''Pick your people, and I'll give them an hour,'' Nixon responded.

Graham selected a group of black leaders, took them to the White House, and Nixon gave them three and one-half hours. ''They let him have it with both barrels,'' Graham says, ''and he sat and took it.''

White House log books, by the way, indicate that Norman Vincent Peale and at least one Catholic bishop spent as much time with Nixon as Graham did. As for overnight visits, Graham estimates that he was a Nixon guest only two or three times, against more than a score of visits with LBJ and his family.

## PLAYING GOD

**The Rumor:**

> *Graham was upset by a magazine cover headline that quoted him as saying, "I can't play God anymore."*

**The Reality:**

I don't think Billy was upset by that. He knew what he meant. But the line has been widely misinterpreted. The statements makes sense in the context in which it was made. The question dealt with salvation and how we know who is truly saved. Billy is quoted as having replied, "I used to play God, but I can't do that anymore." That single sentence was then further condensed and used as the title of the article.

On other occasions, he has been quoted more fully in his effort to make the same point: that he, Billy Graham, is not an arbiter of salvation. He says, "God does the saving. I'm told to preach Christ as the only way to salvation. But it is God who is going to do the judging, not Billy Graham." And again, on the Phil Donahue show from Las Vegas, when asked about the authenticity of publisher Larry Flynt's religious experience, Billy answered: "I don't know who has been born again and who hasn't." In other words: "I can't play God."

## RETIREMENT

**The Rumor:**
> *Billy Graham is sick, disillusioned, tired, or disposed for other reasons to retire from the field of evangelism.*

**The Reality:**

The rumor keeps cropping up. On his sixtieth birthday, Graham said, "I have no plans whatsoever to retire. I plan to go on and preach the Gospel."

A UPI reporter recently wrote, "Although he said a few years ago he would like to reduce the number of his crusades, which have attracted millions throughout the world, he has a full schedule for this year and next and has enough requests for crusades to keep him busy for a decade."

The year of 1979 will probably be one of his most arduous. It will see him preaching in Singapore, Brazil, Australia, as well as several crusades in the United States. Also, he feels that the communist world is opening as a fertile missionary field. "There's a spiritual hunger today," he said. "The entire world has opened up."

In another interview, Graham said, "I don't think I can retire as long as there is a spiritual need, and there will always be one. I'll continue as long as the Lord gives me strength and ability to communicate the Gospel. I'm sure I'll have to retire from the big, massive crusades in the next five or six years. But I feel a responsibility to people all over the world. Before I would let them down, I would rather God killed me."

# SATAN AND BILLY GRAHAM

**The Rumor:**

> *Billy Graham has an obsession that his uncertain health and the controversies which have recently spawned so many headlines have been specifically instigated and manipulated by Satan, in order to subvert the BGEA and all its works.*

**The Reality:**

The word *obsession* originally referred to the act of an evil spirit in possessing or influencing a person. I doubt very much that Graham is possessed by an evil spirit, but I am also aware of his conviction that Satan exists and constantly does his utmost to thwart the work of anyone who seeks to spread the good news of the Gospel. On various occasions, his own work has been attacked.

Several years ago, Graham wrote: "One day I was preparing a sermon on the devil. My original notes were mysteriously lost. I sat down to dictate a new sermon, and the dictating machine caught fire. One thing was certain: The devil did not want me to invade his domain. But I did.

"I also find the devil hinders me when I pray. I have an hour set aside for prayer. These are the hours when the phone rings loudest, visitors come in droves, and my team members seem always to have pressing problems that cannot wait.

"Satan may not appear in person, but he makes himself felt. I once had a painful experience with a ram on my farm. Some aspects of that attack remind me of the devil's tactics. The ram butted me when I least expected it. Before I could regain my feet, he hit me a second time. While I was tumbling down the mountainside, he rushed down and knocked me over a ledge. . . .

"I have found Satan just as aggressive in spiritual matters. But whenever I am aware of his presence, I try to follow the formula offered by a little girl. She said, 'When Satan knocks, I just send Christ to the door.' "

Graham says every thinking person has surely wondered about the devil. The modern concept is that he is a harmless sort of fellow, akin to the leprechaun. We make jokes about him. Cartoonists give him a tail and horns.

"Satan cannot be dismissed so easily," Graham says. "He is mentioned twenty times in the Old Testament and over one hundred times in the New Testament. He is no abstract force. He is a person who walks, talks, debates, deceives, lies, cajoles, tempts, and destroys.

"Almost certainly, he is a handsome devil, attractive and winsome. The Bible says he disguises himself as an angel of light. It also says he is real, active, powerful, wise, crafty, clever, and designing."

In all the universe, the earth is the only place that harbors evil, Graham has said. All the remainder of creation is good, as God designed it. This is the reason that God sent Christ into our world, to combat the devil.

During a sermon preached in a recent crusade, Billy said, "God calls every Christian to march, not onto a religious playground or into a sports field, but into grim, terrible, bloody conflict. The Bible calls the devil many names: deceiver, murderer, accuser, the evil one, the bitterest enemy of God. As followers of Christ, we believe that the way Christ speaks of Satan shows that he is real, a genuine personality, and destructive of every Christian."

Some modern theologians hold that Satan is a holdover from the Middle Ages. Graham disagrees. The Bible says that he has great authority and that "the whole world lies in the arms of the wicked one." He commands a host of evil spirits. The Bible calls this force "the kingdom of Satan."

Today's life-style, with its provocative clothing, amusements, literature, and free-and-easy relationships, is "the greatest smorgasbord of worldly pleasures in all history," says Graham. "Let's recognize that we are involved in a great spiritual conflict and that each of us has a decisive role to play. Like it or not, we must choose sides."

## TAX STATUS OF BGEA

**The Rumor:**
> *The BGEA doesn't pay any taxes.*

**The Reality:**
That's right. In 1953 the association requested tax-exempt status and was recognized as such by the IRS. Not all of the Graham organization's operations, however, are tax exempt. For instance, its publishing- and book-distribution branches, World Wide Publications and Grason Company, pay taxes, just like any other business.

In explaining the tax-exempt status of the evangelical branches of the Graham organization, Graham team members remind you of the original Christian meaning of *the church* as a group of people united for the worship of God through Jesus Christ. Only much later did we come to think of a church as a building. Because the real church is a group of members pledged to worship, to help one another, and to spread the good news of Jesus Christ, the Billy Graham crusades are considered to be a church, even though they have no building as such. But then, neither did Jesus and His apostles.

# VIETNAM

**The Rumor:**

> *Billy Graham took both sides of the issue on the Vietnam War.*

**The Reality:**

Graham always refused to take a position or to comment on the Vietnam War, although time and again in press conferences I heard reporters trying to force him into making a statement.

In 1966, he told me how he had called on the American people to pray for President Johnson, and how he was dismayed to discover that some newsmen had interpreted that as meaning that he backed Johnson's Vietnam policy. Personally, Graham did not ever support or defend the war, but he often made the observation that "equally devout Christians are on both sides of the question." This statement may be the source of the later distortion to the effect that Billy "took a two-sided stand."

## WHEATON CENTER

**The Rumor:**

> *The four-story Billy Graham center at Wheaton*
> *College is to be an expensive monument to the*
> *evangelist.*

**The Reality:**

On the contrary, Graham has made every effort to insure that the building on the Wheaton campus shall not be a monument, but instead will provide inspiration and instruction to those who either visit or study there.

The center has been mentioned elsewhere, but the annual report explains some of its features in greater detail.

It will house a layman's Bible-training program that will use the most modern materials and equipment and will help laymen and laywomen to greater effectiveness in communicating the Gospel.

Already, various conference ministries for North American pastors, Christian workers, and those engaged in special evangelistic programs are being held.

When the building is completed, a part of the first-floor area will be used for visitors and will contain memorabilia of significant crusades and ministries of the BGEA. Each visitor will receive a clear presentation of God's plan for salvation.

A library of over 50,000 books has been acquired. The goal is to make this one of the finest collections of books on evangelism, revival, and missions in the world.

Archives will contain records and other items gathered by Billy Graham in his crusades around the world, including original tapes of the "Hour of Decision," books and magazines in a dozen languages, and so forth.

A graduate school of Bible communications and Christian ministries will be headquartered here. Already, approximately 290 students are at work in master's degree programs. The school will be expanded to accommodate at least 500 students. Eventually, the center will house a full-scale communications laboratory for television, radio, and print media.

## WHITE HOUSE CONNECTIONS

**The Rumor:**

> *Billy Graham has been a White House hanger-on*
> *through the administration of four presidents.*

**The Reality:**

Throughout his career, Graham has had the ear of businessmen, legislators, and community leaders. It is not surprising that, since he had known three of these four presidents before they went to the White House, his associations with them would continue. They were Dwight D. Eisenhower, who Graham has said he knew best; Lyndon Baines Johnson, who he has said "understood preachers," and Richard Nixon.

He did not meet John F. Kennedy until after his election to the White House, and he did play golf with Kennedy occasionally, but the two were not close. Graham knew Jimmy Carter through Carter's work in a film crusade and had been Carter's houseguest in Georgia when he was governor. The rumor that Billy Graham likes to hang out around the White House is ironic in two senses. First, although he was a more frequent visitor to the White House over these four administrations than any other minister, his visits were not nearly so frequent as the public seems to think—they were merely well publicized. Second, while the assumption seems to be that he might have used his relationships with these powerful men, in fact, the relationships have made him subject to charges of guilt-by-association support for McCarthyism, the Vietnam War, and Watergate.

# WHITE HOUSE TAX INTERVENTION

**The Rumor:**

> *Billy Graham has been spared Internal Revenue Service investigations by the intervention of "White House intimates."*

**The Reality:**

Rumor it is. During the Watergate hearings, a White House memo was publicized that indicated the Nixon administration had offered to help Graham with any IRS audit of his personal taxes. But there was no suggestion that he had ever sought such help, or needed it. In any event, he did not accept it. All of his personal financial affairs, including taxes, are handled through the trust department of the First Union National Bank in Charlotte.

## WORLD EMERGENCY FUND

**The Rumor:**

> *Billy Graham has given various sums of money to various causes, projects, or institutions. If contributors support him in order to advance his work of evangelism, how can he conscientiously use part of those funds for the relief of heathen victims of a tidal wave in India? Or for the maintenance of a halfway house for American convicts coming out of Mexican prisons?*

**The Reality:**

Contributions come from many sources, but only a portion of it is marked by donors for evangelistic use. Frequently, a contribution will not be designated for any specific purpose, but given into Graham's hands for disposal subject to his own best judgment. Early in his ministry, he decided that his association should "tithe" its income, giving 10 percent to other evangelistic projects.

In 1973, the association's board approved the formation of a World Emergency Fund, designed to meet critical needs in disaster areas. This was a fund within the association itself, and was started in 1973 at a crusade being held in Minneapolis, with an offering of $72,000. The offering was for the relief of the drought-stricken area of the Sahara in Africa. Since then, all funds given for world relief have come from this fund. No overhead is ever charged against it. Whatever is contributed goes 100 percent for relief.

## L'ENVOY

I am indebted to many people and to many institutions for their assistance. These include librarians and libraries; newspaper reporters and newspapers; press associations and press tycoons; educators and business executives.

My labors initially involved the digging out of facts, confirming them, organizing them, and ultimately of writing them into meaningful sentences. To all who helped, I am everlastingly grateful.

I am especially grateful to a half-dozen co-laborers whose wisdom has been of particular value. These helpers and critics include Dr. Paul D. Steeves, Dr. Kay Arthur Huson, Cardyne Buchanan, Ann Paden, and Evelyn Mantz.

One more name completes this memorial. It is of one who supported the author, from beginning to end, with constant but undeserved draughts of TLC: my friend and my beloved wife, Zelpha.

C.M.

24246